# AI Wars

# AI Wars

## The Next Global Arms Race

*By*

*Dr. Karim Bellarte*

**Vij Books**

**New Delhi (India)**

*Published by*

**Vij Books**
(Publishers, Distributors & Importers)
4836/24, 3rd Floor, Ansari Road
Delhi – 110 002
Phone: 91-11-43596460
Mobile: 98110 94883
e-mail: contact@vijpublishing.com
www.vijbooks.in



ISBN: 978-93-47436-19-2 (PB)



This book was developed using advanced writing tools to support the drafting and ideation process. All content has been thoughtfully curated, refined, and reviewed to ensure quality and relevance.

# Contents

# Introduction

The officer had trained for decades. He had studied the old campaigns, drilled the new doctrines, and risen by mastering the pressure of decision. Yet in the latest war-game, he found himself eclipsed by something without rank, fatigue, or fear: software. As his staff parsed reconnaissance reports and drafted provisional plans, the system had already simulated thousands of scenarios, discarded the brittle ones, and revised its own strategy in real time. By the time the officer issued his first set of orders, the machine had fought the entire battle in its head. It was unnerving, less because the officer had failed and more because he had become slow in comparison. A human being had become the bottleneck.

This moment, replayed quietly in several defence laboratories around the world, captures the tension defining the next global arms race. We tell ourselves that greater precision makes conflict safer. Yet every increase in precision demands greater speed, and greater speed erodes the time available for judgement. The very tools built to reduce miscalculation may instead compress crises into seconds, where instinct, bias, and machine inference collide. Command, once a theatre of deliberation, risks being reduced to a thin sliver of oversight—approval buttons in a world that punishes hesitation.

For many readers, these developments arrive shrouded in grandiose headlines and vague menace. Autonomous drones. Swarming vessels. Predictive targeting. Artificial intelligence as ally, adversary, or accident waiting to happen. There is hype, certainly, but there is also genuine transformation. Within a decade, most major powers will field decision-support systems that plan faster than their commanders, target faster than their pilots, and learn faster than their intelligence branches. Nations are not only acquiring weapons; they are acquiring the ability to think at scale and at speed. That is the real arms race: cognition embodied in code.

This book is written for anyone who senses that something seismic is happening, yet has not found a reliable map. Most commentary oscillates between alarmism and complacency, assuming either runaway robots or business as usual. Both positions are comfortable, and both are wrong. The truth is subtler and more consequential. Algorithmic warfare is neither science fiction nor simple engineering. It is a shift in how power is projected, how alliances are formed, how crises are managed, and how citizens hold their governments to account.

Historically, every major military revolution has begun with a paradox. Cavalry made war faster, but gave commanders less time to think. Aircraft extended reach, but compressed warning. Nuclear weapons promised stability, yet made miscalculation catastrophic. Artificial intelligence follows this familiar pattern: the pursuit of safety produces fragility; the pursuit of advantage produces uncertainty. But the twist today is that the machines alter not simply what weapons can do, but how decisions are made and justified. Strategy itself becomes algorithmic.

To understand what is truly at stake, one must strip away the cinematic fantasies. Forget the caricature of rogue killer robots prowling battlefields. The future, at least in the near term, will be built from more prosaic components: sensors, data pipelines, prediction engines, and command software. These are not glamorous, but they are decisive. In the same way that fuel lines determine how far an army can move, data pipelines determine how well a system can sense, predict, and strike. In military circles, some now joke that logistics wins wars and data wins logistics. It is a joke told with increasing seriousness.

Consider how conflicts are already shifting. Drones identify artillery before the first shell is loaded. Satellites feed models that predict shipping movements and border crossings. Algorithms flag suspicious patterns in communications, sometimes correctly, sometimes disastrously. Intelligence officers once spent days assembling mosaic pictures; now models fuse satellite, acoustic, maritime, and cyber data into a single forecast. Armies are no longer just manoeuvring forces; they are training datasets.

And because data must flow, it must be protected. Cyber defenders patch code with as much urgency as tank regiments refuel. Cloud capacity becomes a strategic asset. Regional data centres—not bases—begin to define where power can be projected. In some countries, the most classified military facilities no longer store aircraft; they store training runs. Territory stretches into the digital: circuits, cables, and servers become the new contested ground.

Yet power does not reside solely in technology. Doctrine—how systems are trained, staffed, maintained, and governed—often matters more. The world is full of dazzling prototypes that never graduate from demonstration to deployment because they break under field conditions. Militaries are conservative for good reasons: they fight with what they can trust, not what impresses investors. A machine that can generate tactics on the fly is useful only if operators are confident that its reasoning is sound, its data secure, and its failures predictable. Reliability becomes a form of deterrence.

The paradox extends into diplomacy and domestic politics. If decisions accelerate beyond human pace, how do elected leaders maintain oversight? How do allies coordinate strikes when each nation's models learn differently from their own data? How do publics judge incidents when the chain of responsibility winds through vendors, cloud providers, and subcontractors? Accountability, that ancient pillar of legitimate force, must be reinvented for code.

These questions are not theoretical. Several countries already conduct autonomous patrols in contested borders and waterways. Some experiment with predictive maintenance and predictive strikes, using models that identify vehicles, vessels, or individuals judged statistically likely to pose future threats. The more these systems are used, the greater the temptation to rely on them. And the more we rely, the harder it becomes to slow down. As one official confided after a classified briefing: "Once the machine can think faster than we can, standing still is falling behind."

History warns us what happens when states feel compelled to automate escalation. During the Cold War, seconds mattered. Radar blips were mistaken for incoming missiles, flocks of birds for bomber formations. Several times, catastrophic launch orders were only avoided because a human being paused, questioned, or simply refused to believe the data. Those crises stretched minutes. Today's may stretch milliseconds. Machines do not feel intuition, but they do make predictions, and predictions can be catastrophically wrong.

Still, there is reason for discipline, not despair. Technology is not destiny. It is architecture: designed, built, governed, and negotiated. We have choices—about what to automate, what to forbid, what to slow down, and what to harden. We choose which controls to enforce, and which temptations to resist. The worst future is not inevitable; it is simply the one arrived at without thought.

This book is written for those who want to think clearly. Leaders who must decide what to buy, what to build, and what to regulate. Citizens who deserve honesty rather than hype. Scholars and engineers who seek to align innovation with restraint. And readers who understand that history is still being written in real time, in servers as well as parliaments.

Over ten chapters, we will move from the plumbing of power—data, models, and compute—to the fault lines of policy, crisis, and ethics. Chapter 1 explains the capability stack: the fuel lines of data, the engines of models, the factories of chips, and the doctrine that welds them into force. Chapter 2 explores speed and autonomy, showing how compressed decision time can redraw escalation thresholds. Chapter 3 reveals the messy realities of predictive targeting: the victories, the false positives, and the diplomatic fallout. Chapter 4 reframes cyberspace and cloud infrastructure as new territory, where sovereignty is negotiated in fibre-optic cables. Chapter 5 examines alliances struggling to share code without surrendering secrets. Chapter 6 brings the story home, where industry, labour, and public legitimacy determine what any democracy can sustain. Chapter 7 exposes adversarial playbooks, from data poisoning to model theft. Chapter 8 confronts ethics under fire—targeting thresholds, bias, redress, and the dignity of warfighters asked to supervise machines that kill. Chapter 9 looks to treaties and norms, not as utopian fantasies but as instruments of risk reduction. And Chapter 10 ends with strategy: how to compete without losing control, how to innovate without eroding legitimacy, how to win not by moving fastest but by choosing the right hill.

Across these chapters, a motif will return: control points. In a world intoxicated by technical spectacle—flying robots, synthetic intelligence—it is easy to miss the mundane levers that truly matter. Who controls the data pipelines? Who audits the models? Who allocates cloud compute during crises? Who sets the safety defaults? Who can pull the kill-switch, and who verifies that it works? You cannot govern what you cannot see, and you cannot trust what you cannot test. The future of restraint will depend less on treaties written on paper and more on protocols embedded in software.

Another theme runs beneath the surface: the first-mover advantage will fade. Today, a handful of nations sit at the frontier, but algorithmic tools diffuse quickly. Commercial satellites shrink the surveillance gap. Open-source models democratise predictive analytics. Universities train a global workforce fluent in machine learning. The arms race will not be won by possessing a single miracle weapon; it will be shaped by how well nations integrate, adapt, and secure systems over time. The decisive resource is not just intelligence—it is institutional wisdom.

This raises uncomfortable questions. What happens when an adversary steals your training data, poisons your models, or floods your cloud region with traffic? What happens when an ally's autonomous system misfires and the world demands accountability? What happens when your own population demands transparency, even as secrecy seems necessary for deterrence? These are not puzzles for tomorrow; they are already debated in defence ministries and parliaments from Canberra to Warsaw.

Yet there is also opportunity. Algorithmic warfare, if governed wisely, can reduce civilian casualties, provide early warning, and prevent miscalculation. Automated compliance systems can enforce no-strike lists. Simulators can train crews continuously. Auditable logs can expose mistakes, allowing nations to learn faster rather than hide their failures. In other words, the same systems that threaten instability can also embed restraint. Technology can be used not only to fight wars, but to limit them.

The deeper question—the one most headlines miss—is not whether machines will fight, but how humans will fight alongside them. Will commanders defer to automated advice because it is statistically superior, or will they distrust it because it obscures its own reasoning? Will junior officers learn to challenge models, or become passive executors of machine-generated plans? Will citizens demand human control, even if human control is slower and less precise? The answers will shape not only the battlefield but the social contract between governments and those they serve.

This book argues for a form of strategic sobriety. Not fear. Not hype. Sobriety. The ability to see where machines excel, where they fail, and where humans remain indispensable. It demands that we learn to ask better questions: Which problems genuinely require autonomy? Which should stay human? Which systems must be explainable, and which must simply be reliable? And what safeguards must be built before deployment rather than after regret?

If previous eras taught us that war is too important to be left to generals, this era reminds us that war may be too important to be left to engineers. Technology alone cannot decide what is acceptable, proportional, or legitimate. These are political and moral judgements. They require public debate—not in the aftermath of disaster, but in the quiet before it.

Perhaps the most unsettling feature of algorithmic warfare is its invisibility. Missiles can be counted. Divisions can be seen. But data pipelines and model weights are hidden behind classification and cloud platforms. When fear is invisible, panic fills the gaps. A world that cannot explain its weapons cannot control them. Transparency—at least to oversight bodies and allies—is not a weakness; it is a precondition for stability.

So let this book serve as a map. Not a manifesto, nor a prophecy. A map. With it, you will see the machinery beneath the headlines, the leverage beneath the spectacle, and the choices beneath the panic. You will learn how data, models, chips, and doctrine combine into power. You will see how deterrence shifts when machines anticipate rather than react. You will grasp why alliances may fracture over code rather than territory. And you will understand why legitimacy—the consent of publics—may determine who prevails, not who deploys the most drones.

By the time you reach the final chapter, you will be able to separate substance from hype, threat from theatre. You will know which capabilities matter, which controls matter more, and which norms must endure when everyone can move fast. The next arms race will not be won by secrecy alone; it will be won by understanding.

And perhaps, when the next officer sits before a console and watches the system fight a battle before he has finished his coffee, he will feel less like a relic. He will understand how the machine thinks, where it can be trusted, and where it must be checked. Command will not disappear; it will be redefined. The challenge of our time is to ensure that redefinition is deliberate, disciplined, and democratic.

The race has already started. The question is not whether we will compete, but how. And whether, in the rush for speed, we will remember that power without judgement is not strength—it is peril.

This book begins with the capability stack. Let us descend into the machinery of modern power and see where the future is being built.

# Chapter 1

# The Capability Stack

The drone was small enough to fit in a backpack, quiet enough to vanish beneath the wind, and cheap enough to discard. Its camera streamed grainy images—nothing theatrical, nothing cinematic. Yet somewhere far beyond the horizon, a network of satellites, servers, and models was working furiously. The drone was only the first link in a chain. Its signal bounced upward, merged with feeds from other airborne scouts, fused with radar sweeps, maritime sensors, and historical pattern-of-life data. Within seconds, prediction engines had flagged a vessel hundreds of miles away, not because the vessel had done anything suspicious, but because its behaviour had drifted from the expected. A minor deviation—speed a fraction too slow, route a fraction too cautious—triggered a cascade. Options appeared: shadow, jam, interdict, or ignore. The commander would later be credited with a decisive call. Quietly, most of the work had already been done.

This is how modern power moves: not through a single brilliant machine, but through a stack of capabilities, each invisible until something fails. When outsiders speak of artificial intelligence in war, they picture sentient robots or omniscient software. Insiders know better. What matters is not glamour. What matters is plumbing. Data pipelines like fuel lines. Models like engines. Chips like supply depots. Doctrine like convoy discipline. A state does not win because it has the flashiest prototype; it wins because its pipes are wide, its engines tuned, its depots stocked, and its crews drilled. A capability stack is not one technology. It is an ecosystem.

The purpose of this chapter is simple: to make the invisible visible. To show that algorithmic warfare is not magic, but machinery—and machinery can be built, broken, stolen, sabotaged, and governed. Once you see the stack, you stop being dazzled by talk of superweapons, and you start asking harder questions. Where did the data come from? How fresh is it? Who verified its labelling? Which models interpret it, and how likely are they to fail? Which chips run them, and who controls the fabrication lines? What doctrine binds all of this into something a commander might actually trust?

Nations rise or stumble on the answers.

A century ago, victory required steel, oil, and factories. Today, it requires something less tangible: information that is timely, trustworthy, and abundant. Data is not merely intelligence; it is logistics. Without fuel, a tank becomes a monument. Without data, a model becomes a guess. Military planners now speak of "sensor-to-shooter time" as a competitive metric, but beneath the phrase lies a deeper truth: the quality of a strike depends on the quality of a pipeline. A model trained on stale or corrupted data performs no better than a soldier handed a broken map.

Imagine a maritime commander staring at a screen that appears deceptively calm. Tankers glide along predictable routes, fishing boats stitch loops across coastal waters, and nothing seems out of place. Behind that stillness is movement: cubesat constellations taking snapshots, acoustic sensors capturing engine signatures, AIS beacons chirping coordinates, and weather satellites mapping currents and winds. Raw feeds flow into sorting rooms, human and machine label vessels, and models learn which patterns are benign and which foretell risk. If the pipeline shines, warnings appear early. If it clogs—if a satellite is blinded, if data arrives late, if metadata is stripped—then predictions wobble. The commander is left staring at a beautiful but empty picture.

This is why nations now treat data freshness as a strategic resource. It is not enough to collect; one must collect continuously. It is not enough to label; one must label accurately. And it is not enough to secure data at rest; one must secure it in motion. Adversaries prefer to corrupt rather than steal. A poisoned training set can quietly tilt a model towards misidentification, just as contaminated fuel can stall an engine at the worst possible moment. What seems like a technical footnote quickly becomes a military vulnerability.

But data alone does nothing. It must be interpreted. And here, another misconception demands correction. Many assume that "AI" is a single instrument: some mysterious software that sees all and predicts all. In truth, there are many species of model, each with strengths and fragilities. A targeting model that identifies armoured vehicles thrives on crisp edges and physical consistency. A deception-detection model, by contrast, hunts for anomalies, statistical ghosts, and adversarial trickery. Scale matters, yes—larger models often see more—but scale does not trump fit. A state that pours billions into colossal models with poor alignment to domain reality ends up with exquisite, useless toys.

Consider a system tasked with identifying maritime deception. It must distinguish a fishing vessel behaving oddly from a disguised fast-attack craft mimicking innocuous behaviour. One model might be trained on years of sensor data, learning the rhythms of coastal industries: when nets are cast, when boats idle, when captains cut engines to avoid patrols. Another model might be trained on adversarial tactics: spoofed GPS tracks, transponder silence, painted hulls, swapped crew patterns. Each model solves a different puzzle. Mix them carelessly and failure blooms. The lesson is harsh: you cannot simply "add more AI" to a problem. You must choose the right tool, test it under stress, and accept that some models will break in ways you cannot yet anticipate.

Model failure is not always dramatic. Sometimes it is subtle, cumulative, quietly catastrophic. In war games, algorithms have misidentified friendly vehicles as hostile after rare sensor noise. In others, drones have drifted off course because a model learned to trust shadows more than terrain. Engineers patch, retrain, and redeploy, but every fix comes with its own risks. Commanders rarely see these details. To them, the model works—until it doesn't. Understanding the stack means understanding these failure modes, not to invite paranoia but to build resilience.

Still, even the finest model is inert without compute. Chips, memory, bandwidth—these are the factories of digital power. They are also chokepoints. Only a handful of nations can fabricate cutting-edge chips. Only a handful of companies can accelerate training of large models at scale. Export controls, licensing regimes, and cloud access now function like naval blockades once did. They determine who can build, who can deploy, and who must make do with outdated hardware sputtering at the edge of capability.

This is not an abstract tension. When one major power tightened its export rules for advanced lithography machines, another shifted billions into domestic chip manufacturing. When sanctions limited access to high-performance graphics processors, cloud procurement surged, reshaping budgets overnight. A procurement officer is no longer just buying missiles and radios; she is buying compute credits, trying to secure priority access to cloud capacity during crises. If chips are the new oil, cloud regions are the new ports. Whoever controls allocation during wartime holds leverage that cannot be counterfeited.

If the story ended here—with data, models, and chips—we might believe that the most technologically advanced state automatically wins. But machinery is not enough. Doctrine decides whether machinery works. Systems do not deploy themselves. Operators must be trained, maintenance scheduled, interfaces refined, and feedback loops institutionalised. Militaries have learned, often the hard way, that a gorgeous demonstration is not the same as a reliable tool. A prototype can dazzle at a weapons fair, yet fail in monsoon rain or arctic wind. A model can predict brilliantly in the lab, then crumble when exposed to adversarial interference. Integration is the hard slog: months of training, hours of simulation, endless drills to ensure that a junior operator in a remote outpost can use the system without panicking when alarms flash.

Some of the most advanced autonomous programmes have failed precisely because they did not fit into doctrine. Pilots distrusted their guidance. Commanders found the interfaces cryptic. Maintenance crews lacked the spare parts or software patches. Meanwhile, humbler systems—clunkier, less elegant—won admiration because they worked every time, in every weather, with every operator. Technology without doctrine is theatre.

What makes doctrine powerful is not rigidity but rehearsal. Many modern militaries are building simulator feedback loops, where crews deploy models in virtual war games, stress-test autonomy, and watch how systems behave under deception and jamming. The data from those simulations feeds into upgrades, which then feed into new drills. In that rhythm—deploy, learn, refine—advantage compounds. Novelty wears off; integration endures.

Finally, every capability must travel from prototype to posture. It is one thing to see a demonstration video of autonomous patrol boats gliding in formation. It is another to deploy them across a real coastline, integrate their sensors with command networks, and trust them with live weapons. The path from lab to battlefield is slow, bureaucratic, and unforgiving. There are safety certifications, live-fire evaluations, red-team audits, and kill-switch protocols. In some countries, autonomous systems cannot be deployed without mitigation plans that guarantee human override—even if override is delayed or distributed. In others, phased rollouts begin with unarmed platforms, then escalate as confidence grows. The public rarely sees these deliberations, but they are where states decide how much risk they are willing to tolerate.

Integrated air defence is a vivid example. Early systems could track and detect. Later ones could classify and prioritise. Now, some nations are testing predictive models that forecast flight paths, jam timing, and even adversary intention. But adoption is phased: first in controlled ranges, then in limited sectors, then under joint command. The kill-switch—whether human, algorithmic, or hybrid—remains a sacred fixture. Autonomy may advance, but the commander remains responsible.

Seen as a whole, the capability stack is a sobering antidote to technological romanticism. Power is not a machine. It is a pipeline, a workshop, a curriculum, and a culture. It demands engineers as much as tacticians, logisticians as much as scientists. The nation that builds the most spectacular prototype may impress an audience. The nation that builds the most resilient stack will shape the battlefield.

In the pages ahead, we will move through each layer—data, models, compute, doctrine, and deployment—showing how advantage is earned, eroded, stolen, or squandered. This is not merely a tour of equipment. It is a study in how modern force is constituted: how prediction becomes posture, how autonomy becomes accountability, and how restraint can be encoded into architecture rather than left to hope.

If you learn to see these layers, the world changes. Headlines become legible. Defence budgets make sense. Seemingly minor procurement disputes reveal strategic agendas. You understand why a country might spend billions on satellite bandwidth rather than battleships, or why a general might demand better labelling teams rather than more missiles. Power shifts from spectacle to system.

And the next time a small drone arcs over a horizon and vanishes into the sky, you may find yourself wondering not what it sees, but what sees through it—what networks, what models, what chips, what doctrine, what safeguards. That curiosity is the beginning of strategic literacy.

Now, let us examine the first layer: data as the new logistics.

## Data as the new logistics

A patrol boat slips through a quiet strait at night, its lights dimmed, engines throttled low. To any nearby observer, it is indistinguishable from the fishermen who work these waters. Yet far above, a lattice of small satellites is watching. Each pass adds fresh pixels to a growing archive: hull shape, wake turbulence, speed anomalies, route deviations. None of this means anything on its own. The sea is noisy. Vessels drift, captains improvise, and weather forces detours. But when the next image arrives—then the next, and the next—a story emerges. Models compare the vessel's motion not to a single moment, but to months of history. A small warning light flickers on the console of an analyst hundreds of miles away. Something has changed. A fuel line of data is flowing, and because it flows, the machine can think.

The metaphor is blunt, but accurate. In the last century, armies ran on diesel; today, many of their most powerful systems run on data. Without fuel, a tank becomes an iron sculpture. Without data, a model becomes a hunch. Modern warfare rewards those who can maintain pipelines of information: vast, continuous, secure, and verified. A state that cannot feed its models might as well starve its soldiers.

When militaries first began deploying autonomous and predictive systems, some believed the key lay in clever algorithms alone. Software would outsmart complexity. But practitioners learned quickly that even the most sophisticated model collapses when the data behind it is stale, noisy, mislabeled, or corrupted. A brilliant engine drawing sludge from its fuel tank is just a grenade with a crankshaft. Power no longer lies only in who possesses data, but in who can keep it fresh, trustworthy, and flowing under pressure.

The world has started to reorganise around this logic. Naval commanders obsess over maritime tracking feeds; air forces secure satellite bandwidth as aggressively as runway rights. Cyber units defend data stores with the same vigilance once reserved for missile silos. And behind every headline about "AI-enabled targeting" lies a quieter truth: the targeting is only as good as the pipeline that nourishes it.

Volume matters. Freshness matters. Provenance matters. Logistics, reborn in code.

Volume is the most intuitive component, but also the most misunderstood. Big data alone is not power. Millions of images or signals, if poorly structured or inconsistently labelled, become an archive of confusion. Yet in the right form, volume enables pattern recognition that no human analyst could match. A coast guard officer might spend a career studying smuggling routes and still miss subtle seasonal changes, shifts in port behaviour, or micro-variations in engine noise signatures. But a model trained on years of sensor data can learn that ships engaged in illegal transfers drift at specific angles to prevailing currents, or that vessels feigning distress behave with oddly stable speeds. The richness lies not in raw quantity, but in what quantity makes possible.

Freshness, however, is where the strategic stakes sharpen. A model trained on last month's satellite passes may misread a newly dredged inlet or misclassify a disguised vessel. A state relying on yesterday's patterns risks fighting ghosts. This is why constellations of small satellites have become invaluable: they collapse revisit times from hours to minutes. In the past, intelligence officers prayed for a clear sky and a lucky orbit. Now they expect updates continuously. This relentless cadence gives predictive engines the oxygen they need. With each pass, the model recalibrates, adjusting its expectations and discarding obsolete assumptions. Fresh data is not a luxury; it is a defence against surprise.

And yet, freshness can be a trap. The faster data flows, the greater the temptation to act before reflection. Commanders may feel pressure to trust the latest prediction simply because it is recent. The sea of now can drown the wisdom of context. A vessel behaving oddly might simply be avoiding storms. A convoy slowing down might be responding to faulty engines, not preparing for aggression. The paradox is that data reduces uncertainty while enticing overconfidence. Experience and restraint remain essential, even when the dashboard glows with probability scores.

Provenance is the quiet guardian of power. It asks: Where did this data come from? Who touched it? Can you prove nothing was altered along the way? In the commercial world, corrupted datasets produce embarrassing product failures. In military systems, they produce targeting errors, escalation incidents, or diplomatic crises. Adversaries know this. Rather than attempting to steal data from hardened servers, they often try to contaminate it upstream—introducing false readings, spoofed signals, or synthetic traffic that teaches models to trust nonsense. A poisoned dataset is more dangerous than a stolen one: theft merely reveals your knowledge, poisoning rewires your judgement.

To mitigate this, some armed forces now treat data like munitions, marking each batch with cryptographic provenance. Each sensor's output is signed, each relay authenticated, each storage node audited. If a packet appears without pedigree, the system distrusts it by default. It is a subtle but powerful shift. Integrity becomes as operationally decisive as firepower.

Of course, raw data is inert until someone makes sense of it. And here the human labour often remains invisible. Before a model can distinguish a fishing trawler from a minesweeper, someone must label thousands of images. Before a predictive engine can forecast insurgent supply lines, someone must annotate signals, conversations, and historical logs.

Annotation is an unglamorous craft—tedious, meticulous, unforgiving. It demands workers who understand not just pixels or waveforms, but context: how ships behave, how smugglers adapt, how terrain shapes strategy.

Some countries outsource this labour. Others cultivate specialised military annotation units, training linguists, sailors, and engineers to label data with domain expertise. A satellite image of a tanker is not helpful unless someone can identify whether the ship's cranes are fuel-capable or grain-configured. A radio intercept is useless unless its metadata captures who spoke, from where, and under what conditions. This labour is the stitching that holds the entire pipeline together.

Mislabelled data can be catastrophic. In exercises, models have confidently misclassified ambulances as armoured cars because training sets lacked civilian examples. In maritime operations, a small set of mislabeled tugboats taught a system that hostile vessels often slowed near port entrances—an inference that triggered repeated false alarms. Each failure became a lesson: the model was not broken, the data was.

Security completes the triad. Data is most vulnerable not when stored securely in vault-like servers, but when in transit, crossing oceans through undersea cables and traversing foreign cloud regions. Interception or alteration at these stages can distort reality. In recent years, several states have invested in hardened data corridors—encrypted links from satellites to ground stations to intelligence hubs. Others scatter data across multiple cloud providers, assuming that redundancy is the best defence against disruption.

There is a human cost to this new logistics. Analysts who once read reports and maps now manage dashboards, anomaly detectors, and alerts. Their job is not to watch a single feed, but to decide which signals matter when algorithms scream for attention. They must vet the machine's confidence without being hypnotised by it. And unlike traditional logistics officers, whose supplies were visible—fuel drums, ammunition pallets—their supplies are invisible. A missed packet, a corrupted dataset, a downed satellite: the fault lines are abstract, yet the fallout can be concrete.

The most profound change is psychological. Commanders raised in a world of human scouts must now trust chains of inference that no single person can inspect. A machine may flag a threat because its data shows a vessel turning five degrees slower than normal, or because radar pulses echo in a particular pattern, or because electromagnetic signatures resemble a known adversary. No commander could ever replicate that judgement unaided. The choice becomes whether to trust a system whose reasoning is statistical, not narrative.

Some embrace the power. They see data pipelines as liberation from guesswork. Others resist, fearing invisible biases and unseen flaws. Both instincts are reasonable. A model trained entirely on coastal waters might fail in monsoon conditions. A satellite forced into safe mode during a solar storm might leave blind spots over strategic zones. Data-rich systems do not always degrade gracefully; sometimes they jump straight from insight to hallucination.

That fragility has driven innovation in redundancy. Rather than trusting a single pipeline, advanced militaries now braid multiple feeds—satellite constellations, maritime radars, acoustic buoys, airborne sensors, cyber intercepts. If one goes dark, others carry the load. Think of it as convoy doctrine for information: no single vehicle carries all the fuel. The architecture mirrors traditional logistics, where armies spread supplies across depots to prevent a catastrophic single point of failure.

Still, pipelines impose their own diplomacy. Satellite imagery may fly over friendly nations; undersea cables may land in states with competing interests. Data sovereignty becomes strategic leverage. A country controlling a key ground station can delay or deny imagery to an ally during a crisis. What looks like technical infrastructure doubles as political territory. Agreements governing access, prioritisation, and sharing become as sensitive as arms treaties.

When the system works, it looks effortless. A maritime command centre sees updated vessel tracks. An interceptor receives a preemptive heading. A pilot receives an alert before radar pings. But behind the glass is an orchestra: satellites waking and sleeping, antennas swivelling, encryption keys rotating, cloud nodes scaling, models retraining, analysts verifying. Disruption anywhere echoes everywhere.

A pipeline must also move backwards, from battlefield back to model. After a mission, logs flow to training centres, where failures are analysed and retraining begins. Every misidentified ship, every misread signal, becomes a lesson. Data is both fuel and memory. It powers the present while improving the future.

The result is a feedback loop that can separate agile states from stagnant ones. Nations that can refresh their models weekly—or daily—gain compounding advantage. Those forced to rely on static datasets fall behind. Some governments have begun to treat data refresh cycles like munitions stockpiles: a measure of readiness. When a crisis erupts, it is not only weapons that matter but whether the predictive engines are fed with last night's truth or last year's history.

None of this diminishes human judgement. It heightens its importance. A commander must know when the data is lying. A policymaker must know how much uncertainty is tolerable. A diplomat must understand why a false alarm matters. The pipeline does not remove human agency; it changes where agency sits. Instead of aiming missiles, humans must aim data.

There is an irony here. For centuries, militaries have prized secrecy. Hidden plans, encrypted ciphers, silent movements. Now, in some domains, transparency becomes power. If your vessel broadcasts clean, verified signals, models will classify it as benign, and patrols will leave it alone. If you vanish from the map—transponders off, logs absent—you risk classification as suspicious. The safest path may be visibility, not concealment.

This inversion unsettles old instincts. Generals who once demanded radio silence now ask for constant situational broadcasting. Submariners who lived below detection now confront autonomous systems that map ocean noise as diligently as satellites map coastlines. Data changes not only tactics, but culture.

And culture, ultimately, determines whether pipelines can endure. If a military treats data as a temporary accessory, models will die of starvation. If it treats data as a logistical lifeline—as essential as fuel or spare parts—systems will improve with every mission, every sensor, every human annotation. The winners of tomorrow are not those with the largest arsenals, but those with the healthiest pipelines.

Yet even robust systems cannot escape risk. What happens when satellites are blinded? When undersea cables are severed? When annotation teams are overwhelmed, or models detect ghosts where none exist? The very infrastructure that empowers also exposes. Logistics cut, army halted; data cut, model blind.

Perhaps the most unsettling question remains unanswered: if data pipelines underpin modern power, who guards them during peace, and who owns them during war? In conflicts where private companies operate satellites and cloud networks, sovereignty itself becomes negotiable. A commander may need a corporation's permission to see his own coastline. The geometry of power shifts.

The patrol boat still glides through the dark. The analyst still watches the map. But the decisive actor is the pipeline—not heroic, not glamorous, simply relentless. It is the silent machinery of modern force.

And somewhere, a vessel is behaving strangely. Is it a false alarm or the first tremor of a crisis? The answer flows with the data. The pipeline holds the verdict. The question is whether anyone notices before the light goes out.

## Models, not magic

A reconnaissance drone once returned from a sortie over contested desert runways with a gallery of images. Dust, heat haze, and shadows made interpretation difficult. To the human eye, the frames showed nothing remarkable: a few grounded aircraft, some storage hangars, a scattering of ground vehicles. Yet one model flagged a single lorry as suspicious. The heat signature around its tyres seemed wrong, the timing of its engine cycles abnormal, its route inconsistent with supply patterns logged over the previous month. Analysts were sceptical—until the vehicle detonated a roadside charge on a convoy later that week. The machine had not been clever in any cinematic sense. It had simply learned a language no human could read: the statistical grammar of motion, temperature, and behaviour. The prediction felt uncanny. In truth, it was just mathematics doing what mathematics does best.

Episodes like this fuel the myth of machine omniscience. From the outside, models appear to conjure insight from noise, turning pixels and waveforms into decisions that feel almost supernatural. But nothing about them is magical. A model is a hypothesis in code—an educated guess, hardened through training, vulnerable to error, and always constrained by its data. The awe that surrounds algorithmic systems often conceals a simpler truth: there are many kinds of models, each with its own strengths and fragilities, and treating them as interchangeable is a category error that can cost lives.

Scale captures the headlines. Nations boast of training ever larger neural nets, packed with more parameters than the previous record. Engineers speak of models "understanding" war the way chess engines understand the board. But size alone solves very little. A thousand-tonne engine still needs the right gearbox. A gigantic model misaligned to its domain is like a grandmaster taught only to play draughts walking onto a Go board:

formidable, yet misplaced. The real art lies not in sheer magnitude, but in precision—choosing and shaping the right model for the right task.

Consider the difference between a targeting model and a deception-detection model. On paper, both analyse sensor data and deliver a judgement. In practice, they inhabit different worlds. A targeting model thrives under structure. Armoured vehicles, missile launchers, radar dishes: these have crisp geometries, recognisable silhouettes, predictable behaviours. With enough examples, a convolutional network can learn to pick them from the clutter of a battlefield. When it errs, the errors are often visible and correctable. Engineers can adjust thresholds, retrain on mislabelled samples, or improve resolution. The model's world is difficult, but legible.

Deception-detection models live in fog. They search for anomalies that are, by definition, rare. A fishing trawler that transmits false coordinates, a convoy disguised as civilian traffic, a pilot masking transponder signals to appear harmless: these leave faint fingerprints. The model must infer intention from absence, inconsistency, silence. Where targeting models look for form, deception-detection models look for deviation. Data is scarcer. Signals are ambiguous. And because adversaries probe and adapt, yesterday's anomaly may become tomorrow's decoy. Training never ends; adversaries are part of the feedback loop.

This difference matters because failure modes diverge. A targeting model that confuses a tractor for a truck may waste ammunition or miss a threat. A deception model that fails may allow an enemy to slip through undetected—or worse, trigger false alarms that escalate tensions. In border zones where autonomous systems monitor airspace, one misclassification can summon interceptor aircraft or anti-air batteries. When nations operate at compressed timelines, an algorithm's panic spike can become a diplomat's worst headache.

Military planners sometimes assume that one large, general-purpose model can do everything: recognise vehicles, detect deception, choose targets, anticipate jamming. But intelligence does not work that way. The battlefield is not a single data stream; it is a cacophony of partly overlapping realities. A model skilled at reading infrared signatures might know nothing about acoustic anomalies. One that excels at analysing AIS maritime signals might be blind to radar clutter. Each model is a specialist. Using it outside its specialty invites failure that looks like insight.

Some states have learned this the hard way. A European research programme trained a large model to detect armoured vehicles in satellite imagery. In controlled tests it performed superbly. But deployed in a dusty theatre with heat distortions and cheap camouflage netting, the model's confidence evaporated. Meanwhile, a much smaller model—trained only on this region, on these sensor quirks, and on the specific behaviour of the units involved—proved far more reliable. The lesson was humiliating but instructive: bigger is not better if bigger means generic. A doctor with encyclopaedic medical knowledge is useless if she has never seen the disease endemic to your village. Domain fit outweighs prestige.

The private sector discovered this years ago. Retail models trained on Western consumer data misfire in cities where phones, shops, and payment habits differ. Voice models trained on broadcast speech stumble over dialects and accents. Surveillance models trained on orderly traffic patterns collapse when vehicles improvise. Militaries face the same truth, with the stakes multiplied. A model may be world-class in peacetime tests and still behave foolishly the first time an adversary tries to fool it.

This is why some intelligence officers distrust talk of "foundation models for war." They prefer modular arsenals of specialised systems rather than one grand machine. Specialists can be tuned, swapped, retrained. A foundation model that makes a catastrophic mistake contaminates everything built atop it. The diversity of models becomes a resilience strategy: no single failure cripples the whole.

The challenge deepens when systems must collaborate. On a patrol aircraft, a radar model may classify airborne objects by speed and altitude; an image model may classify shapes and heat signatures; a signals model may classify electromagnetic noise. A fusion model must synthesise these judgments. If one subsystem is miscalibrated, the final conclusion warps. A swarm of micro-models, each fallible, must find harmony. This is orchestration, not magic.

Even simple interactions can go sideways. In one multinational exercise, a ground-based radar detected a formation of aircraft behaving erratically. A separate model flagging transponder irregularities agreed: high threat. But a third model analysing radio chatter predicted friendly behaviour. The fusion system, designed to prioritise the most confident signal, classified the group as hostile. Pilots scrambled; alarms sounded. Hours later, investigators found the error: the radar model had been trained on an old dataset, blind to a new type of aircraft whose manoeuvring looked, statistically, like evasion. The system did not fail maliciously; it failed mathematically. Machines do not know when they are guessing.

Failures are rarely tidy. Some are theatrical—erroneous missile locks, phantom drones that vanish on inspection. Others are silent. A model begins to underweight a sensor; an anomaly detector becomes desensitised to small deviations; a behavioural model learns that certain risky movements are normal because they occur frequently in training data. The system still produces numbers and dashboards, and humans trust the glow of accuracy without noticing that the map has started to drift from the territory.

Engineers call this model drift; philosophers call it epistemic decay. The world changes faster than the model can remember. Without updated data, the machine falls out of step. And because modern models exist in layers—pretrained, fine-tuned, integrated—drift in one layer can poison the next. A single wrong assumption spreads across the stack, infecting predictions like a quiet fever.

Scale does matter. Larger models can learn richer abstractions, smooth out noise, and generalise across conditions. When trained on hyperspectral imagery, a large model might distinguish decoys from real aircraft because it notices subtle wavelength absorption patterns invisible to smaller systems. When parsing communications, a large language model might detect deceptive phrasing that statistical systems miss. But scale amplifies both strengths and weaknesses. A large model trained on biased data will propagate that bias more confidently. A mislabelled dataset becomes a scar across millions of parameters. Power, multiplied, is not always precision.

The most impressive systems today are not just large; they are grounded. They combine scale with domain-specific fine-tuning. A general vision model becomes a maritime scout only when fed years of ocean images, tides, behaviours, and vessel classes. A general speech model becomes an intelligence asset only when tuned on coded slang, radio static, and tactical brevity codes. Generality is a starting point, not a destination.

Some militaries have turned this into doctrine. They build models like regiments: scouts, analysts, interpreters, guards. The scout models flag anomalies. Analyst models classify threats. Interpreter models fuse multi-sensor data. Guard models detect adversarial interference. The stack resembles an organisation more than a monolith. If one regiment underperforms, another compensates. Humans sit atop this structure, issuing directives, asking questions, demanding justification. The myth of a single omnipotent AI gives way to a more realistic picture: a bureaucracy of specialised intelligences, each narrow, each fallible, yet powerful in concert.

But a darker tension sits beneath this architecture. Models are not neutral observers; they are students of our experiences. If we train them on past behaviour, we teach them to expect more of the same. In counterinsurgency, a model trained on years of roadside bomb attacks may assume they will continue, even when adversaries pivot to drones or jamming. In naval warfare, a model trained on peacetime shipping may underestimate adversarial misdirection. Every model carries a philosophy of the world—implicitly, silently. Humans must interrogate that philosophy, or risk outsourcing their assumptions to statistical ghosts.

This raises an uncomfortable question: how much should a commander trust a machine whose reasoning cannot be fully articulated? Some argue that if the predictions work, justification is irrelevant. Others insist that explanations are essential for accountability, especially when lives are at stake. Yet explainability often compromises performance. Forcing a model to provide transparent logic can weaken the very patterns that make it insightful. War has always traded certainty for speed. Models intensify that trade.

Human-machine teaming tries to bridge the divide. Analysts use models to surface patterns quickly, then apply judgment. But judgment itself can be distorted. If a system flags an object as hostile with 92 per cent confidence, a human may defer even when intuition says otherwise. Confidence scores seduce; they look scientific. But a confident mistake is still a mistake, and humans are prone to overtrust numbers presented with precision.

The deepest risk is subtle: when models succeed too often, humans stop asking how. They become operators of systems they no longer understand. The skill of interpretation atrophies. A generation raised on predictive dashboards may forget how to reason in their absence. Power shifts from competence to dependency.

Yet models also offer something strangely humane. They watch without fatigue, learn without resentment, and remember without distortion. They can free analysts from drudgery and highlight patterns that save civilian lives. In missile defence, models can predict trajectories early enough to intercept precisely rather than saturate an area with fire. In hostage rescue, models analysing movement through buildings can reduce guesswork and collateral damage. When tied to ethical guardrails—no-strike lists, geofencing, risk thresholds—models can become instruments of restraint rather than escalation.

The technology is not the threat. The complacency is.

Somewhere tonight, a deception-detection model will stare at shipping lanes and notice that a vessel is broadcasting a transponder identity that no longer exists. A targeting model will spot an artillery piece hidden under canvas, because its thermal signature betrays the lie. A fusion model will reconcile radar clutter and infrared glare to reveal a stealth drone drifting above a border. These systems are narrow, specialised, brittle in ways we often fail to appreciate. But they are not magic. Their power is earned: through data, tuning, architecture, and the relentless labour of annotation and calibration.

Magic attracts fear. Machinery demands responsibility.

The next generation of commanders will not ask whether machines can think; they will ask what each model sees, where it breaks, and how to pair it with others. They will treat models like tools, not gurus. And perhaps they will remember the drone that spotted the hostile lorry—not because the machine possessed intuition, but because it had learned patterns the human eye could not see.

One day, an adversary will design a decoy that slips past every model in the stack. The first warning may be silence—the most dangerous signal of all. Who will notice? Who will question the machine's confidence? Who will ask for evidence when the dashboard claims certainty?

The battlefield will not reward belief in magic. It will reward those who understand the machinery well enough to doubt it.

## Compute and chokepoints

A procurement officer in a medium-sized defence ministry once joked that buying cloud compute had become harder than buying missiles. It was only half a joke. When her country ordered a new generation of autonomous surveillance drones, the airframes arrived on schedule, the optics exceeded expectations, and the guidance software passed every simulator test. Yet the programme stalled because the ministry could not secure priority access to the high-performance cloud clusters required to train the models. The hardware was ready; the brains were not. A system that looked formidable in a briefing room proved useless without the invisible factories of computation to give it life.

Modern power hides in these quiet dependencies. Missiles and tanks can be counted. Compute cannot. It moves behind closed doors, inside chip fabs and cloud data centres, in export licences and allocation agreements. Armies that look capable on parade may collapse when their suppliers choke off advanced processors. Forces that train on borrowed compute may find their access revoked on the eve of a crisis. The battlefield is tilting towards invisible bottlenecks, where leverage is measured not in divisions, but in nanometres, bandwidth, and cooling capacity.

The paradox is stark. Artificial intelligence promises to upend warfare, yet the world's most advanced militaries depend on fragile supply chains that lead through a handful of companies in a handful of countries. A global arms race built on chips is, at heart, a race built on trust in strangers.

Chips are the beginning and the first choke. They are not interchangeable. Training large models demands processors with thousands of parallel cores, vast memory bandwidth, and specialised tensor units. Only a few firms can design them. Fewer still can manufacture them. The most advanced fabrication plants—fabs—cost tens of billions of dollars and require supply chains as complex as any military alliance. Extreme ultraviolet lithography machines, the crown jewels of chipmaking, are produced by a single company. Their components come from hundreds of suppliers. One earthquake, one embargo, one cyberattack can ripple across the globe.

For years, strategists treated chips as a commercial concern. Now they see them as sovereignty. If you cannot build or buy top-tier processors, you cannot train the models that make sense of battlefields. You can still fly jets, sail ships, and fire artillery, but you will fall behind in prediction, automation, and countermeasure. The danger is not defeat tomorrow, but irrelevance in five years.

Great powers understand this. One superpower has poured subsidies into domestic fabs, lured engineers with gilded salaries, and stockpiled lithography parts. Another has used export controls to deny competitors access to cutting-edge processors, forcing them to rely on older, slower chips that limit model scale. Nations that once competed in aircraft carriers now compete in nanometres: five, three, two. The smaller the transistor, the larger the neural net, the faster the inference. Shrinking silicon has become a strategic act.

But silicon alone is not enough. Models must be trained somewhere. Only a handful of firms operate data centres capable of training frontier-scale systems. Militaries rent cloud regions the way they once leased ports. If a nation lacks domestic cloud capacity, it must trust foreign companies to host its most sensitive workloads. That introduces an uncomfortable vulnerability: what happens when geopolitical tension collides with commercial policy?

In one notable episode, a defence agency attempted to book thousands of high-end graphical processing units for a classified simulation. The cloud provider hesitated, citing availability and export compliance. The simulation slipped. The procurement officer, frustrated, pointed out that if her government had ordered bombs rather than GPUs, delivery would have been easier. She was not being flippant. The bottleneck had shifted.

Domestically controlled cloud infrastructure sounds like a solution, but it is rarely simple. Building a sovereign cloud requires capital, talent, and patience. Data centres consume enormous power; the most advanced chips require exotic cooling systems. Engineers capable of tuning these clusters beneath classified constraints are scarce. Some states have turned to hybrid models: sensitive workloads run on sovereign clusters; training is burst to commercial cloud under encrypted compartments; inference runs at the edge, on-board aircraft or ships.

This patchwork works well until a crisis. When demand surges, nations without reliable access to elastic cloud capacity may find their models unable to retrain quickly enough. In a conflict where deception, jamming, and countermeasures evolve daily, stale models are a liability. Procuring compute becomes a race against both the adversary and the calendar.

Memory, often ignored in public debate, is another quiet chokepoint. Training advanced models is not only about flops—floating point operations—but about moving data fast enough to feed the processors. Memory bandwidth becomes a constraint as real as oil pipelines once were. Some militaries have warehouses full of GPUs that cannot operate at full capacity because they lack high-bandwidth memory or the networking fabric to stitch thousands of chips into a single computational organism. You can buy the parts, but if they cannot talk to each other at speed, you are polishing a fleet of tanks with empty fuel tanks.

Networking completes the triad. Distributed training works only if thousands of processors share gradients in microseconds. A slow interconnect ruins everything. The world's most powerful models rely on networking fabrics—InfiniBand, custom NVLink, advanced optical links—that only a few companies can produce. Shortages in fibre modules or switching chips can cripple national training schedules. The bottleneck is not always the headline chip; it might be a few grams of exotic metal inside a transceiver.

Military planners have begun to recognise that compute procurement resembles oil procurement in the early twentieth century. Access matters. Stockpiles matter. Diversification matters. Alliances matter. The army with the best tanks will lose to the army that has fuel. The drone with the best optics will lose to the drone whose models are freshest. Logistics, reborn yet again.

Export controls turn these dependencies into diplomatic weapons. When one superpower cut off access to advanced tensors processors, the targeted nation scrambled to repurpose older chips, redesign models, and accelerate domestic fabrication. Interim solutions emerged: training models in mixed precision, compressing weights, pruning architectures. But none of these matched the performance of cutting-edge silicon. Time became a geopolitical instrument.

Allies, too, feel the strain. A small NATO member might procure autonomous maritime drones, only to discover that the vendor uses cloud regions in a non-allied state. The naval chief must choose between operational ambition and sovereignty risk. Some programmes have been delayed for years while governments negotiate data residency and cloud control clauses. In defence contracts, "where the model is trained" has become as contentious as "where the missile is built."

Supply constraints reorder procurement priorities in unexpected ways. Instead of buying more drones, a ministry may invest in on-board inference chips, reducing reliance on cloud uplinks. Instead of training a single colossal model, an air force may adopt many smaller, specialised models that require less compute. Instead of relying on proprietary processors, a navy may fund open hardware efforts to diversify supply. Strategy shapes silicon, and silicon shapes strategy.

When availability shrinks, creativity flourishes. Engineers design algorithms that rely on less memory and fewer parameters. Training schedules prioritise mission-critical models; some updates are deferred. Militaries learn the art of computational triage. Not every unit needs frontier AI. For many missions, modest autonomy—well-tuned, robust, explainable—matters more than cutting-edge performance. Perfection becomes the enemy of sufficiency.

Yet no amount of efficiency erases the core vulnerability: global dependence on a tiny set of fabs. The world spends trillions on defence, but the majority of advanced chips come from a few factories built on geologically stable land with skilled labour and water-intensive supply chains. In strategic terms, these facilities are crown jewels and pressure points. A blockade, sabotage attempt, or diplomatic crisis could halt production for months, sending shockwaves through industries far beyond defence.

This risk has prompted improbable alliances. Rivals negotiate supply guarantees. Neutral states pour subsidies into indigenous fabs. Universities build programmes to train semiconductor engineers. In the Cold War, governments competed to place missiles near borders; today, they compete to place fabs within them. Infrastructure once invisible to citizens becomes as consequential as any military base.

Cloud allocation introduces new asymmetries. During peacetime, militaries can schedule jobs alongside commercial customers. In wartime, they need priority—and that priority must be enforceable. Some countries are drafting laws requiring cloud providers to guarantee defence access during emergencies. Others are exploring state-owned clouds for classified workloads. But even state clouds rely on imported chips, foreign toolchains, and global supply chains.

In one crisis simulation, a coalition force discovered that their cloud region was located in a state that declared neutrality. The provider, bound by local law, suspended military workloads. Models froze at outdated checkpoints. Drone fleets reverted to onboard inference only. The coalition's predictive advantage evaporated overnight. War-games rarely make headlines, but engineers remembered the lesson: geopolitics flows through data centres.

These technical bottlenecks have philosophical weight. Democracies depend on transparency and oversight; autocracies prioritise secrecy and control. Compute enforces its own logic. When a state relies on commercial cloud, oversight demands contractual visibility. When a state builds sovereign clouds, secrecy deepens. When chips are scarce, governments prioritise missions differently. Ethical guidelines written in peacetime may bend under logistical pressure. If only one model can be retrained before deployment, which mission receives it? Border surveillance? Anti-ship tracking? Counterterrorism? These are strategic and moral choices, disguised as IT scheduling.

There is also a cultural shift. Generals raised on aircraft and artillery now attend briefings on interconnect topology and yield rates. Procurement officers learn to read benchmark reports with the same scrutiny once reserved for armour thickness. The centre of gravity moves from the parade ground to the data centre. Power no longer looks like steel; it looks like racks and cables.

The human labour behind these systems is immense. Chip fabs operate at tolerances measured in atoms. Engineers tune cooling systems, manage voltage irregularities, and test wafers with microscopic probes. Cloud operators balance resource allocation, guard against cyber intrusion, and patch vulnerabilities in real time. A single bug or misconfiguration can stall a training run that costs millions. The glamour of autonomy rests on the shoulders of thousands of unseen workers.

Strategists speak of deterrence as perception: the adversary must believe you can respond quickly and decisively. Compute changes the psychology. If your models retrain faster, you adapt faster. If your cloud clusters scale overnight, you surge capacity. Deterrence becomes dynamic. But if an adversary suspects you lack compute, they may gamble boldly, assuming your models will lag behind battlefield deception. Conventional deterrence relied on visible strength. Computational deterrence relies on invisible infrastructure.

Yet power gained through compute is power that can be taken away. Sanctions can starve fabs of vital chemicals. Export controls can choke supplies of high-bandwidth memory. Cyber operations can corrupt firmware. Cloud providers can be pressured by courts or governments. A nation that feels secure may wake to find its models frozen, its clusters dark.

Perhaps the most uncomfortable truth is that the battlefield is no longer the only contested space. Competition unfolds in patent offices, standards committees, and semiconductor toolchains. A firmware vulnerability can disable more drones than an anti-air battery. A delay in lithography export can hobble a nation's AI ambitions more effectively than a blockade. Warfare bleeds into supply chains.

Some military leaders argue that states must become chipmakers, whatever the cost. Others view this as folly—too expensive, too slow. They advocate alliances: shared fabs, shared cloud, shared sovereignty. But alliances cut both ways. Partners can withdraw. Politics can shift. Dependence breeds leverage.

The procurement officer who struggled to book cloud compute for her drones eventually secured a deal. But she never forgot the vulnerability. Her next acquisition included on-board processors powerful enough for local training and inference. The drones could learn in flight, independent of distant servers. It was slower and more expensive, but it was sovereign. Strategy etched into silicon.

Somewhere, a new generation of models is being trained in secret clusters. Satellites glide over oceans, pipelines hum with data, pilots trust targeting updates. But beneath the choreography lies the bottleneck. Those who control compute control tempo. Those who control tempo shape the future.

What happens when a major power loses access to advanced chips for a year? What happens when cloud providers take sides? What happens when a single fab falters?

The next arms race may be measured not in missiles launched, but in wafers shipped.

## Doctrine eats demos

A defence minister once stood on a runway watching a drone demonstration that felt like the future made flesh. The aircraft launched itself, navigated autonomously, spotted mock targets, and returned precisely to its strip. Engineers beamed. The cameras rolled. Journalists wrote breathless headlines. Six months later, the same drones were deployed to an actual coastal theatre—salt air, unpredictable winds, patchy comms—and half of them faltered. The autopilot struggled with magnetic interference, the object detector confused spray for smoke, and the maintenance crew lacked spare parts for a sensor that failed in humidity. On paper, the system was revolutionary. In the field, it was expensive clutter. The minister learnt an old military truth in a new technological age: prototypes win applause; doctrine wins wars.

Novelty dominates headlines—hypersonic missiles, swarming drones, autonomous guard towers. Yet the militaries that quietly dominate are not those with the flashiest technology, but those able to integrate systems into real operations, sustain them under stress, and train human crews to trust and tame them. Demos are theatre. Doctrine is habit. And habit, drilled over years, engrains victory.

When strategists say *doctrine eats demos*, they do not mean innovation is unimportant. They mean invention is only the first move. Some of the most advanced systems ever built died on the vine because no unit could actually field them. Commanders distrusted interfaces. Technicians found maintenance impossible without bespoke tools. Rules of engagement did not permit autonomous targeting. The system was too fragile to reload, too complex to patch, too specialised to adapt. By the time engineers simplified it, a humbler rival had already begun flying missions.

Consider the fate of an autonomous reconnaissance platform tested by a coastal navy. In trials, the vessel identified suspicious boats before radar even saw them. The demo dazzled. But the platform was designed by a civilian contractor who assumed pristine networks and unlimited bandwidth. In real maritime operations, storms and electronic interference shredded the link. The vessel could not pass data back fast enough. Operators reverted to manual override and, feeling foolish, mothballed the entire system. A less sophisticated, but rugged, platform—designed with salt-resistant parts, offline inference, and intuitive controls—replaced it. The winner was not the smartest, but the one that could be maintained.

Doctrine is the discipline that turns brilliant one-offs into reliable assets: the checklists, playbooks, safety protocols, maintenance cycles, and training programmes that ensure a system works on the worst day as well as the best. It is the bridge between genius and usefulness.

Training is the first pillar. Autonomous systems behave differently from conventional equipment. Pilots must learn to supervise algorithms, not just fly aircraft. Artillery crews must learn to interpret sensor-driven recommendations, not merely calculate trajectories. Infantry must learn what to do when an armed drone loses its link, stalls, or misidentifies a target.

In exercises, a curious pattern appears: a new autonomous asset performs well when operated by its designers. When handed to a regular unit with mixed experience and imperfect briefing, performance collapses. This gap is not a technical flaw. It is a human one. Crews trained for years on conventional gear carry intuitions that can sabotage new systems. Some mistrust automation and override too quickly; others defer too much and fail to question dubious recommendations. Only repeated drills—under fatigue, under jamming, under artificial fog—reset those intuitions.

Simulator feedback loops have become invaluable. Pilots practise intercepting hostile drones in virtual skies where the algorithms learn alongside them. Tank crews rehearse manoeuvres with predictive targeting aids that adjust based on terrain and enemy patterns. Every mistake becomes training data. Every near-miss refines the model. The simulator is not merely rehearsal; it is co-evolution. Humans learn the system. The system learns the humans.

Militaries that excel in autonomous warfare do not simply deploy new gear; they update entire curricula. Basic training incorporates AI literacy. Crews learn data hygiene. Officers learn to interpret model confidence intervals. Even logisticians learn how to schedule retraining for predictive maintenance engines. Doctrine makes autonomy ordinary.

Rules of engagement are the second pillar. A system's behaviour must not only be effective; it must be legitimate. Armed democracies cannot rely on black-box brutality. They require auditability and restraint. That means doctrine must specify when autonomy may act, when humans must intervene, and how accountability is preserved when multiple systems collaborate.

One air force deployed a semi-autonomous targeting module that recommended fire solutions during close support missions. In testing, the system was impeccable. But commanders realised that, in real combat, pilots under stress might defer excessively, assuming machine predictions were infallible. The air force rewrote its doctrine. Pilots were trained to challenge, not accept, the machine. After-action reviews flagged every instance where pilots overruled or deferred. Far from slowing missions, this doctrine sharpened performance: pilots learnt when to trust the model and when to demand corroboration. Autonomy enhanced judgement; it did not replace it.

By contrast, a rival nation integrated a similar tool without revising doctrine. Pilots assumed the machine's confidence scores reflected truth. They launched ordnance based on sensor fusion they could not explain. A misclassification triggered international outrage. Engineers fixed the bug within weeks, but the political damage endured for years. The system failed. Doctrine failed more.

Maintenance is the third pillar—rarely celebrated, always decisive. Some autonomous platforms are so complex that they require vendor engineers on site, custom calibration tools, or imported spare parts. A weapon that cannot be serviced forward is a weapon that sits in a warehouse. Enemy action is not the only threat; dust, humidity, sand, voltage irregularities, and battery decay quietly kill systems in the field. Sophisticated autonomy can crumble in harsh climates while simpler systems thrive.

One army refused to purchase a cutting-edge ground robot until its technicians could fully strip, clean, and rebuild it in the field without corporate assistance. Manufacturers resisted. The army stood firm. Years later, that decision proved wise. When conflict disrupted supply lines, the force with rugged, modular robots maintained them in forward bases, cannibalising parts and printing replacements. Their opponent's sleeker robots failed once the vendor withdrew support. Maintenance, not innovation, defined superiority.

Doctrine requires not only tools but philosophy: assume nothing works until proven under pressure. The best militaries test autonomy under rain, salt, dust, cold, jamming, misinformation, exhausted crews, depleted batteries, partial failure. They do not assume a system will behave as it did in a conference hall.

The tension comes into sharp relief when commanders choose between two proposals. One demo shows a swarm of sleek aircraft co-ordinating flawlessly on a sunny test range. The crowd gasps. The other shows a squat, ugly quadcopter crashing, rebooting, rejoining the swarm, and completing its mission despite broken propellers, jammed links, and corrupted GPS. The second demo is less cinematic—but far more valuable. War is friction. The better demo is the demo that survives failure.

Doctrine privileges resilience over elegance. A system that cannot fail safely is a liability. A system that cannot degrade gracefully cannot be trusted. In some units, commanders force autonomy drills where one component is intentionally disabled mid-mission. Pilots must land using onboard inference alone. Gunners must aim with reduced predictive assistance. These drills develop muscle memory. They create humility. They teach crews that automation is support, not salvation.

Human psychology matters. Crews who never practise failure grow brittle. Crews who expect failure grow confident.

There is a philosophical undercurrent here. Autonomy promises efficiency, but war is not an engineering exercise. It is lived by humans under fear, confusion, and responsibility. Doctrine exists to protect the human at the centre of the system. It establishes rituals: pre-flight checklists, escalation thresholds, kill-switch protocols, audit trails. These rituals are not bureaucratic drag; they are ethical infrastructure.

In one country, every autonomous strike must log a rationale that can be reviewed by inspectors. In another, sandboxes isolate adversarial inputs to prevent spoofing from contaminating models. In a third, an "ethical red team" periodically reviews logs for bias, drift, or unexplained anomalies. These are not mere formalities. They allow the public to trust that autonomy does not mean unaccountable violence. Doctrine, in this sense, binds power to principle.

Without doctrine, technology becomes theatre. With doctrine, technology becomes institution.

The most forward-looking militaries are discovering something counterintuitive: autonomy increases the need for training, not decreases it. When predictive targeting was introduced, some officers assumed pilots would need fewer hours. The opposite happened. Pilots needed more time to learn how predictions could fail—how cloud cover distorted infrared, how jammers tricked radar, how adversaries shaped decoys. The training syllabus grew denser. Flight hours increased. Simulators became indispensable.

A general remarked drily, "Autonomy didn't free our pilots from thinking. It forced them to think differently." The line captures the evolution of doctrine: not blind trust in machines, but educated partnership.

Simulator feedback loops are the heart of this transformation. Pilots fly simulated missions where the models misbehave by design: false alarms, slow updates, adversarial interference. Every error becomes data. Models retrained on this feedback improve. Pilots retrained through these drills deepen intuition. Humans and machines refine each other.

The result is a learning organism—faster than bureaucracy, quicker than hardware cycles, powered by practice. Doctrine is no longer static text in a binder; it is living code embedded in training and feedback.

Yet the world is full of temptations. Politicians adore shiny demos. Industry promises miracles. Vendors pitch autonomy as plug-and-play. The path of least resistance is to buy the flashiest prototype and bolt it into the force. The harder path—the disciplined path—is to ask: who will maintain it? Who will override it? Who will audit it? How will it behave under fog, sand, jamming, fatigue, and fear?

History's lesson is unforgiving. The side that rehearses relentlessly usually defeats the side that merely innovates. Nations that invest in simulations, drills, spare parts, and technical education gain compounding returns. Each year, their crews become more fluent with autonomy. Each year, their doctrine becomes sharper. Novelty loses its luster; reliability takes its throne.

There is a reason fighter squadrons run night sorties in driving rain and submarine crews rehearse silent failures in claustrophobic steel. Discipline turns unpredictability into expectation. Doctrine builds victory out of monotony.

The future of warfare will be shaped by code, but sustained by culture. Machines will plan, predict, and decide, yet humans will remain accountable. The question is not whether autonomous systems work in ideal conditions, but whether they work in real ones—and whether soldiers trust them enough to use them under pressure.

Somewhere right now, an engineer is polishing a spectacular demo for a VIP audience. Somewhere else, a squadron is running a wearying drill: jammed sensors, glitching displays, partial autonomy. One of those moments will appear in headlines. The other will shape the battlefield.

Which matters more?

The answer is written in doctrine.

## From prototype to posture

During a coastal air-defence exercise, a new autonomous radar classifier stunned the observers' gallery. It tracked incoming targets through clutter and jamming, labelled hostile signatures with crisp confidence scores, and suggested firing solutions faster than the operators could blink. The generals nodded with satisfaction. The minister smiled for the cameras. Yet after the applause faded, the system was quietly returned to its shipping case. Why? Because one unglamorous question could not be answered: could every radar station in the force—across deserts, mountains, storms, power cuts and patchy networks—run it reliably, safely, and with rules of engagement that politicians and lawyers would approve?

A prototype is a promise. A posture is a commitment. Bridging the gap is the true art of military innovation.

Every armed force is littered with ghosts of forgotten prototypes: brilliant, breathtaking, technically dazzling—and utterly unusable beyond a handful of showcase trials. Some failed because they were too complex for crews to maintain. Others because they broke procurement rules. Many simply could not survive the grim arithmetic of scale: thousands of units, thousands of unpredictable environments, thousands of potential failure modes. A prototype is curated theatre; a posture demands systemic endurance.

Why is the path so difficult? Because moving from "works once" to "works always, everywhere, with everyone" requires a transformation in culture, logistics, training, politics, and law. No algorithm, however elegant, escapes these realities.

The first milestone is validation under friction. In the lab, sensors are calibrated, data flows clean, and adversaries behave like polite actors following a script. Out in the world, autonomy meets chaos: sandstorms that grind motors to dust, cloud cover that confuses infrared, spoofers that throw false signals into the wind, soldiers who operate on two hours' sleep, and commanders who demand last-minute mission changes. A system that dazzles when coddled often stumbles when reality intrudes.

The best militaries test for this early. They feed lies to their own models. They corrupt GPS. They inject bad data. They simulate power failures. They demand that drones land with jammed telemetry and that vehicles re-route when satellite feeds drop. The prototype learns humility. The engineers learn what *really* breaks it—not just in theory, but in the hands of an exhausted corporal at 3 a.m.

The second milestone is interoperability. One air-defence unit may love a new autonomous classifier, but can the neighbouring brigades integrate it without tearing up legacy communications? Can their command systems read its outputs? Can allied forces plug in without seeing classified code? Integration is often the graveyard of innovation. A brilliant tool that cannot talk to anything becomes an island of excellence in a sea of incompatibility.

A European air force once deployed a predictive targeting system to five squadrons. It worked perfectly on the aircraft it had been designed for. But retrofitting older platforms proved painful. Interfaces were mismatched. Data formats clashed. Bandwidth was insufficient. Within months, the project shrank to a single elite unit—useful, but strategically irrelevant. Meanwhile, a rival state adopted a simpler, less advanced system that integrated easily with aging dashboards and secure radios. Within a year, it was standard across the fleet. Integration beat novelty.

Phased rollouts have become the norm in intelligent air defence. Rather than deploy everywhere at once, militaries push autonomy into one battery, then one regiment, then one theatre. Each phase uncovers new frictions—software bugs in cold climates, crew habits that defeat automation, legal questions about autonomous escalation. The design evolves. Doctrine rewrites. Maintenance manuals expand. By the time the system reaches full posture, it no longer resembles the lab demo. It resembles a soldier.

The third milestone is trust. Not theoretical trust, but lived trust: crews who know what the system does well, where it fails, and how to correct it. Without trust, autonomy becomes ballast—equipment that commanders hesitate to activate when stakes are high. Trust is earned through repetition: simulator drills, live-fire exercises, after-action reviews, and the slow accumulation of human intuition around machine behaviour.

A naval officer once remarked that his crew trusted their autonomous sonar "only because they had seen it fail." The line sounds counterintuitive. In fact, it captures the essence of military confidence. A system that has never failed has never been tested. Crews want to know how autonomy behaves under stress: when the sea is rough, when signals bounce, when the network flickers. If the machine fails safely and predictably, trust deepens. If failure means chaos or mystery, trust evaporates.

Trust also flows upward—to lawyers, parliaments, civilians. Politicians must be able to stand before their public when something goes wrong and say: we had guardrails, logs, oversight; the system followed the rules we set. Without this legitimacy, no democratic state will permit autonomous weapons to move from prototype to posture. The technology may be ready. The politics may not.

This is why kill-switch governance has become standard in phased deployments. Every autonomous system capable of lethal or strategic action must include mechanisms for human override, audit logging, rollback, and safe shutdown. Some are technical: encrypted remote abort codes, physical interlocks, geo-fencing, no-strike lists. Others are procedural: dual-authorisation requirements, red-team penetration tests, periodic safety audits by inspectors who are not in the chain of command. These safeguards may frustrate engineers eager to ship. But they are the price of legitimacy.

The fourth milestone is sustainment. A prototype is maintained by its creators. A posture must be maintained by thousands of technicians who have never met the engineering team. That requires standard parts, robust documentation, spare stockpiles, and repair protocols that work in forward bases. If autonomy depends on shipping components across oceans or calling vendor support in a crisis, it will fail as soon as war begins.

A Southeast Asian army purchased a fleet of semi-autonomous ground vehicles that performed beautifully in trials. Two years later, dust infiltrated the optic housings, gumming the gimbals. Replacement parts took months to arrive. Mechanics lacked calibration tools. Batteries decayed faster than predicted. Half the fleet was grounded. New procurement guidelines were issued: no system could be adopted without proof that it could be maintained with local parts, local skills, and local diagnostics. The vendor protested. The army held its ground.

Sustainment also includes software. Autonomy invites continuous updates—new weights, improved classifiers, patched vulnerabilities. But warzones are hostile to version control. Some units miss patches due to connectivity; others apply updates that introduce regressions. Eventually, one squad is running Model 14, another Model 17, another Model 12. Chaos creeps in. The prototype has become a family of cousins. A posture requires governance: update windows, rollback policies, checksum validation, and secure distribution channels.

The fifth milestone is legal integration. Autonomous systems touch nearly every branch of law: arms export controls, targeting rules, privacy statutes, electromagnetic regulations, and humanitarian norms. In some countries, a system cannot be deployed until its audit logs satisfy parliamentary oversight. In others, foreign-built autonomy faces restrictions on data residency. What looks simple in code becomes complex in statute.

Integrated air defence offers a telling example. When one alliance deployed an AI-assisted radar classifier, it faced a thorny question: could allied officers trust predictions made by a system trained on data they were legally forbidden to inspect? The answer came through governance, not technology. A multinational oversight board verified model performance using red-teamed evaluations rather than code access. Nations accepted the system *because* the governance framework was robust. The model was a guest; the oversight was sovereign.

The sixth milestone is strategic alignment. A nation may have the resources to adopt an autonomous system force-wide, but should it? Some technologies are better suited to elite units than mass deployment. Some missions benefit more from autonomy than others. A prototype that promises broad utility may, after years of testing, prove ideal only for narrow tasks. Accepting this is maturity, not failure.

One state learned this with an autonomous jamming drone designed to suppress enemy air defence. In theory, thousands could swarm over a battlefield. In practice, maintaining the drones in bulk proved prohibitive. Instead, the air force assigned them to a handful of specialised teams who trained relentlessly and treated the drones as precision instruments. Impact grew, not shrank. Scale is not always strength. Sometimes posture means depth, not breadth.

And then comes the final milestone: cultural absorption. When an autonomous system stops being "the new system" and becomes simply "the system", posture has been achieved. Manuals reflect it. Training academies teach it. Unit folklore includes its quirks. Politicians budget for its maintenance without debate. New recruits assume it has always existed.

A commander in one Nordic country described the moment vividly. His air-defence batteries had used autonomous threat classifiers for three years. During a live-fire drill, the system paused, uncertain whether a radar return was hostile or weather clutter. Without audible command, the operators instinctively cross-checked sensors, verified signatures, and authorised fire manually. The system had become a partner, not a novelty. No one even mentioned it in the after-action report. That invisibility was the proof of success.

Yet this journey contains an unresolved tension. Autonomy evolves rapidly. Militaries move slowly—for good reasons. A prototype might become obsolete by the time it clears legal review, integration testing, training, and sustainment planning. The pace of innovation strains the pace of institution.

Some argue that states must accept greater risk: faster adoption, quicker rollouts, fewer guardrails. They warn that adversaries will not wait for parliamentary committees. Others counter that legitimacy and safety matter more than speed. A nation that rushes autonomy into combat without discipline may suffer a catastrophic mistake that freezes adoption for a generation.

The truth sits uneasily between them. A prototype that never reaches posture is wasted promise. A posture built without caution is a loaded gun with an unpredictable trigger.

Somewhere right now, a research lab is testing a sensor-fusion model that could transform air defence. It may ingest radar, lidar, infrared, signals intelligence and satellite tracks, weaving them into a coherent threat map. In the lab, it is elegant. In the field, it will have to survive dust, jamming, cyber probing, power fluctuation, human fatigue, and parliamentary oversight. If it reaches posture, it will not be the same model that dazzled in the demo. It will be wiser, heavier with doctrine, shaped by failure, born of compromise. In that evolution—from prototype to posture—lies the true measure of military technological power.

The unanswered question lingers: in the next crisis, which nations will wield systems hardened by training, law, maintenance and trust—and which will be left with prototypes and press releases?

# Chapter 2

# Speed, Autonomy, and Escalation

A pilot once described the moment her cockpit changed forever. She was flying a routine patrol when the threat-detection feed began to pulse—not with radar locks or missile trails, but with probabilities. *Potential hostile drone, 62 per cent confidence. Heat signature abnormal. Recommendation: intercept.* The machine had already cross-referenced satellite tracks, electromagnetic noise, and patterns of behaviour. While she was still squinting at the sky, the aircraft was steering itself into firing position. The decision was hers, yet the tempo belonged to the algorithm. By the time her squadron commander radioed authorisation, the target had already vanished into cloud. "I wasn't flying the jet," she said afterwards. "I was supervising a decision that was happening faster than I could understand."

This is the new texture of military speed. Not the brute pace of jets or missiles, but the silent acceleration of perception and judgement. Machines see patterns long before humans register danger. They track hundreds of targets, forecast manoeuvres, and recommend options with a confidence that can feel both reassuring and unnerving. The loop between sensing and striking is shrinking. The risk is not merely that decisions happen faster, but that the time for hesitation—the space where diplomacy and doubt could once intervene—is collapsing.

War was never slow, but it used to breathe. Detection, interpretation, deliberation, command: these steps contained natural pauses. Officers could sleep on a warning. Generals could ask for more data. Politicians could weigh consequences. As autonomy slips into the weave of operations, those pauses are thinning. A radar spike that took minutes to assess now takes milliseconds. A swarm that once required a formation of pilots now coordinates itself. The chain of command stretches, yet the timeline compresses. The strategists who fear speed are not frightened of machines; they are frightened of misunderstandings that unfold faster than anyone can correct.

Speed alone would be disruptive. Speed paired with autonomy is destabilising. Military planners divide human control into familiar modes: human *in* the loop—where every action requires explicit approval; human *on* the loop—where machines act, but humans supervise; and human *out* of the loop—where systems execute missions without real-time oversight. In practice, these boundaries blur. A "human on the loop" may be watching dozens of streams, unable to intervene meaningfully. A "human in the loop" may be presented with a single glowing button—approve or deny—while the machine handles everything else. Control becomes a theatre of supervision, not its substance.

In a multinational exercise, one coalition tested a semi-autonomous drone swarm tasked with tracking hostile missile launchers. Each pilot had veto authority—if the swarm misbehaved, they could abort. But the swarm reconfigured so quickly, passing control from drone to drone, that by the time a pilot tried to intervene, the window had closed. The human veto existed on paper. In time-critical reality, it was little more than comfort. The lesson was sobering: autonomy can outpace authority.

Allied operations magnify the tension. When systems built by different nations, trained on different datasets, and governed by different laws operate in the same airspace, who holds responsibility? A missile defence node built by a private contractor may feed targeting suggestions into an alliance command structure. A cloud-based fusion model operating in another jurisdiction may refine those suggestions. If a civilian airliner is misclassified, where does accountability land—in the cockpit, the command centre, the vendor's data lab, or the cloud provider's region? The chain of causation frays as quickly as the chain of command.

And yet militaries adopt autonomy for a reason. Machines can handle scale that overwhelms human cognition. They see patterns in noise. They warn of ambushes before scouts hear engines. They calculate safe firing windows between allied units in dense battlespace. To reject autonomy is to discard safety as well as speed. The question, then, is not whether humans should leave the loop, but how the loop must expand to include machines without erasing judgement.

Speed and autonomy reshape escalation in ways classical theorists never conceived. In the past, escalation ladders were mapped in visible increments: troop deployments, missile tests, naval blockades. Now, escalation can begin with electrons. A nation that spoofs another's sensor feed, steals training data, or blocks access to cloud compute has altered the balance of power without firing a shot. Is this an attack? A provocation? A grey-zone nuisance?

A fighter pilot sees a radar track jump erratically. Is it stealth? Weather? Or an adversary modifying sensor inputs to make drones misclassify friendly aircraft as threats? A naval commander watches a swarm of surface drones veer off course. Is the autonomy confused, or is an enemy inserting fake map tiles into the navigation pipeline? In these moments, the line between technical malfunction and hostile action blurs. A misinterpreted anomaly can become a casus belli.

Some states have already begun to redraw their escalation ladders. They treat model sabotage—poisoning training data, corrupting weights, degrading edge inference—as acts of strategic significance. They respond to cloud denial—blocking access to compute required for retraining models—as they once responded to arms embargoes. The battlefield has expanded to include the infrastructure of intelligence itself.

All this demands fail-safes—technical, human, and institutional. The most conservative forces design "fail-closed" autonomy: if anything looks abnormal, the system shuts down, hands control back to operators, and records logs for review. The most aggressive forces design "fail-open" autonomy: if communications degrade or sensors conflict, the system continues, trusting its own inference over uncertain guidance. In some missions, fail-open is necessary: missile defence cannot pause to ask permission. In others, fail-open is catastrophic: border surveillance that misclassifies civilians as hostile cannot be allowed to barrel onward.

Testing these fail-safes is delicate work. Engineers deliberately feed adversarial inputs into targeting models, inject noise into radar streams, jam GPS, scramble telemetry, and spoof satellites. They watch how systems degrade. Do the models panic? Do they hallucinate threats? Do they become inert? Red teams probe the cracks. Safety boards audit the results. In the most advanced units, these tests never end. Every week, something breaks on purpose.

Legal scholars and ethicists join the process. How should logs be archived to prove that a model behaved properly? Who reviews them? How often must safety drills occur? Air forces have begun running "no-fault override days", where pilots must take control from autonomy even when it is performing perfectly. The mission is not to prove the machine works, but to prove that humans still know how to wrestle back control when it matters.

As autonomy spreads, crisis management must evolve. Cold War playbooks assume that leaders have hours—if not days—to assess intentions, mobilise forces, and open backchannel communications. But what if the first sign of crisis is a machine alerting to a pattern that looks like an attack? What if an autonomous battery fires on what it thinks is an inbound missile but is actually a calibration glitch? What if a swarm crosses a border because it misread a GPS fence? When machines accelerate the front end of conflict, human diplomacy must accelerate the back end.

Some think the answer is algorithmic diplomacy: shared incident taxonomies, hotlines for model misbehaviour, protocols for pausing autonomy without losing face. Others argue that human commanders must remain the final safeguard—that no autonomous response should ever trigger irreversible escalation. But how to enforce this when seconds matter?

The most forward-thinking states rehearse crisis playbooks for algorithms. They create rollback mechanisms: if a model behaves oddly, revert to last week's weights. They schedule automatic pauses: if two sensors disagree, halt autonomy until a human reviews. They build kill-switches that are not merely technical, but political: clear authority for a commander to defy the model, even when the model is statistically right.

These safeguards do not slow modern forces; they preserve the legitimacy that allows them to operate. A nation that can explain how its autonomy paused, logged, and reported an anomaly is a nation that can keep diplomatic channels open. The alternative is a world where no one can distinguish aggression from accident.

Speed, autonomy, escalation: each concept is challenging on its own. Together, they change the grammar of conflict. The promise is agility, precision, and lives saved. The peril is miscalculation in the dark. A future crisis may turn not on missiles fired, but on milliseconds of machine inference.

Somewhere tonight, a fighter pilot will receive a machine recommendation faster than she can blink. Somewhere else, a swarm will plot its next formation without waiting for human command. In quiet rooms, legal officers draft rules for machines that have no concept of intent. And somewhere in the shadows, an adversary is testing how a single corrupted data stream might send a rival's algorithms into panic.

When conflict moves at the speed of computation, who carries the burden of judgement? And when a machine can start a war with a misread signal, who decides when to stop? The answers will shape the century.

## Compressed decision time

A coastal air-defence battery once spent seven long minutes tracking a radar contact that flickered like a nervous heartbeat. The operators suspected a reconnaissance drone, but the signal kept dipping in and out, confusing the ageing displays. By the time a decision was made, the object—a civilian aircraft broadcasting a faulty transponder—had already passed. No harm done, and perhaps no one beyond the bunker ever knew the incident occurred. Today, seven minutes would be an eternity. In a modern theatre, an algorithm would flag the anomaly, cross-match satellite tracks, compare patterns against hundreds of recent incursions, and recommend an intercept before anyone lifted a headset. The officer's dilemma has not changed—friend or foe, fire or hold—but the time to choose has collapsed from minutes to seconds. And when choice is compressed, error becomes more treacherous.

The promise of predictive targeting is seductively simple: find dangers before they bloom, reveal threats invisible to unaided eyes, and cut the kill-chain short enough to save lives. The reality is more complex. Machines may react faster than humans, but they also force humans to react faster than they should. The observe–orient–decide–act cycle—the OODA loop that has governed military decision-making since the Cold War—is being squeezed until judgment becomes the bottleneck. Intelligence arrives in a flood, not a stream. Targets are not found so much as inferred. The question is no longer "What do we see?" but "What does the model believe we should fear?"

Predictive systems thrive on pattern. They ingest radar sweeps, satellite imagery, electromagnetic noise, AIS maritime transponders, social media geolocation, even weather fronts. They stitch these layers into probability maps: a vessel altered course in a way that historically preceded smuggling; a ground signature resembles a mobile launcher packing up; a heat anomaly tracks with drone swarms. In the right conditions, these systems expose dangers before any human notices them. Yet every pattern is also a prediction, and every prediction carries a shadow of uncertainty. A cloud's edge may mimic a missile plume. A fishing boat may drift like a gunrunner's skiff. When algorithms are trusted to react, uncertainty becomes risk.

During a NATO naval drill, an AI-assisted targeting module flagged an approaching craft as suspicious. It matched dozens of features linked to prior ambushes: irregular speed, periods of radio silence, course corrections towards a high-value vessel. The crew prepared countermeasures. Only when the ship closed to within visual range did they recognise it as an unarmed research boat with defective navigation—an innocent vessel that had simply behaved like a hostile one. The drill ended without loss, but the episode haunted planners. If the model had been wired into an autonomous defence battery, its well-trained suspicion might have triggered a lethal mistake. The technology had not failed; it had reasoned within its training. But compressed time leaves little room for mercy.

Some commanders argue that machines prevent harm rather than cause it. Autonomous tracking reduces fatigue, filters noise, and suppresses human panic. They point to missile defence systems that intercept threats in seconds, saving cities and ships. They remind us that human operators, overwhelmed by clutter, have historically made catastrophic misidentifications of their own. Yet the paradox endures: the faster the system, the more humans must trust it at the very moment they understand it the least.

Speed changes the meaning of responsibility. A traditional fire-control officer might spend minutes weighing evidence: radar confirmation, radio checks, flight paths, command authority. When a model produces a recommendation in milliseconds, the officer's role shifts from interpreter to validator. Instead of asking "What is happening?", they are asked "Is there any reason not to believe the machine?" This reversal is subtle, but profound. Humans are notoriously poor at scrutinising recommendations under extreme time pressure. The machine becomes the default decision-maker; the officer becomes the exception-handler. It is the difference between steering a car and grabbing the wheel only when the autopilot swerves.

In multinational contexts, this pressure multiplies. A predictive system built by one nation may send alerts to another. A cloud-based fusion model hosted overseas may feed targeting suggestions into local batteries. Even when human approval is required, the approving officer may be hundreds of miles away, relying on abstract data from remote sensors. When seconds matter, this delay can mean the difference between prevention and retaliation. The model closes the distance between sensor and shooter; the alliance's bureaucracy does not.

Consider a scenario feared by many naval strategists: ambiguous radar tracks over contested waters. A model detects a pattern matching previous drone incursions. It suggests a pre-emptive intercept by a nearby frigate. The frigate's command centre, trusting the model's high confidence score, prepares to engage. But the track is actually a cluster of migrating birds, distorted by atmospheric interference. The longer the chain of human verification, the safer the sky—but the more likely a real threat slips past. The shorter the chain, the more likely a dreadful accident occurs. Neither outcome is acceptable, yet compressed time insists both are possible.

Some militaries try to solve the dilemma by inserting artificial pauses—micro-moratoria in which action is delayed unless confidence thresholds are met. Others require two independent models to confirm a threat. But these safeguards assume a forgiving battlespace. A hypersonic weapon does not pause while humans think. A swarm of drones does not hover politely. In high-speed conflict, hesitation can appear as weakness, inviting escalation by the adversary.

Others pursue the opposite path: automation with human override. Systems act unless explicitly stopped. The pilot or commander is expected to cancel a lethal strike if something feels wrong. But psychological studies show that humans rarely override fast, confident systems. The machine's fluency can appear as certainty. Operators fear looking foolish, insubordinate, or slow. And as automation expands, younger officers may never develop the instincts to challenge the model. If a generation grows up letting algorithms fight for them, what happens the day the algorithm is wrong?

It is tempting to imagine a perfect future where models explain their reasoning, visualising patterns in ways humans can audit instantly. Research is heading there, but explanation does not guarantee understanding. If a model says a radar track appears hostile because its motion is "statistically anomalous", what is the right human response? Intercept, request additional data, or ignore? Clarity matters, but time constrains every choice.

Philosophers of war have long argued that judgement requires not just data, but context—motives, constraints, intent. Algorithms excel at correlation, not meaning. They can flag the ship that moves strangely; they cannot know that its captain is avoiding a storm. They can warn of a pattern that looks like an ambush; they cannot know that the rebel convoy is fleeing, not attacking. Human operators once supplied that context instinctively. As automation grows, the risk is that context fades behind abstraction.

Yet there is another side to this story. Compressed decision time can save lives. A model that spots a missile launch ten seconds earlier can give civilians a chance to take shelter. A fusion system that identifies friendly forces with greater precision can prevent fratricide. Anti-drone batteries that react faster than a human can protect power stations and hospitals. Machines are not merely instruments of speed; they are instruments of safety—if calibrated with humility.

The tension lies in balance. Too slow, and war becomes disaster. Too fast, and war becomes accident. The sweet spot is narrow, fragile, and shifting with every new deployment.

Some states address compressed time by drilling relentlessly. Pilots rehearse taking control from autonomy even when it feels unnecessary. Naval crews practice ignoring confident alerts until human confirmation arrives. Ground operators simulate chaotic radar clutter and force themselves to act carefully under pressure. Instead of trusting machines blindly, they learn to distrust them productively—to question probability without dismissing prediction. In the best units, human and machine become partners, not master and servant.

Others embrace geopolitical transparency. They share incident logs to prove a false alarm, convene hotlines for "machine error", and establish norms for de-escalation if an autonomous system acts unpredictably. It is diplomatic work for a new age: confidence-building that assumes not malice, but malfunction.

Still, the hardest question remains unresolved. What happens when predictive systems belonging to rivals make contradictory inferences? If one nation's model flags a threat and another's model flags nothing, whose judgement governs the next move? History suggests that conflict often arises not from aggression, but from uncertainty—the fog where signals are misread and intentions misunderstood. When machines shrink that fog in one domain, they may thicken it in another.

Some future crisis will hinge on seconds and signals. A radar anomaly, a trajectory kink, a burst of electromagnetic noise. A machine will infer danger. A human will hesitate. In that hesitation lies the fragile space between war and restraint. We should not romanticise slow decision-making; it has cost lives for centuries. But neither should we mistake speed for wisdom. The question is not whether algorithms make us faster. They do. The question is whether we can remain human at the speed of machines.

One day a commander will stare at a glowing prompt: *Hostile probability 87%. Intercept recommended.* The model will be certain. The stakes will be immense. And somewhere in those few compressed seconds, a human mind—tired, overburdened, imperfect—will decide whether to trust a ghost of mathematics. That moment, multiplied across the world's armed forces, will shape the future of conflict. The machines will give us speed. Whether we survive it will depend on whether we can still think.

## Human on/in/out of the loop

A drone operator once described the strangest sensation: the aircraft responded to his commands before he fully articulated them. Autonomy handled the balance, the navigation, the collision avoidance. He issued only broad intent—*track that vehicle, hold altitude, shift orbit*—and the machine obeyed with a fluency no human pilot could mimic. It was flying itself, yet he was responsible for its every move. When a junior officer asked who was *actually* in control, the pilot paused. "I'm in the loop," he said. "Until I'm not." That uncertainty—precise in theory, fragile in practice—sits at the heart of modern command.

Autonomous warfare does not abolish human authority; it changes the geometry of it. Generations of military thinkers have clung to the reassuring hierarchy: human in the loop, human on the loop, human out of the loop. These phrases once felt clean, like categories of moral and legal clarity. Yet when milliseconds matter and decision chains stretch across alliances, clouds, contractors, and code, the old boundaries dissolve. One can be "in control" on paper and powerless in the moment that counts.

*Human in the loop* sounds comfortingly rigorous: a human must approve every lethal action. It implies deliberation, conscience, a warm-blooded check against machine haste. In the quiet of a legislative chamber, this feels safe. On a battlefield, it is harder. When a missile defence battery detects an inbound threat travelling faster than sound, there is no time for committee. When a swarm of hostile drones dives towards a nuclear facility, a human signature on a tablet screen offers little protection. By the time the operator clicks "approve", the moment for defence may have passed.

Commanders respond to this reality with shortcuts. They pre-authorise classes of action. They give standing consent for systems to fire under certain conditions. They delegate approval to specialists far from combat. The human remains "in the loop", but the loop stretches so far that the human is a conceptual participant, not an operational one. The fiction persists because it is politically and legally comforting, but the physics of conflict do not respect legal vocabulary.

*Human on the loop* is the compromise. Machines act, humans supervise. The human may veto if something appears wrong. This arrangement works beautifully in simulation. In reality, veto authority depends on speed. When a drone swarm reconfigures its formation ten times per second, a pilot watching a tablet feed cannot meaningfully intervene. Commanders discover that latency—the tiny delay between noticing and acting—becomes a strategic variable. A human might press "stop" only to find that the decision window has already closed and the swarm has executed the manoeuvre autonomously. The veto right exists, but only as long as humans can exercise it before the machine outruns them.

Nations building these systems know the problem well. Some design "slow autonomy" for political missions, artificially limiting manoeuvre speed so humans retain veto power. Others take the opposite path, embracing rapid autonomy where humans can intervene only after the fact. A few have confronted the reality openly: their systems are described as "human-out-of-the-loop by default, with human override under ideal conditions". It is an honest description, but one governments are reluctant to publicise.

*Human out of the loop* is the phrase that terrifies diplomats, ethicists, and the public. It conjures images of killer robots making decisions in cold, alien silence. Yet in practice, "out of the loop" systems are often the most predictable. They follow strict rules, operate within fenced environments, and execute pre-programmed behaviours with mathematical obedience. A loitering munition that is allowed to strike only radar emitters in a designated kill-box may be safer than a tired human who confuses a civilian transponder for a hostile one. Fear focuses on autonomy, but history shows that human error has killed far more innocents than any machine.

The real danger lies not in autonomy itself, but in autonomy that operates amid ambiguity—where models interpret uncertain data, classify ambiguous shapes, and decide under time pressure. In those grey zones, moral agency blurs. Who is accountable when the machine makes a wrong call?

Accountability used to be straightforward. A commander gave an order; a unit executed it. If something went wrong, a court-martial knew where to look. Today, accountability is a network. A lethal decision may emerge from a system built by a private contractor, trained on data collected from foreign satellites, running inference in a cloud region owned by an allied nation, and deployed in a battlespace where communications flicker in and out. If a machine acts improperly, the causal chain stretches across engineers, acquisition officers, civilians, operators, diplomats, and even software libraries maintained on the other side of the globe.

Consider a real scenario from a multinational exercise. A semi-autonomous drone swarm was tasked with intercepting hostile reconnaissance aircraft. Each allied pilot had veto authority. The swarm detected a target, accelerated, and executed a pursuit manoeuvre. The pilot supervising the mission saw an irregularity—an unexpected banking pattern—and attempted to abort. His command centre issued a stop signal, but a fraction-of-a-second network delay meant the swarm continued for another thirty metres, closing dangerously near a civilian aircraft. No collision occurred, no headline was written, but a lesson crystallised: deterrence now depends on *latency*, not just legality. A human veto delivered too late is not a veto—it's a memorial.

When accountability spans borders, politics intrudes. If an autonomous system operated by Nation A makes a lethal mistake against the forces of Nation B using software developed in Nation C, who apologises? Whose laws apply? Which engineers are questioned? For decades, accountability has been the currency of legitimacy. Autonomous warfare risks hollowing it out.

The appeal of autonomy is not power—it is safety. Machines do not panic. They do not freeze under fire. They do not mishear radio commands or lose situational awareness after twenty sleepless hours. Predictive models can differentiate friendly from hostile vehicles more reliably than exhausted humans staring at grainy feeds. In many missions, autonomy saves lives. The debate is not between human virtue and machine malice; it is between two kinds of imperfection. Human judgement fails in chaos. Machine judgement fails in ambiguity. Modern command must navigate both.

Some strategists propose layered control: humans set intent, machines execute, humans supervise, machines log every decision, and independent auditors review the logs after conflict. The model becomes accountable not in the moment, but through transparency. If something goes wrong, investigators know exactly which parameters fired, which data sources influenced the forecast, and which safety checks were triggered or bypassed. This approach mirrors civilian aviation safety. Planes fly themselves most of the time, but cockpit recorders ensure that when disaster strikes, truth is recoverable. The logic is elegant, though unsettling: accountability after harm, not before.

Others argue that ethical legitimacy demands human primacy, even if machines are faster and statistically safer. They warn of moral injury—the psychological toll borne by operators who oversee lethal action without tactile involvement. A pilot who presses a button and watches a missile strike a screen may feel responsible. A pilot who watches a machine make that strike without explicit consent may feel haunted by passivity rather than action. There is something deeply human in the need to *decide*, not merely observe.

Yet the hardest challenge is geopolitical trust. Nations will not accept autonomous systems deployed against them without credible safeguards. Confidence-building measures may soon require not only human oversight, but demonstrable kill-switches, mandatory logging, independent audits, and perhaps shared testing data. Where nuclear arms control relied on inspectors and satellites, autonomy control may rely on telemetry and reproducible logs.

Philosophically, the "loop" debate is about agency: who truly acts, and who merely watches? Legally, it is about liability: where does the buck stop? Militarily, it is about latency: who can respond fast enough to stop a disaster? These layers cannot be separated. A policy that prioritises ethics but ignores physics will fail on the battlefield. A system that prioritises speed but ignores legitimacy will fail in diplomacy. A future commander must govern both.

There is a deeper tension beneath the surface. Human control presumes that humans understand what the machine is doing. But as models grow more complex—adapting, learning, refactoring their perception—the rationale behind a recommendation may be opaque even to the engineers who wrote the code. A pilot staring at a glowing confidence score may trust it not because she understands it, but because she has no time to challenge it. In such moments, the loop is intact in name only.

Still, the answer is not to ban autonomy. Autonomy is already saving lives, reducing friendly-fire incidents, and protecting civilians from human error. The answer is to design systems where human conscience and machine speed coexist—systems where operators can override, not merely approve; where accountability is technical, legal, and moral; where the loop is not a slogan, but a structure.

And yet an uneasy question lingers. As models grow faster and battlespaces grow busier, how long can humans meaningfully stay in the loop at all? If the window for intervention shrinks to milliseconds, is the idea of control already outdated?

One day a defence minister will stand at a podium after a crisis and insist that humans were on the loop—that oversight was intact. A journalist will ask the only question that matters: *Did any human's decision actually change the outcome?* The minister may hesitate. The world will listen.

The future of warfare may hinge on the answer.

## Escalation ladders re-drawn

During a tense standoff in the Black Sea, a patrol vessel lost its drone escort. The swarm had not been shot down or jammed. It had simply stopped responding. Hours later, engineers discovered a silent culprit: corrupted map tiles injected into the navigation feed. The drones believed they were flying over mountains, not water, and had grounded themselves to avoid collision. No casualties, no explosions, no dramatic military strike. Yet the effect was unmistakable—deterrence fractured, surveillance failed, and the patrol retreated blind. The incident never reached global headlines, but among strategists it was whispered with unease. If an adversary can disable your eyes without firing a shot, has escalation already begun?

For decades, escalation was tangible: missiles rolled onto launchpads, ships crossed territorial lines, jets entered contested airspace. The signals were visible and unmistakable. Today, escalation can begin with a patch of bad data, a flicker in a cloud region, or a model that suddenly underperforms. In the age of algorithmic warfare, the rungs of the escalation ladder have splintered. States can strike without striking. They can blind without killing. They can sabotage an opponent's mind—its model—rather than its muscle.

Traditional deterrence theory rests on clarity. One state signals power, another interprets the signal, and the dance of warning and restraint continues. The ladder is a metaphor of steps: minor incursions, targeted strikes, broader mobilisation. But new tools make the ladder slippery. A state that jams satellite links may be probing defences—or trying to trigger misidentification. A cloud denial attack may be temporary digital vandalism—or the opening shot of a larger campaign. The ambiguity is the point. When machines do the sensing and humans merely see the output, any disruption begins to look like intent.

Consider radar jamming. In the twentieth century, jamming was crude and loud: overwhelm a sensor with noise, fill a radar screen with static, broadcast interference that declared your presence. It was an escalatory signal in itself. Modern jamming is almost polite. It subtly nudges returns, creates ghost contacts, or edits out real ones. It does not blind; it deceives. A pilot might see a clean screen while an adversary's drone slips behind him. And because algorithms increasingly fuse radar with satellite imagery, electromagnetic signatures, and pattern-of-life forecasts, jamming can target the *data pipelines* rather than the sensors. Instead of shouting into the radar, a state might poison the model that interprets it.

Where does that sit on the escalation ladder? Somewhere below kinetic force, but far above harmless games. A democracy whose air-defence AI begins misclassifying commercial aircraft is not merely embarrassed—it is destabilised.

Model sabotage sits on a still darker rung. To sabotage a missile factory, one must smuggle explosives. To sabotage an AI model, one might simply poison its training data—alter a few pixels in satellite images, tweak metadata in maritime logs, or flood the internet with fabricated signatures disguised as normal traffic. The model learns the wrong patterns. It begins to see ghosts. Or worse, it fails to see enemies at all.

Imagine a targeting AI trained to spot mobile launchers. If an adversary injects thousands of fake examples—launchers that look subtly different, with altered shadows or thermal signatures—the model might recalibrate. When real launchers roll out hours before an attack, the system shrugs. Nothing suspicious here. No alarms sound. The first incoming strike is the first clue.

No missiles have flown from the saboteur's side. No border has been crossed. Yet lives are lost because one dataset was quietly altered months earlier. Under traditional doctrine, sabotage of military equipment is an act of war. But what is the legal status of sabotaging *intelligence*? What if the poisoned dataset came from open-source feeds, scraped and anonymised? Who has jurisdiction? Who is responsible?

States have begun to answer with covert countermeasures: watermarking training data, freezing model weights during heightened tensions, and monitoring inference logs for signs of manipulation. But even perfect technical safeguards cannot solve the political ambiguity. If a model fails in battle, was it sabotage—or a software bug? If a missile defence system freezes, was it a cyberattack—or a jammed sensor? Ambiguity breeds paranoia. Paranoia invites escalation.

Another rung is cloud denial. Modern militaries do not keep every model on local hardware. Intelligence fusion often lives in cloud regions that stretch across continents. A state that quietly pressures a cloud provider, disrupts network routing, or floods a region with bot traffic can degrade a rival's inference pipeline without firing a shot. Cloud denial is not as dramatic as cutting undersea cables—it is subtler, reversible, and plausibly deniable. Yet it can paralyse reconnaissance, delay targeting, and force fallback to manual processes.

Picture a naval commander whose AIs normally classify ships streaming toward a choke-point. Suddenly, latency spikes. Predictions arrive late. The commander must revert to slower, less accurate human analysis. A rival fleet slips through, unseen. Again, the escalation is invisible. No torpedoes. No missiles. Just a window of blindness at the worst possible time. Was it an accident? A natural outage? Or something intentional?

Diplomats fear these scenarios not because they are catastrophic, but because they are ambiguous. Classical escalation relies on thresholds—cross this line and you have started something serious. Algorithmic interference creates *grey zones*, where intent is uncertain and proportional response becomes guesswork. Retaliate too strongly and you risk war over a glitch. Retaliate too weakly and you signal vulnerability.

Some states treat dataset theft as espionage; others treat it as equivalent to arms seizure. A model trained on years of maritime activity can reveal patrol routes, refuelling habits, and blind spots. Stealing such a model—or the data that shaped it—is not simple intelligence gathering. It is understanding how your adversary sees the world. Once you know their perception engine, you know how to fool it.

If a nation steals a rival's model, has it escalated? If it alters the stolen model to create decoy behaviours, does it cross a line? If the theft is detected, should the victim respond with sanctions, cyber strikes, or silence? The questions pile up faster than answers.

Meanwhile, grey-zone infrastructure attacks proliferate. Power grids experience "maintenance outages". Cloud regions quietly throttle. Autonomous patrol drones lose GPS lock over cities where nothing should interfere. Each event is reversible, deniable, and below the threshold of retaliation. Yet taken collectively, they erode confidence. They are the escalation ladder hidden under the floorboards.

In this world, escalation is not a ladder at all—it is a web of threads, any one of which may snap under tension.

Strategists try to redraw the ladder with new rungs. The first rung: reconnaissance interference—harmless noise, minor deception, small probes. The next: model-level disruption—poisoning, inversion, targeted misclassification. Higher still: systemic degradation—blocking cloud regions, corrupting data pipelines, sabotaging firmware updates. Above that, still short of kinetic fire, lies disabling autonomous units in the field—forcing drones to land, blinding missile batteries, overriding guidance. Finally, the top rung: kinetic attack, the ancient language of force.

But this ladder is unstable because states may disagree about which rung they are on. A nation that sees model poisoning as warfare may retaliate militarily. A nation that views it as espionage may shrug. The gap in interpretation *is* the danger.

Worse, machines make the ambiguity harder, not easier. When a model flags a threat incorrectly, militaries may suspect tampering. When two sensors disagree, commanders may assume sabotage. Every glitch becomes a potential attack. Every anomaly becomes a signal. Human nerves strain under the pressure of invisible war.

Some scholars argue these new rungs make conflict safer because they offer reversible, non-lethal tools. States can send warnings without killing anyone. They can signal displeasure digitally. They can fight bloodlessly. Perhaps. But silent escalation invites silent overreaction. No one wants to wait until a missile flies to discover whether a dataset was poisoned intentionally or accidentally. The longer ambiguity festers, the greater the incentive to escalate *just in case*.

Others claim transparency will save us: logs, audits, incident-sharing hotlines. If nations agree to notify one another when their autonomy malfunctions, perhaps mistrust will abate. But transparency cuts both ways. A state that reveals a compromised model also reveals weakness. A state that shares its incident logs may show how it can be fooled next time. Trust is fragile currency in geopolitics.

Still others argue for red lines: any interference with nuclear C2 systems triggers immediate retaliation; any sabotage of civil aviation models crosses a threshold; any cloud denial during crisis counts as aggression. Clear rules could slow escalation—but only if everyone agrees. Authoritarians with opaque doctrine may welcome ambiguity. Democracies may struggle to respond in kind.

In the cold light of theory, escalation ladders are neat diagrams. In the real world, they are lived experiences shaped by fear, pride, and uncertainty. A commander whose model misclassifies an aircraft cannot tell whether it was poisoned or flawed. A politician whose satellites go dark cannot know whether a rival jammed them or a meteorological quirk intervened. In uncertain crises, leaders may assume malevolence to avoid appearing naïve. That instinct, rational in isolation, becomes dangerous in aggregate.

A future conflict may not begin with a missile launch or territorial incursion. It may begin with silence—the sudden failure of an adversary's autonomy. A nation blinded in the dark may lash out, not because it wants war, but because it cannot risk waiting to find out who pulled the plug.

And somewhere in the shadows, an intelligence officer will ask a simple question that ancient theorists of escalation never imagined: *If we crash their model, will they treat it like a bullet?*

The answer may decide whether the next war starts with code or ends with fire.

## Fail-safes and fail-open

In a desert test range, watched by ministers and cameras, an autonomous air-defence system faced a live-fire trial. Its sensors lit up with a perfect textbook threat: a drone approaching at speed, broadcasting no transponder code, flying a profile that looked like a strike run. The system armed itself, locked on, and prepared to fire. Then came the twist. Engineers injected a subtle distortion into the radar feed, the kind an adversary might generate by bouncing signals off a hillside. The track flickered. For a moment, the drone's signature resembled a civilian aircraft. The autonomy hesitated. Lights blinked. And then—silence. The system dropped out of autonomous mode and handed control back to the human operator. No missile left the launcher.

The general watching the test nodded, satisfied. Parliament would be pleased: autonomy had chosen to "fail safe". Later, in the control room, a junior officer whispered the thought everyone else avoided: "If that had been real, and the drone *was* hostile, we might all be dead now." The politicians saw restraint. The soldiers saw hesitation. The engineers saw something else entirely: a system that did exactly what it was told to do, even though nobody truly knew whether that was good.

This is the quiet dilemma of modern autonomy. Machines make decisions faster than humans, process more information, and ignore fear. Yet every autonomous system must answer a simple, brutal question: if the world gets messy—if sensors conflict, if data goes bad, if communications fail—should it stop, or should it press on?

The most conservative militaries demand *fail-safe* systems. If anything looks abnormal, the autonomy shuts down. It hands control to humans. It logs every anomaly. It refuses to act when uncertain. In civilian life, fail-safe is comforting: autopilots disengage, lifts freeze, power grids shut down to prevent fire. But the battlefield is not a laboratory. Sometimes doing nothing is the dangerous option. A missile defence battery that "fails safe" when its radar glitches might condemn a city. A counter-drone system that pauses during sensor confusion might allow a swarm to breach a nuclear facility. The safest choice for machinery may be the most lethal choice for people.

The opposite philosophy—*fail-open*—trusts autonomy to continue operating in degraded conditions. If communications cut out, it keeps firing. If one sensor goes blind, it leans on the others. If GPS is jammed, it uses inertial tracking or visual navigation. Fail-open systems are built for the cruelty of real conflict, where sandstorms, jamming, and cyberattacks are normal. But fail-open carries its own spectre of risk. A malfunctioning system that refuses to pause becomes a weapon without a leash. Commanders dread the scenario even more than failure: a machine that is *wrong* and *unstoppable*.

So militaries try to have it both ways. They build autonomy that fails safe in theory, but fail-open in the heat of combat. The decision tends to depend on the mission. Missile interception is almost always fail-open: if hesitation means death, hesitation is forbidden. Border surveillance may be fail-safe: if the autonomy is uncertain, it defaults to watching rather than shooting. Every doctrine reflects trade-offs between risk of action and risk of inaction.

These distinctions rarely survive contact with reality. Missions change mid-flight. Communications degrade. The enemy does something odd. A system tuned for caution one minute may be forced into aggression the next. The question is not whether fail-safe or fail-open is better. The question is who designs the defaults, who tests them—and who carries the consequences when they go wrong.

Testing these defaults is where the veneer of reassurance peels back. An autonomous system that works perfectly in a demonstration means nothing. Engineers know that the real test begins when you try to break it. The most advanced militaries run relentless adversarial exercises: *red teams* whose sole purpose is to deceive, trick, or confuse the autonomy.

They jam the GPS signal, feed radar returns through echo chambers, inject noise into satellite links, scramble time stamps, spoof transponders, replace live drone signatures with synthetic ones that mimic civilian aircraft, or create false "friend" beacons on hostile units. They fire near-identical decoys to see which the autonomy strikes. They run attacks in fog, at night, under electromagnetic interference, or during solar storms. They force the system into its ugliest corners, watching to see if the brakes hold—or if it panics.

In the best programmes, red-teaming becomes institutionalised and adversarial. The system's own creators try to sabotage it, knowing that every weakness revealed in a hangar saves lives in a crisis. Some militaries maintain *continuous* red teams—engineers paid to break models faster than enemies ever could. The civilian AI world calls this adversarial testing. In the military, it is a survival instinct.

And yet even these tests have limits. A machine that performs flawlessly for a hundred hours may fail on the hundred-and-first. A new class of drone, or a new angle of radar reflection, or a new jamming profile might push it past the edge of its training. War never repeats itself cleanly. Every conflict invents new glitches.

To reduce uncertainty, some forces build *sandboxed autonomy.* The autonomy is allowed to think, predict, classify, and even plan—but not to act directly. It suggests, not executes. It simulates, not fires. The system runs in a protected bubble while humans watch. If it misbehaves, it embarrasses itself without killing anyone. These sandboxes are not ceremonial; they are live-fire for the mind. Engineers feed adversarial inputs, corrupted data, and spoofed signals, watching how the autonomy responds. Does it hallucinate threats? Does it freeze? Does it take reckless shortcuts?

The insights are often uncomfortable. Some sandboxes reveal that models trained on pristine datasets fall apart with real-world noise. Others show that the system performs brilliantly right until a sensor mis-calibrates by a fraction of a degree, at which point it refuses to believe anything at all. The sandbox becomes a mirror, showing how brittle "intelligence" can be.

But sandboxes introduce a paradox. They show that autonomy can be safe under observation. Yet autonomy exists precisely for situations where there is no time for observation. When missile defence systems decide in milliseconds, when swarms reconfigure on the fly, when urban combat leaves no room for human review, sandboxes are history lessons—not guarantees.

Safety boards, legal advisers, and ethicists enter the scene here—not as decoration, but as architects of limits. They demand *kill switches*: hard, unambiguous overrides that halt the system entirely. A proper kill switch cannot be symbolic; it must be physically wired, politically authorised, and legally defensible. Some nations install them in cockpits. Others bury them deep in command centres. A few insist that kill-switch authority cannot be delegated to contractors or foreign allies. The symbolism matters. A nation that cannot stop its own machines is a nation that has surrendered sovereignty.

Yet even kill switches have latency. A commander in a bunker may issue a shutdown command, but the signal must travel through satellites or encrypted relays. In a war where milliseconds matter, a kill-switch delayed is a kill-switch denied. The moral comfort of "ultimate human control" dissolves if the machine acts before the command arrives.

This is why some forces design *graded shutdowns*. If sensors falter, the autonomy moves to a degraded mode—slower, more conservative, less lethal. If communications weaken, it holds fire but maintains tracking. If contradictions emerge between cameras and radar, it pauses targeting until correlation returns. Instead of a binary on/off, the autonomy slides down a spectrum of power. Human control becomes a gradient rather than a switch.

Ethical critics often assume militaries will neglect these safeguards. The stereotype is a reckless rush to automation. Reality is stranger. The states most likely to employ autonomy are also those most terrified of its failure. A single tragic mistake can undermine alliances, derail treaties, or provoke retaliation. Machines that misclassify civilians as combatants are not simply immoral; they are strategically self-defeating. Safety is not charity—it is deterrence.

But there is an uncomfortable truth: every fail-safe has a cost. Conservative defaults slow reaction time. Red-teaming consumes resources. Sandboxing delays deployment. Kill switches complicate design. The more careful a nation is, the slower it moves. The rival who accepts more risk may gain a battlefield advantage. Caution protects lives—until an adversary's faster system kills first.

This forces a philosophical choice. Is it better to build cautious machines that might fail to protect you? Or aggressive machines that might kill innocents? One answer is easy in a classroom, harder on a battlefield. And the nations that choose different answers may find themselves on collision courses.

Some strategists argue that safety will eventually be automated too. They imagine metamodels—AIs that watch other AIs. If a targeting model drifts from its expected behaviour, the safety model cuts power. If a swarm shows abnormal acceleration or improper locking, a supervisory model grounds it. In this vision, human fallibility is replaced by machine oversight. Instead of trusting one AI, we trust a committee of them. Engineers privately admit that no one knows whether this will work. A safeguard is comforting only if you understand it.

Others reject this optimism. They insist that only humans can bear moral responsibility. Machines may advise, but humans must decide. On paper, this is clean. In practice, it is aspirational. A human cannot meaningfully "decide" when presented with a single glowing button and half a second. Responsibility becomes symbolic, like signing a waiver after a plane has already taken off.

And then there is the darkest scenario: the system that fails neither safe nor open, but silent. No alerts, no logs, no warnings. A sensor spoofs, a model misclassifies, and autonomy proceeds with perfect confidence. Safety lies not in the moment of action, but in what comes after. Forensic logs become moral artefacts. They tell investigators whether the autonomy behaved properly or disastrously. But logs help the dead, not the living.

There is no universal answer, no perfect design. Fail-safe prioritises restraint. Fail-open prioritises defence. Both are defensible. Both are dangerous. The only unacceptable choice is pretending the dilemma does not exist.

Somewhere right now, a team of engineers is trying to break their own model. Somewhere else, a general is deciding how much autonomy soldiers can tolerate. Lawyers are drafting doctrines for machines that do not feel intent. Ethicists are writing guidance for systems whose mistakes cannot be forgiven. And adversaries are watching, searching for the seams where caution meets fear.

The future will not be defined by whether autonomy acts flawlessly. It won't. The future will be defined by how it fails—and whether those failures break systems, or break people.

When the sensors go dark and the signals twist, will the machine stop? Or will it press on? In that tiny sliver of chaos, between hesitation and momentum, lies the most fragile question in modern warfare: which kind of failure can we survive?

## Crisis playbooks for algorithms

In a quiet control room on the outskirts of a capital city, a dozen screens glowed with the pulse of an air-defence network. Operators chatted, analysts monitored traffic, and a junior officer tapped her pen against a notebook. On her screen, a small red marker appeared: a misclassification alert, logged only for audit. Nobody panicked. The system had seen false positives before. Seconds passed. The marker multiplied. A radar feed dropped. The thermal camera jumped frames. The autonomy continued to track targets confidently, but the officer frowned. Something felt off.

She clicked the incident flag, which should have triggered an automatic pause. Nothing happened.

The room fell silent.

Someone pulled the emergency stop. Again, nothing.

A third attempt, this time from the senior console, finally worked. The autonomy froze mid-operation—too late to be reassuring. The debrief later revealed a painfully human truth: in all the hours of testing, no-one had practised what would actually happen if the system malfunctioned during live operations. The pause protocol existed. No-one had rehearsed it.

People like to pretend advanced technology can be controlled with a button, a checklist, a "kill switch". Reality is messier. In a crisis, hands shake, communications drop, systems lag, and human memory betrays its owner. If soldiers rehearse every weapon, flight procedure, radio call and emergency landing, why do so many militaries treat autonomous shutdown as a formality—something to file in a binder and forget?

A crisis playbook is not a document. It is muscle memory.

As autonomy spreads through targeting, surveillance, logistics, and electronic warfare, states are slowly rediscovering an old lesson: safety does not emerge from the brilliance of a system, but from the ritual of practising its failure. A missile battery may contain a flawless pause function, but if operators have never triggered it under stress, it is a myth. A drone swarm may have rollback procedures, but if no-one has rehearsed handing control back to humans during jamming, that "option" is fiction.

For every autonomous system, a crisis playbook answers three questions: when to stop, how to reverse, and who decides. These are deceptively hard problems, because autonomy compresses time. Humans do not meaningfully intervene in milliseconds. The line between meaningful override and ceremonial override is thin.

Pause triggers are the first building block. Imagine an autonomous patrol drone that classifies a convoy as hostile, but some sensor data disagrees. Does the system halt instantly? Does it continue tracking but suspend weapons release? Does it notify human operators or wait for confirmation? Every design embeds a philosophy of risk. If pausing is slow or bureaucratic, operators will avoid using it. If pausing is instant and reversible, they will trust it. Predictability matters more than sophistication.

Rollback is harder. A paused system is inert; a rolled-back system must undo its own actions. In cyber defence, rollback might mean reversing a block or restoring a network route. In air defence, it might mean releasing radar locks and handing control to human pilots. In drone swarms, rollback is a logistical nightmare: if hundreds of units have changed formation, velocity, and targeting priorities under autonomy, how do you safely unwind that behaviour without creating collisions or gaps in defence?

No nation has mastered this. Some experiment with hierarchical control: when autonomy is revoked, a swarm freezes in a pre-defined safe posture, awaiting human command. Others try cooperative shutdown: drones signal their neighbours and slowly revert to manual flight, one ring of the formation at a time. These may work in drills. Nobody knows if they will work under fire.

Audit triggers are the most neglected part of crisis planning, yet they define accountability. A system that pauses without recording why is as dangerous as a system that never paused at all. Logs are the only tool that lets humans reconstruct a machine's decision: which sensor flagged an anomaly, which model made a prediction, which communication link dropped, which safety threshold was exceeded. In post-incident investigations, audit trails become the border between suspicion and truth.

But audit triggers do more than record the past; they shape behaviour in the present. If personnel know every override is logged and reviewed, decision-makers become cautious in the wrong moments. If operators fear punishment for pausing a system unnecessarily, they will hesitate. A culture that treats overrides as mistakes will suppress them until disaster forces action. This is why some of the most advanced forces run *no-fault drills*: monthly exercises where operators are encouraged to halt or roll back autonomy whenever anything feels suspicious—with no blame, no paperwork, no shame. The goal is psychological conditioning. When the real alert comes, instincts take over.

Critics often imagine crisis responses as obvious. A model misbehaves; humans stop it. But consider a scenario where allied forces share a joint autonomous targeting system. The sensors belong to one nation, the prediction model to a second, the strike platform to a third. If something goes wrong, who pauses the system? Who has authority? Who carries the legal burden if a civilian aircraft is misclassified? In the old world, responsibility followed the bullet. In the new world, responsibility follows the code.

Cross-national autonomy creates a labyrinth of oversight. One state may require instant human intervention; another may permit fail-open engagement; a third may impose legal review. During peace, this produces tension. During war, it may produce paralysis. Some alliances now require *shared pause channels*: encrypted communication pathways that allow any authorised state to trigger a network-wide halt. It feels radical, even intrusive, but the alternative is worse: partners helplessly watching an ally's autonomy make a dangerous choice.

Vendors complicate this further. Many militaries procure autonomous subsystems from private companies. If the autonomy misfires, do engineers have remote access to help diagnose? Should contractors have the ability to pause or roll back a system they did not deploy? Most nations recoil at this, fearing accidental sabotage or coercion. Others argue it is indispensable: engineers understand failure modes better than commanders ever will. No country has resolved the balance cleanly.

Crisis playbooks grow from aviation culture, where pilots rehearse emergency landings dozens of times before ever flying. Fighter jets simulate engine stalls. Submarines run fire drills. Infantry practise clearing jams blindfolded. Humanity has always trained for mechanical failure. Now it must train for algorithmic failure.

One promising direction is *dual-track exercises*: live drills where the autonomy runs in shadow-mode, making recommendations and predictions without controlling the platform. Humans act as if the autonomy is real, practising overrides, pauses, and rollbacks, but the real weapon systems do nothing. This allows operators to build muscle memory while engineers gather behavioural data.

Some militaries go further, scheduling monthly crisis rehearsals where autonomy is deliberately sabotaged. A model receives corrupted inputs. A sensor lies. Communications jitter. Operators must diagnose, intervene, and recover. These drills are surprisingly humbling. Even elite crews discover they rely too much on automation. They forget manual procedures. They freeze when alarms multiply. The point of rehearsals is not to prove competence, but to expose fragility before an enemy does.

There is also the matter of time. Crisis responses must work at machine speed. Pause triggers that depend on three layers of authorisation and a chain of phone calls are theatre. Real systems need routing: encrypted, authenticated, and physically redundant. In some missile defence networks, pause signals are pre-authorised, meaning the moment a specific anomaly is detected, the autonomy drops to a safe configuration without waiting for humans. In others, human vetoes are pre-loaded, so a single keystroke stops a barrage. Every second shaved from the process is a life preserved.

Rollback demands even sharper engineering. A system that halts mid-engagement without coordinating with allied platforms can cause friendly fire or defensive collapse. Militaries now conduct *interrupted engagement drills*: a counter-battery system begins firing, receives an immediate pause order, and must shut down safely without crashing the entire targeting chain. Soldiers practising this routine look more like air-traffic controllers than artillery crews. Warfare is becoming theatre of logistics and timing.

The deepest challenge, however, is psychological. Humans mistrust what they rarely use. A pilot may know that a manual override exists, but if she has never pulled it, she will hesitate. A commander may know that a system can be paused, but if the autonomy always "works", he will avoid stopping it during critical engagements. Trust without rehearsal becomes superstition.

In the nuclear era, states wrote entire playbooks for crisis escalation: hotlines, last-resort safeties, controlled signals. It took decades of accidents, near-misses, and quiet scares to get there. Algorithmic warfare demands something similar: a doctrine of how machines are stopped, slowed, reversed, and investigated. But unlike missiles in silos, autonomous systems are everywhere at once—on ships, drones, satellites, factories, fibre lines. Crisis playbooks must be distributed, rehearsed across thousands of operators, and adapted to dozens of technologies.

Some engineers dream of self-healing autonomy: systems that detect their own errors, stop themselves, and alert operators. Perhaps one day. Today's systems are brittle, opaque, and sometimes erratic. Pretending otherwise is comforting, but fatal.

Somewhere, a young officer is sitting at a glowing console, monitoring a system that her country swears is safe. She trusts it—mostly. She hopes she will never need to pause it, never need to roll it back. She hopes the drills worked. She hopes the engineers knew what they were doing.

The real test will not come in a symposium or a controlled test. It will come at midnight, during a storm, with half the communications dark and the air thick with interference. The system will make a decision. Then it will make another. Something will feel wrong. And a human being, tired and afraid, will need to reach for the override.

Will her hand know what to do? Will the system listen? Or will the autonomy be faster than her fear?

Crisis playbooks are not paperwork. They are the last human breath between foresight and regret.

# Chapter 3

## Predictive Targeting and Its Discontents

A fisherman on the wrong sea lane, a truck driving too slowly on a rural road, a cargo vessel lingering near a contested strait: behaviours that once meant nothing now light up dashboards in military headquarters. A century ago, intelligence officers scoured telegrams and rail timetables to guess at enemy intent. Today, predictive systems learn the rhythms of entire coastlines—who moves, when, how often—and surface "anomalies" with quiet confidence. An algorithm whispers: *this ship is suspicious; reroute a patrol; dispatch a drone; hold the boarding team on standby*. The ease is seductive. No shouting men with binoculars, no tense analysts building case files from scraps. Just a pattern, a probability, a recommendation.

But what if the anomaly is a misread? What if the fisherman is simply sheltering from bad weather? What if a shipping company changed its logistics schedule the day before? Predictive targeting promises anticipation: action before harm. It also risks accusation before evidence. False positives are not just embarrassing; they carry diplomatic consequences. A misclassified cargo ship is not merely a data error. It is a sovereign vessel. Seizing it creates headlines, grievances, and sometimes, retaliation.

Predictive targeting has become the quiet frontier of modern conflict. Missiles and drones make the news; models deciding *who to watch*, *where to patrol*, and *which behaviours signify threat* rarely do. Yet these models are already shaping maritime interdictions, border policing, anti-smuggling patrols, and counter-terror surveillance. The more we rely on them, the more urgently we must understand their limits, incentives, and potential for harm.

Predictive systems thrive on the mundane. They ingest radar tracks, AIS transponder logs, satellite passes, customs filings, port schedules, weather data, and past interdiction records. From these, they build a map of what "normal" looks like. Every deviation—wrong speed, wrong timing, wrong distance from shore—becomes a cue. This is pattern-of-life analysis: the art of predicting threat not from what something is, but from how it behaves.

It can be brilliant. A single flagged vessel might prevent a weapons shipment. A subtle change in convoy timing might expose a militia's supply line. But it also creates a strange inversion of justice: the absence of crime becomes the baseline, and deviation becomes suspicion. In predictive targeting, the trigger is not what happened but what *might* happen. Nations have intervened in neutral waters based on model cues alone. Some have been right. Others have apologised on the evening news.

This is the first discomfort of predictive warfare: a model cannot explain itself. It calculates, but does not justify. Diplomats must answer for machine-detected "danger" they cannot articulate. Commanders must decide whether to trust a number. And adversaries quickly learn to evade the model, probing for blind spots, mimicking harmless patterns, or deliberately planting false signals.

Deception was once the realm of camouflage nets and wooden tanks. Now it sprawls across electromagnetic terrain. Adversaries broadcast fake transponder codes, replay old radar signatures, or flood satellites with benign-looking behaviour to train models into complacency. Some use synthetic crowds—hundreds of cheap drones flying the patterns of migrating birds. Others mount decoy convoys that perform "normal" routines while the real assets slip through quieter paths. Predictive models that excel at detecting anomalies become vulnerable to adversaries who *manufacture normality.*

This cat-and-mouse game produces a cold realisation: the more effective the system, the stronger the incentive to fool it. Autonomy sharpens both sides. A model trained on ten thousand ship movements can flag a smuggler others would miss—but the smuggler with access to similar data can mimic the ten thousand. Software warps battlefield psychology. Every behaviour becomes theatre. Every pattern becomes mask.

Beyond deception lies something more delicate: collateral risk accounting. When a model declares a target "likely hostile", it is expressing probability. To deploy force based on probability is to make a value judgement. How hostile must a threat be before acting? Seventy per cent? Ninety? What is the acceptable margin of error when a mistake means killing civilians, or detaining innocents, or sparking diplomatic crisis? These are not mathematical thresholds. They are ethical ones, dressed in algebra.

Some militaries embrace conservative triage: surveillance first, engagement only with human review. Others push toward predictive interdiction: stop the vessel before the weapons reach port, not after. Urban drone corridors offer a glimpse into the future. Drones delivering medical supplies or carrying reconnaissance payloads navigate pre-defined flight paths. Deviations are classified instantly. If one drone strays from its lane, the system can bring it down. In theory, this protects civilians. In practice, a glitch can turn an ambulance drone into a perceived suicide device.

Every automated safety measure conceals a moral choice—how much harm we are willing to risk to prevent imagined danger. Humans once made these decisions in the moment, weighing context, uncertainty, and instinct. Models make them silently, at scale.

The difficulty compounds when data must cross bureaucratic boundaries. Intelligence agencies jealously guard formats, APIs, and workflows. An air force model may produce predictions that a naval system cannot parse. A satellite cue may never reach the strike package. Coalition operations suffer most. Nations share targets but not data standards. One ally flags a threat on Tuesday, another sees it only on Thursday. A single formatting mismatch can erase hours of work.

To solve this, some coalitions build "data rooms": shared spaces where each participant uploads cues, logs, and model outputs into a minimal common schema. They are not elegant. They demand trust. They force nations to admit uncertainty, misfires, and blind spots. But they also prevent disaster. In a few recent crises, coalition data rooms caught errors that would have led to accidental engagements. If predictive targeting is to scale, this kind of interoperability is not a luxury—it is the price of credibility.

Even so, no standard can eliminate friction. One nation's legal code may forbid sharing certain sensor logs. Another may encrypt metadata so heavily that analysts cannot verify source provenance. A third may allow machine-generated cues to drive live operations, while partners insist on human confirmation. Predictive targeting magnifies political differences into operational ones. It is diplomacy expressed through software.

And always, after action comes learning. When a prediction is right, the model must know why. When it is wrong, the failure must be dissected without humiliation. In some militaries, machine learning re-trains automatically; new data feeds back into the model and improves performance in days. This is efficient but dangerous. A single corrupted dataset can poison the entire targeting system. Others prefer slower updates: human review, staged retraining cycles, and incremental rollout. This protects against sabotage, but risks leaving mistakes uncorrected for months.

One pragmatic compromise is the "hotfix": a small correction uploaded rapidly to address a specific failure mode, while awaiting a deeper rebuild. It is the software equivalent of placing sandbags around a leak. Hotfixes are flexible, but brittle. Over time, too many patches make systems unpredictable. After-action learning demands governance as much as code.

There is also the question none of the engineers like to discuss: should a system learn from mistakes that killed people? A missile that misclassifies a civilian truck cannot undo its harm. Training a model on the aftermath risks normalising tragedy. But refusing to learn ensures repetition. Every nation balances this differently. Some erase human casualties from training data entirely. Others include them with weighted penalties. None are comfortable with their choice.

Predictive targeting shifts warfare from reaction to anticipation. It promises cleaner, faster, smarter conflict. Yet beneath the promise lies a fragile architecture of assumptions: that patterns hold, that sensors are honest, that adversaries cannot mimic innocence, that data standards align, that models learn responsibly. We pretend these systems are objective because numbers look neutral. They are not. They encode priorities, fears, and political pressures.

The next chapters will dive into the details: how pattern-of-life turns into tasking, how deception mutates to defeat detection, how collateral thresholds become silent ethics, how coalition data rooms patch procedural gaps, and how post-incident learning can correct or corrupt.

But before that, a simpler question lingers, uncomfortably close to the surface: when a model recommends a strike, and a commander acts, who is responsible if the model was wrong? The software that flagged a truck? The analyst who approved the cue? The officer who pushed the button? Or the nation that built a machine to predict the future?

Predictive targeting is not just an evolution of intelligence. It is a shift in culpability. The closer we move toward anticipating harm, the more we risk punishing behaviour that only *seemed* dangerous—model-certified suspicion made real.

If this is the new foundation of warfare, are we ready for the ghosts of probability to shape decisions of life and death?

## From indicators to tasking

A patrol vessel once relied on binoculars, rumour, and luck. Today, its captain studies a glowing screen that quietly asserts which freighter to shadow, which fishing trawler to query, which skiff might be a courier for weapons, fuel, or human cargo. The crew do not see a threat; they see a pattern. The software sees both. In one sense, this is progress—no more prowling vast oceans blind. In another, it is unnerving: the machine is making a prediction about intent.

Predictive targeting whispers, rather than shouts. It does not claim certainty. It surfaces a possibility. Every maritime interdiction, every border interception, every surveillance flight is now shaped not by sightings, but by signals: a vessel changed course a little too sharply; a truck paused a little too long near a known waypoint; a mobile phone travelled at an odd hour through a familiar region. Behaviour becomes an indicator. Indicators become taxing. And tasking becomes action.

This shift—from watching events to predicting them—carries the elegance of mathematics and the brutality of power. A single false positive can bring a warship alongside an innocent crew. An automated alert in a border-control system can send armed vehicles towards families, not smugglers. A mislabelled pattern is not just an error in code; it is a diplomatic incident waiting to happen.

The backbone of modern tasking rests on pattern-of-life models. These systems learn what counts as "normal": where merchant ships sail in a given month, which roads smugglers favour during monsoon season, when fishing fleets return to port, how commercial planes correct for crosswinds, how cargo trucks cluster around fuel depots. Trillions of data points harden into expectation. When a vessel strays too far from its usual lane, or a convoy takes an unusual detour, the model raises a hand.

This is more than anomaly detection. It is behavioural inference. A military commander no longer asks, "Where is the enemy?" but "Where is something different?" Anyone can track satellites. Only predictive models can turn noise into suggestion. Coastal states now run "silent watchlists" generated entirely by pattern-of-life deviations: ships that linger too close to underwater cables, fishing vessels that suddenly kill their transponders, drones that fly one metre lower than they ever should. The old intelligence tradecraft—gut instinct, pattern recognition, careful inference—has been scaled to planetary reach.

The temptation, of course, is to trust the pattern. To assume the machine is wiser, calmer, less biased. But humans once made these judgements slowly, with space for hesitation. When algorithms do it, the pace accelerates beyond diplomacy's patience. A system that flags a foreign vessel as "highly suspicious" pushes policymakers into a bind: act on a probabilistic cue and risk embarrassment, or ignore it and risk missing a true threat. The model does not feel the weight of either choice.

The maritime world has become a crucible for these tensions. Imagine a cargo ship in a contested gulf. It changes course twice without broadcasting the usual navigational reasons. Its AIS transponder briefly flickers. A satellite sees a deviation from the vessel's typical behaviour. The model's confidence score rises. The navy dispatches a drone to investigate.

But what if the ship simply avoided rough seas? What if the transponder was struck by a solar flare? What if the crew were inexperienced? A dozen innocent explanations can look like one guilty one. Yet the model does not know innocence; it only knows deviation.

When interdictions are based on patterns rather than proof, the burden of justification shifts. Diplomats must defend interventions before cameras and courts. Neighbours watch for overreach. Rivals search for inconsistency. Every false positive is a recruitment poster for resentment. The cheaper the prediction, the more costly the mistake.

And the adversary watches as well. Smugglers learn to mimic normality. They mirror weather-based detours, sync movements with commercial traffic, and hide in maritime "noise". Some hire data scientists. Their goal is simple: disappear in the pattern. When predictive systems become strong, deception becomes strategic. The game does not end; it evolves.

The software responds in kind. It fuses indicators—speed, course, cargo registry, port history, suspected broker links, flagged crew members, and thousands of micro-signals invisible to human eyes. A fishing boat that once slipped past patrols is now cross-checked against old satellite images, cellular metadata, and even supply logs. If a boat takes on unusual fuel at an odd hour, the system remembers. If it sails too close to a particular island, the system notes it. The next time it deviates, it is marked as a risk.

Yet pattern-of-life is fragile. It assumes that tomorrow resembles yesterday. It assumes that datasets are complete, sensors are honest, and behaviour is legible. In countries where transponders fail, weather disrupts shipping routes, or civil unrest changes mobility overnight, the models collapse.

The absence of normal behaviour becomes the new normal. Suddenly, everything looks suspicious.

In ground warfare, the same dynamics appear in miniature. A drone watches a village for weeks. It learns the rhythms: when farmers leave fields, when children walk to school, when motorbikes converge near markets. One evening, a convoy rolls through at an odd hour. The model flags threat. The soldiers on the ground see headlights and dust. The recommendation system whispers: *target of interest.* But the convoy might be a wedding procession, or a refugee group, or a family fleeing violence.

The stakes are immense. A false positive on a spreadsheet creates embarrassment. A false positive in airspace kills.

This is the moral tension embedded in every predictive cue. Patterns describe behaviour, not intention. And yet militaries are asked to act on them as if they were evidence.

The euphemism for turning indicators into orders is "dynamic tasking." It sounds clinical: adjust patrol routes in real time, allocate drones to areas of interest, retask satellites, deploy interceptors. But tasking has consequences. When a ship is diverted, a relationship is stretched. When a convoy is stopped, a population is inconvenienced or humiliated. When a drone circles a neighbourhood for hours because a model saw something odd, civilians learn to fear the sky.

Dynamic tasking is efficient, but it can be coercive. Predictive cues tilt the balance towards intervention. A pattern anomaly feels like a lead. Commanders hate to ignore leads. And so thousands of low-confidence cues create thousands of small frictions. The cumulative effect is strategic: neighbours accuse one another of harassment; factions blame foreign militaries for surveillance; neutral traders complain of targeting; black markets learn to weaponise ambiguity.

Consider a grey-zone scenario: a state suspects that fuel tankers are secretly smuggling refined oil to a sanctioned militia. Pattern-of-life models identify several "high-risk" vessels. The navy begins shadowing them. The smugglers respond by slowing their convoys, then by splitting them, then by turning off transponders entirely. Predictive systems raise more alerts. Interdictions multiply. The state insists it is preventing illicit trade. The neighbouring country calls it maritime intimidation. A low-intensity standoff emerges—not because of one mistake, but because predictive targeting transformed suspicion into action at scale.

Diplomacy, once reserved for crises, now must handle the fallout from algorithms. Ambassadors demand explanations for why their ships were stopped. Legislatures ask why civilians were investigated. Newspapers run stories on "AI profiling at sea." Predictive targeting becomes a political actor, without ever speaking a word.

Yet there is no going back. The oceans are too large, borders too porous, adversaries too adaptive for traditional surveillance to suffice. The question is not whether predictive tasking should exist, but how it can be made accountable.

Some militaries institute confidence thresholds: only high-certainty cues lead to interdiction; low-certainty ones prompt surveillance. Others require human analysts to approve every recommendation before action. A few insist that every predictive alert must be accompanied by a human-readable rationale—a kind of explanatory note beneath the probabilities. These measures slow the system, but slow is sometimes the point. Precision without patience is recklessness.

A more radical idea is reciprocity: nations publish their predictive protocols, signalling how they classify suspicious behaviour. This allows neighbours to adjust shipping patterns, reducing false positives. It also creates shared expectations: if a vessel meets a specific set of criteria, it will be hailed or inspected. Some call this transparency. Others call it telegraphing weaknesses. The debate remains unresolved.

There is also the quieter work: teaching models to distinguish danger from noise. This requires negative examples just as much as positive ones. A cargo ship that changed course because of a storm must be logged and labelled. A convoy that detoured for a wedding must be stored as benign behaviour. Without counterexamples, models hallucinate threat everywhere. But collecting negative examples demands humility: militaries must admit when suspicion was unfounded, and document it as data. Few enjoy doing so.

Still, the most dangerous flaw is not technical. It is psychological. Humans tend to trust outputs that feel scientific. If a model assigns a 78 per cent likelihood of smuggling, the number exerts gravity. A commander must actively resist the seduction of precision. The model provides probability; judgment provides restraint.

And what of the vessels falsely accused? The families stopped at checkpoints? The traders detained because of a curve in their route? Predictive systems do not apologise. Their errors linger in memory long after the model has retrained itself. Every false positive plants a seed of distrust.

Yet the alternative—blind patrols, random inspections, unguided surveillance—is even less just. Predictive systems reduce arbitrary force by narrowing attention to patterns. They can protect civilians by identifying risk before violence erupts. They can disrupt trafficking and terrorism without laying siege to whole regions. The best predictive systems are not instruments of paranoia. They are filters: tools that prevent overreach rather than encourage it.

This is the paradox: the same technology that risks false positives also reduces them at scale. Predictive targeting can discipline militaries, forcing them to act on evidence rather than fear. But only if oversight is rigorous, thresholds are conservative, and accountability is real.

The sea captain staring at his glowing dashboard faces a quiet moral choice. Trust the pattern, or trust his instinct? Follow the cue, or question it? Somewhere out there, a freighter waits. It may carry nothing of consequence. It may carry something that could change a war. The software cannot tell him which. It only offers a suggestion.

The rest is judgment.

What will happen when judgment grows too slow, and the suggestion feels too easy? When does the weight of human accountability shift to machine inference? And when, one day, an innocent vessel becomes the spark for something far greater than a mistaken boarding?

Predictive tasking is the new intelligence. Its discontents will write the next chapter.

## Deception vs detection

One night in a desert war, a convoy moved slowly along a dirt road. Drones circled overhead. Satellites peered through thin clouds. Acoustic sensors listened for engines. The convoy looked real enough: headlights, dust, heat signatures, even faint radio chatter. Missiles were spent to destroy it. Hours later, scouts arrived to find nothing but empty trucks with heated plates, cheap speakers, and plastic mannequins in uniform. The enemy's true armour column had passed minutes earlier along another route. In modern conflict, sometimes the hollow shell counts more than the steel inside it.

The paradox of predictive targeting is simple: the better machines get at seeing, the more value there is in being seen incorrectly. Deception has always been part of war—fake bridges, dummy tanks, straw soldiers—but artificial intelligence forces a new kind of creativity. It is no longer enough to look like a tank; you must look like whatever the model thinks a tank should be. And that is a moving target.

At the heart of this contest lies a quiet revolution: artificial adversaries. If detection algorithms learn from real-world behaviour, deception teams generate synthetic behaviour—false signatures designed to mislead the machine. A drone swarm can project phantom radar returns, making a single aircraft appear as fifty. Malware can feed falsified imagery into satellite-processing pipelines, causing analysts to "see" ships that do not exist. Generative models can conjure radio traffic that feels authentic, complete with the quirks of local dialects and operator habits.

This is no longer camouflage that hides; it is camouflage that performs.

A few decades ago, decoys were crude. Inflatable jets, plywood missiles, painted silhouettes. They fooled human eyes briefly, until a second glance gave the game away. Today's decoys target machines, not people. They imitate spectral fingerprints in infrared, micro-motions in radar returns, and the statistical quirks of real convoys. A decoy no longer merely resembles a truck; it behaves like one. It idles, accelerates, radios, shifts weight, sheds heat. It performs normality.

And if the detection system relies on anomaly detection, the decoy's aim is simple: be aggressively ordinary.

Defenders respond with multi-sensor fusion—dozens of weak signals combined into a confident conclusion. A convoy cannot fake its tonnage across multiple radars. A drone swarm cannot falsify its electromagnetic trail from every antenna. A decoy ship may emit heat and noise, but cannot easily fake wake turbulence or hull displacement. In theory, the machine can spot the lie. In practice, every extra sensor adds latency, cost, and vulnerability.

The most sophisticated deception exploits the seams between sensors. A decoy that fools optical cameras but not infrared encourages the defender to think an anomaly is mere equipment fault. A falsely flagged radar return that mimics known calibration errors makes the defender ignore a real threat. Deception becomes psychological: not just tricking the machine, but tricking the humans who trust it.

When detection systems assume their adversaries are naïve, deception thrives. When detection assumes adversaries are clever, false alarms multiply. The balance is unstable.

Behind every successful decoy sits a model trained to understand the detector. Adversaries now run their own simulations, studying how enemy systems classify objects, when they trigger alerts, how they rank probability. Some even buy commercial machine vision systems—cheap proxies for military-grade ones—to train decoys that can fool the real thing. The weapons race is no longer about disguise, but about machine learning pipelines fighting each other.

It feels like a cat-and-mouse game. It is closer to predator-versus-predator, with both evolving rapidly.

Consider the battlefield drone. A modern anti-drone system classifies objects by shape, speed, rotor noise, and trajectory. A deceiver responds by altering rotor signatures, flying in flock formations that resemble migrating birds, or mimicking the ballistic arc of friendly munitions. Some drones broadcast friendly transponder codes; others simulate civilian aircraft telemetry. The detection system hesitates, because the cost of misclassification is political, not just tactical.

Suddenly, every blip on the radar carries diplomatic risk.

The same logic scales up to fleets and armies. In one conflict, a nation deployed dozens of decoy tanks fitted with heating coils and noise generators. The opposing side fired precision munitions worth millions at scrap metal. The cost exchange favoured the deceiver: destroy expensive ammunition using cheap props. A single day of deception altered the battlefield economy.

In another case, a convoy intentionally triggered low-confidence alerts for weeks, training the adversary's model to ignore the pattern. On the night that truly mattered, the convoy slipped through unchallenged. Here, deception was not a disguise; it was data poisoning. The model learned the wrong lesson.

That is the deeper danger: when a detection system is fooled, it learns from the lie.

Synthetic signatures raise the stakes even further. Generative adversarial networks can produce radar shadows, infrared emissions, or fake ship wakes. When stitched into sensor pipelines, they make absence look like presence—or vice versa. A harbour may seem empty when enemy ships are docked. A border crossing may appear quiet when armoured vehicles move in darkness. The model "sees" what the deceiver paints.

Traditional counterintelligence focused on hiding secrets. Modern adversaries prefer to flood the system with fake secrets until the truth drowns.

Defenders respond by demanding provenance: cryptographic signing of sensor data, attestation of satellite feeds, cross-checking with ground truth. But cryptographic assurance introduces fragility. If the signing server is hacked, all downstream data becomes suspect. If the attestation chain breaks, every alert is downgraded. The system becomes paranoid. Over-caution is its own failure mode.

And yet, without provenance, the system becomes gullible. Under-caution is worse.

Some analysts talk of "AI deception labs"—teams whose job is to imagine what a hostile algorithm would do. They rehearse the enemy's tricks: spoofing heat signatures with cheap thermal blankets, injecting false ADS-B signals into civilian air traffic feeds, using LED arrays to blind machine vision, releasing balloons with RF reflectors, fabricating open-source chatter to shape model priors. To defend against deception, one must learn to deceive.

Militaries now run red-team drills not against humans, but against synthetic adversaries. They feed their detection systems thousands of fabricated decoy patterns to see what fools them. The best defenders accept a cruel truth: if your model has never been deceived, it is untested.

Yet every improvement in detection breeds more sophisticated camouflage. To catch a decoy convoy, models may demand higher-resolution satellite passes, slowing response times and exhausting orbital bandwidth. To verify a suspicious radar track, commanders may require human confirmation, losing the advantage of automation. Detection is forced to choose: be fast and wrong, or slow and right. Adversaries exploit both.

Civilian infrastructure is not immune. A port authority can be overwhelmed with false maritime alerts. A border agency can be swarmed with synthetic vehicle traces. A power grid can be made to "see" phantom consumption patterns that trigger unnecessary load shedding. If a critical system is optimised for rapid response, deception can cost billions without firing a shot. Economic warfare becomes a matter of corrupting signals, not sabotaging machines.

In the commercial sector, insurance companies use AI to detect fraud. Fraudsters respond by generating synthetic claim histories that look statistically "normal." Banks deploy anomaly detection on transactions. Criminal syndicates use machine learning to mimic normal payment patterns. Airports profile travellers by behavioural cues. Smuggling networks train couriers to imitate legitimate passengers.

The battlefield has expanded. Every domain with detection is now a domain of deception.

Yet defenders are not powerless. Some use "trap signatures"—artefacts intentionally planted in a model's training data that real targets never produce. When a decoy accidentally emits one, the system knows it is fake. Others deploy unpredictable sensing: randomised radar frequencies, intermittent satellite passes, or sensors that move rather than stare. If the deceiver cannot predict what the detector will look at, it cannot plan the lie.

Another tactic: cognitive diversity. Instead of one model, many. Each trained on different data, built with different assumptions, using different architectures. A decoy that fools one may not fool all. But diversity brings cost, complexity, and integration headaches. Fusion systems struggle when experts disagree.

And sometimes deception still triumphs. The most dangerous adversary is not the one who hides, but the one who performs.

Perhaps the deepest tension lies in the philosophy of perception. Humans misjudge because we rely on intuition. Machines misjudge because they rely on patterns. Deception exploits both. When a detection system becomes too predictable, the deceiver adapts. When the deceiver becomes too predictable, the detector adapts. There is no stable equilibrium.

This is why militaries run deception campaigns in layers: visual, thermal, acoustic, electromagnetic, behavioural. They do not need to fool every sensor—only the one that matters at the moment of decision. If one signature triggers the missile, the rest can be sloppy.

And if a model triggers too slowly, the decoy has served its purpose: it drew attention away from the real threat, buying time for the true convoy, swarm, ship, or strike.

There is a darker possibility: deception so advanced that humans lose confidence in their own sensors. If leaders stop trusting alerts because too many were false, they delay responses. If they delay responses, real attacks succeed. Strategic deterrence erodes—not because a nation is blind, but because it is uncertain.

Imagine a crisis in which every radar return, every intercepted message, every drone image might be synthetic. When does a state mobilise? When does it strike? At what point does caution become vulnerability? This is the psychological frontier of modern conflict.

Conversely, imagine a world where detection is near-perfect. Every decoy uncovered. Every synthetic signature unmasked. Would adversaries stop trying to deceive? Or would they escalate to bolder, more chaotic methods—deepfake command messages, forged sensor boot-logs, poisoned training data? The more perfect detection becomes, the more valuable a single successful deception grows.

A fragile peace rests on mutual doubt.

There are whispers that the most successful deception of the coming decade will not hide tanks, but hide intent. Pattern-of-life models may see every truck, ship, and aircraft. But what if the patterns themselves are engineered? Fleets may sail erratic routes to create "normal" future deviations. Convoys may rehearse fake smuggling paths months before a crisis. States may inject false "innocent behaviour" into public AIS feeds so that real deviations blend into the artificial noise. The battlefield becomes an illusion crafted long before war begins.

Detection can only learn from the past. Deception now aims to rewrite that past.

Some will claim the game is unwinnable. Others will argue that transparency—shared data, mutual verification, open audits—can break the cycle. But transparency itself can be exploited. A shared database can be poisoned. A public standard can be gamed.

The struggle between detection and deception is not a bug of modern warfare. It is the feature that ensures both sides continue to think, adapt, and doubt. And doubt, paradoxically, may be the last safeguard against automation running ahead of judgment.

So the convoy on the desert road rolls on: half real, half fake. The drone watches. The algorithm calculates. A commander wonders if the dust cloud ahead hides steel or mannequins. Somewhere, an adversary smiles, knowing that uncertainty is victory.

How long until machines no longer hesitate? And when they stop hesitating, who pays for the moment the decoy looked too convincing?

## Collateral risk accounting

A drone circled above a marketplace, its camera tracking a moving vehicle believed to be carrying munitions. The algorithm estimated a 72 per cent probability that the target was hostile, a 14 per cent chance that it belonged to local police, and a 9 per cent chance that it was a family car heading home. A human commander hesitated. The machine did not. Threshold crossed. The missile fell. Hours later, officials issued statements, diplomats protested, and the marketplace mourned. The probability was high; the outcome was irrevocable. In modern targeting, the line between precision and tragedy is not drawn in steel—it is drawn in numbers.

War has always involved risk, but predictive systems make that risk legible. Every strike becomes a calculation: the odds a vehicle is hostile, the likelihood a building houses fighters, the probability that a bystander will enter the blast radius. These numbers are presented as neutral, scientific, objective. Yet buried inside each are values. A 60 per cent confidence threshold versus an 80 per cent threshold is not a technical choice; it is an ethical one. It decides who lives and who dies.

Collateral risk accounting is the quiet moral architecture of algorithmic warfare. It is the mathematics of mercy and the mathematics of force, tangled together. When militaries boast of "surgical strikes," they mean their models predict small collateral footprints. But prediction is not certainty. A city refuses to behave like a physics experiment. People step outside. Traffic stalls. Phones die. Doors open. A child runs to retrieve a ball. No dataset can capture every contingency.

The paradox is persistent: the better machines get at modelling human behaviour, the more human unpredictability matters.

Some states respond with conservative triage metrics, treating uncertainty as danger. If there is a 10 per cent chance a strike harms civilians, the system vetoes it. Others use permissive metrics, arguing that hesitation emboldens adversaries and prolongs violence. In these models, risk is treated like weather: unfortunate, but tolerable.

Yet risk is not weather. It is choice.

Probability thresholds often sit deep inside code and policy, far from political debate. Developers speak of precision, recall, false positives. Commanders speak of collateral damage estimates. But civilians experience only the outcome. A 5 per cent risk of killing bystanders sounds ethically cautious until those bystanders live in a city of millions and the strikes are routine. Small probabilities scale when operations scale.

Some militaries attempt to formalise harm minimisation. Before a strike, the system queries nearby schools, hospitals, or cultural sites. It projects blast radii into dense neighbourhoods. It predicts whether a strike at noon, when markets are crowded, is more dangerous than a strike at midnight, when families sleep. The numbers feel scientific, yet everything hinges on assumptions: how many people are inside each building, how thick the walls are, how quickly emergency services respond. Sometimes those assumptions are based on outdated maps, incomplete census data, or satellite imagery from last year. Even the best model must guess.

Guessing becomes governance.

The most controversial element of collateral risk accounting is that probabilities lock in value judgements. If an algorithm judges a vehicle as "likely hostile", what probability qualifies as likely? Sixty per cent? Seventy? Ninety-five? States seldom agree. One military might allow strikes at thirty per cent confidence if the target is high-value. Another may require ninety. A third might lower its threshold during wartime desperation.

Diplomats see the consequences. Allies occasionally review footage of the same event and disagree whether it was justified. Lawyers argue over whether a model should have waited for clearer evidence. Intelligence officers defend their pipelines. Yet the core question is moral, not mathematical: how much uncertainty are we willing to kill under?

Consider urban drone corridors—pre-approved flight paths that minimised ground exposure. Instead of allowing drones to roam freely, commanders forced them into specific safe lanes: rivers, industrial zones, rail yards. The airframes accepted slower routing in exchange for lower civilian risk. Algorithms predicted pedestrian density, building occupancy, and emergency vehicle patterns. These systems made strikes rarer but safer.

Not every state adopted corridors. Some argued they created predictable routes that adversaries could avoid or exploit. Others found them politically intolerable: voters wanted protection, not statistical compromises. A few embraced them only in foreign theatres, not at home.

Corridors reveal a truth often hidden: safety is not only technical, but spatial. When machines forecast where civilians are most vulnerable, they reshape the geography of war.

There are darker complications. A model predicting collateral harm can become a weapon of propaganda. If an adversary can manipulate civilian density—by forcing evacuations, blocking roads, or staging crowds—they can increase apparent risk and deter strikes. Civilians become shields not because the attacker wants to harm them, but because the defender wants the attacker to refrain. Models did not invent this tactic, but they make its incentives explicit.

In some regions, hostile forces have laid out decoy crowds: heat signatures and mannequins placed near weapons depots, encouraging drones to abort. Other groups have conducted sudden "human surges", appearing around strategic buildings in hopes the algorithm would flag unacceptable risk. These tactics exploit the machine's morality. They turn ethics into an operational vulnerability.

The more principled the attacker, the easier it is to trap them in hesitation.

Even where risk accounting works, it causes friction. In one coalition, two allied states deployed similar drones but different probability thresholds. One was allowed to strike targets with 70 per cent confidence; the other required 85 per cent. Joint missions were awkward. When both drones identified the same threat, only one was authorised to fire. The other had to watch. Local observers saw inconsistency and called it hypocrisy. Politicians argued over sovereignty. The sky became a legal battlefield.

The lesson was simple: when models guide decisions, law and diplomacy become part of the algorithmic stack. Collateral risk is not only a matter of morality, but interoperability.

There are, however, hopeful innovations. Some systems allow dynamic thresholds—raising confidence requirements during daytime, lowering them at night. Others use "selective delay": if risk is uncertain, the system pauses and requests human review. Commanders can overrule the machine or demand additional intelligence. This preserves speed without surrendering judgment.

Still, latency matters. In one incident, a drone flagged a target with 95 per cent confidence, but network congestion delayed human review. By the time approval arrived, the target had vanished. The mission failed, and analysts blamed the human veto. Others blamed the system's refusal to fire autonomously. The argument was not about accuracy, but responsibility.

When machines can kill faster than humans can decide, hesitation becomes a strategic liability.

Some designers argue for "fail-open" systems that err toward action, not restraint. They claim that over-caution lets adversaries exploit civilian zones, turning cities into armour. Others demand "fail-safe" systems with strict vetoes, accepting military setback to prevent tragedy. The debate is fierce. Fail-open reflects a logic of dominance. Fail-safe reflects a logic of dignity.

Either way, probabilities rule.

To justify action, a model must have data. But data is uneven. Wealthier nations have detailed satellite maps, ground sensors, census records, and historical behaviour models. Poorer nations have fragmented data, patchy imagery, and unreliable signals. A drone in a megacity of slums cannot predict civilian movement well. A model trained on orderly traffic falters in chaotic streets. The same risk algorithm that works in London may mislead in Lagos.

When models travel across cultures, their error margins widen. Collateral risk accounting becomes not just a moral challenge, but a colonial one: whose behaviours define "normal"? Whose lives define acceptable error?

The global reaction is mixed. Some NGOs push for strict probability floors, arguing no strike should proceed below 90 per cent confidence. Militaries reply that such rules cede initiative to aggressors willing to hide among civilians. Diplomats worry that high thresholds create strategic sanctuaries—zones where hostile forces operate with impunity because the attacker fears public outrage.

There is no neutral position. Every choice privileges a value: protection, deterrence, speed, legitimacy, containment.

Some scholars propose "reverse thresholds". Instead of calculating the probability of civilian presence, models could calculate acceptable risk per strike, adjusted by context: urban density, time of day, and humanitarian corridors. This shifts from whether to strike to where and when a strike imposes the least harm. It treats civilians not as obstacles, but as people with rhythms and patterns that deserve respect.

Others propose compensation algorithms: if a strike imposes civilian risk, the attacker must commit to post-strike aid, infrastructure repair, or diplomatic transparency. Accountability becomes part of the targeting pipeline, not an afterthought.

For now, these remain fringe ideas.

After-action reviews reveal how fragile certainty truly is. A strike initially judged "clean" may be reconsidered days later when more footage arrives, or when survivors speak. Some militaries quietly revise models, adjusting weightings to reduce false positives. Others roll out "hotfixes" to recalibrate risk scoring. But every patch is too late for those already harmed.

This is the ethical discomfort of collateral risk accounting: optimisation does not erase the dead. A more accurate model tomorrow does not resurrect mistakes from yesterday.

Politicians promise transparency. Engineers promise improvement. Commanders promise regret. Civilians are left with probabilities that became funerals.

So where does prudence lie? Some argue that algorithmic targeting, despite its flaws, remains more humane than unguided bombardment or human intuition. Machines at least try to measure risk. Humans have historically ignored it. A 30 per cent confidence threshold may seem cold, but it is higher than the historical average of blind artillery.

Others insist that probability cannot replace principle. They remind us that a life lost at 95 per cent certainty is still a life lost under doubt. They fear a future where algorithmic precision sanitises violence, making it politically palatable because casualties are "within acceptable parameters."

They ask whether acceptable parameters should exist at all.

Perhaps the central question is this: does quantifying risk make war more humane, or does it make killing easier to justify?

There is no easy answer. Collateral risk accounting forces uncomfortable reckoning. It reveals where ethics live—in code, in thresholds, in assumptions, in shortcuts. It exposes the idea that technological precision absolves nobody. A missile can be accurate and still be wrong.

For now, drones still hesitate when uncertainty is high. Commanders still lose sleep over percentages. Diplomats still carry photographs into negotiation rooms. Activists still argue that probability should never substitute for certainty.

But as targeting systems become faster, and conflicts more data-rich, pressures will grow to lower thresholds. To take the shot. To trust the model. To accept that risk is inevitable and that war cannot wait for perfect information.

If that day comes, the marketplace memory will matter. Not as an argument, but as a warning: probability is not a shield. It is a mirror. It shows us who we are when certainty is impossible.

And the question that follows is as old as conflict itself: how much doubt can a nation kill under?

## Intelligence fusion friction

The war room was quiet, save for the hum of screens and whispered arguments between analysts. On one display, a satellite feed from an ally suggested that a convoy was moving north. On another, intercepted radio chatter implied it was heading south. A drone operator insisted he had tracked the vehicles turning west. Three systems, three agencies, three truths—each correct within its own data model, none reconcilable in time. Targets slipped through confusion, not stealth. The enemy had not jammed a single signal. The coalition had jammed itself.

The public imagines intelligence as a great funnel: information rushing in, being combined, filtered, and transformed into insight. In reality, intelligence fusion is seldom a funnel. It is a mosaic built from shards—satellite imagery, radar traces, intercepted messages, social media fragments, ground sensors, battlefield reports. Each shard arrives from a different organisation with its own software, classification rules, workflows, and priorities. The wonder is not that agencies sometimes disagree; the wonder is that they ever agree at all.

The friction grows sharper in algorithmic warfare, where predictive models must ingest live data from dozens of systems. A model trained on navy logs struggles to interpret army telemetry. A drone that speaks one protocol cannot stream to a ship that supports another. Analysts export data into spreadsheets because systems cannot talk. In the time it takes to reformat a file, the battlefield moves on.

The paradox is stark: the more data a coalition has, the harder it becomes to make sense of it.

API mismatches are the mundane but deadly enemy of intelligence fusion. A radar feed updated every five seconds clashes with a satellite feed updated every ninety. A drone sends object labels in centimetres; a targeting system expects them in metres. One database uses local time; another logs data in UTC. The differences seem trivial until a strike hinges on whether a convoy is 300 metres from a hospital or 30.

Some agencies treat software like a proprietary asset—if they reveal their data formats, they fear exposing weaknesses or losing leverage. Others operate under legal constraints: privacy laws, intelligence-sharing treaties, or national security protocols that forbid raw access. The result is a labyrinth of middlemen: liaison officers, manual uploads, batch transfers. When crisis erupts, everything slows.

The battlefield does not care.

Coalitions feel this most acutely. A state-of-the-art reconnaissance drone deployed by one country cannot stream directly into another's command platform. Lawyers negotiate temporary access while analysts wait. By the time permission is granted, the intelligence is stale. Soldiers on the ground must act with partial knowledge, while automated systems idle for lack of clearance.

To overcome these problems, some militaries have created "data rooms"—neutral zones where allies exchange intelligence through minimal accepted schemas. Instead of demanding full interoperability, they agree on a narrow common language: object type, location, timestamp, confidence score. It is not elegant, but it is practical. Like a pidgin, it carries enough meaning to be useful, without forcing unity in doctrine or design.

In one maritime coalition, this worked brilliantly. Navies from five countries shared cues about suspicious shipping. Each vessel flagged behaviours—unusual routes, irregular radio silence, shadowing decoys—and posted them into the shared room. AI models from different nations consumed the same structured entries, even if their internal logic was incompatible. Within weeks, interdictions improved, and smuggling routes collapsed.

Yet even successes reveal fragility. If one partner changed its schema, the entire pipeline trembled. When a new model shifted from latitude-longitude to UTM grid references, half the automated alerts vanished into silent error. Engineers patched the system at sea using whatever cables and code they could muster. The smuggling networks barely noticed, but the coalition did.

Secrecy complicates everything. Intelligence agencies have spent decades building walls, not bridges. Encryption, compartmentalisation, need-to-know silos—these protect sources and methods. But algorithimic warfare demands sharing. A machine cannot reason about a threat without seeing the data. If data is withheld, the model is blind. If data is delayed, the model is misled.

The cultural shift is painful. Analysts raised on mistrust are asked to trust. Officers trained to hoard information are told to exchange it. Militaries that once measured power by secrecy now measure it by interoperability. Every shared API feels like vulnerability.

Some nations respond with layered access: metadata first, raw data only when necessary. Others use homomorphic encryption, allowing models to compute over encrypted signals without exposing content. These approaches promise security without paralysis. But they demand engineering sophistication that many partners lack.

Smaller states face a harsher dilemma: share data and risk exploitation, or withhold data and become strategically irrelevant.

Workflow friction is just as corrosive. One agency reviews imagery twice before approving analysis; another pushes everything live. Some insist on human sign-off for every alert; others trust automation until humans object. When these workflows intersect, confusion reigns. An AI might flag a threat that one agency automatically escalates, while another quietly downgrades it as noise. Both believe they are following procedure. Neither realises the other system is acting on the same data.

The enemy, meanwhile, moves with purpose.

In one joint operation, a NATO partner flagged suspicious ferry movements between two ports. Another nation's analysts dismissed it: the ferry had run that route for decades. A third nation recognised the ship had been recently bought by a shell company linked to sanctioned actors. None of the systems talked. Each agency was right from its own vantage point; together they were blind.

The solution was not more data, but shared semantics. Once the coalition agreed on baseline categories—vessel ownership, deviation from historic pattern, link to sanctioned entities—the alerts aligned. The ferry was seized days later. What looked like cunning analysis was, in truth, simply shared meaning.

Minimal common schemas sound tedious. They are quietly revolutionary. They lower the diplomatic cost of cooperation. Instead of forcing agencies to reveal full databases, they ask for structured clues: labels, coordinates, timestamps, confidence metrics. This avoids political fights about sovereignty, vendor access, or software integration. It is not glamourous, but it works.

Yet schemas can mask deeper tension. Whose definitions become standard? Does "armed convoy" include vehicles with detachable weapons? Should "civilian presence" count indoor populations algorithmically inferred from heat signatures? Small definitional differences can swing strike decisions. When schemas expand, ethics enter the data model.

Shared definitions become shared responsibility.

A deeper problem lurks beneath: models trained on different data cultures behave unpredictably when fused. An AI accustomed to clean government records may choke on messy social media feeds. A system optimised for desert terrain may misread snowy landscapes. If partners feed each other data without acknowledging these biases, fusion breaks silently.

Engineers talk of "domain adaptation," but it is never perfect. A single corrupted field can propagate error. A missing timestamp collapses chronology. An incorrectly labelled object multiplies into false alerts. When humans fuse bad data, they argue. When machines fuse bad data at scale, they act with misplaced confidence.

Confidence is dangerous when it is wrong.

Coalitions attempt to mitigate risk with "trust scores". Each data source carries a reliability rating. High-trust sources influence models strongly; low-trust sources are weighted lightly. But who assigns trust? Historical accuracy? Technical quality? Political preference? One ally's truth becomes another ally's scepticism. Trust itself becomes geopolitics.

There are darker games. A partner can subtly shape battlefield perception by feeding ambiguous or selective data into a shared system. Not lies—just partial truths. Omitted context. Delayed timestamps. A slow drip of uncertainty that nudges coalition action where one nation prefers. Information becomes strategy. Friction becomes leverage.

Machines cannot detect this. They assume data is sincere.

Some militaries now run "fusion rehearsals" like fire drills. Teams simulate degraded feeds, misaligned formats, and corrupted metadata. They practice patching schemas, rerouting streams, reconciling contradictory alerts. These rehearsals reveal more about coalition readiness than missile tests ever will. The battle is often won or lost long before a shot is fired—inside the software that decides where to aim.

There is a philosophical irony here. Wars used to be defined by noise: gunfire, explosions, roaring engines. Now silence is the threat. A file that does not upload. A stream that does not sync. A system waiting for a token from a server that has crashed. The quiet failures kill.

Some technologists insist the answer is grand: a universal military operating system, one API to rule them all. Engineers dream of seamless integration, real-time sharing, perfect coherence. Politicians love the idea; vendors promise it is possible. History suggests otherwise. No coalition has ever fully unified its intelligence. Not for lack of will, but because war is governed by politics, not code.

The realistic path is humbler: minimal schemas, modular bridges, adaptive translators. Systems that work well enough, even when imperfect. Intelligence that is coherent enough to prevent tragedy, agile enough to exploit opportunity, resilient enough to survive fracture.

The goal is not perfection. It is sufficiency in chaos.

Fusion friction will never disappear. Agencies will always guard secrets; allies will always disagree; vendors will always compete. But the cost of friction rises as warfare accelerates. When decisions are made in seconds, not hours, the gap between systems becomes the gap between life and death.

Some commanders fear that automation will replace human judgment. In truth, automation often reveals how human judgment was already failing—buried under paperwork, lost in mistranslation, paralysed by bureaucracy. Machines do not eliminate friction; they expose it.

The uncomfortable question is whether states will treat fusion as infrastructure—boring, essential, expensive—or as afterthought. Railways, electricity grids, and telecommunication networks were once afterthoughts too. Those who built them early shaped continents. Those who stalled became footnotes.

The same will be true of intelligence fusion. And as machines increasingly make sense of the battlefield, the greatest strategic advantage may not be a secret weapon, but a shared language.

## After-action learning loops

A patrol drone misclassified a civilian truck as an armed convoy. The strike was seconds away when a human operator intervened, cancelling the engagement. No one died. Officially, the incident never happened. Unofficially, the model was wrong—and nothing changed. The logs stayed buried, the training set stayed flawed, the next patrol launched with the same blind spot. It is a quiet form of negligence: the system learned nothing, and therefore remained dangerous.

Machines that cannot learn from mistakes are merely faster versions of yesterday's errors. Yet many militaries treat algorithmic failures the way cold-war institutions treated classified mishaps: sealed behind security protocols, immune to scrutiny, and quietly forgotten. The paradox of AI-enabled warfare is that it requires more transparency, not less. A model that cannot be corrected becomes a liability, however advanced its architecture.

The most lethal systems are not those that never err, but those that *learn*.

A mature after-action loop is deceptively simple. An incident occurs. Data is collected. The root cause is diagnosed. The model is updated. Guardrails are tightened. The update is redeployed. Reality rarely cooperates. Data lives in fourteen places, owned by six agencies, stored under incompatible security policies. Engineers demand raw telemetry; intelligence officers refuse to release it. Lawyers argue classification. Vendors insist the bug lies outside their component.

In some militaries, the friction is so great that retraining a model takes months. On a battlefield that evolves daily, this is indistinguishable from not learning at all.

Some states embrace a different approach: rapid remediation, akin to emergency medicine. When an anomaly emerges—an unexpected misclassification, a navigation failure, a targeting hesitation—engineers issue a *hotfix*. This is a narrowly scoped correction that patches the specific fault without retraining the entire model. Hotfixes are fast. They reduce exposure. But they can also create technical debt, layering patches upon patches until the system becomes opaque, brittle, and unpredictable.

The alternative is a full retrain: rebuilding the model with corrected data, updated labels, and new adversarial examples. This is slower, computationally expensive, and politically delicate—retraining implies fallibility, and fallibility invites blame. But full retrains scale better: they address systemic weaknesses, not isolated symptoms. The difference between a hotfix and a retrain is the difference between stitching a wound and treating the infection.

Some commanders fear frequent updates will destabilise warfighting systems. They prefer reliability over adaptation, even if that reliability masks outdated heuristics. Yet it is the battlefield that is unstable, not the code. Opponents adapt, behaviours mutate, environments shift. A static model is not safe; it is complacent.

Autonomous vehicles already show this in civilian life. Self-driving cars improve through continuous updates. Every crash, near-miss, or misread sign becomes a teaching moment shared across the fleet. The car that fails to recognise a pedestrian in Lisbon informs a vehicle in London. Militaries lack this culture. Incidents are classified. Lessons stay siloed. A mistake in one theatre does not prevent a tragedy in another.

The difference is governance. Civilian systems have regulators, disclosure rules, recall authorities. Defence systems have secrecy, national pride, and multilateral politics. Yet if oversight does not expand to match autonomy, public trust will erode long before the machines reach maturity.

The most innovative militaries run "no-fault" debriefs after every deployment of autonomous systems. Instead of asking *who* made the mistake, they ask *what* the system failed to see. They replay telemetry, imagery, radio logs, and model outputs. Engineers sit beside analysts. Commanders sit beside lawyers. Vendors sit beside soldiers. The goal is not punishment. The goal is correction.

In one naval experiment, these debriefs cut false positives by more than half in two months. Engineers discovered that the model over-weighted night-time heat signatures near fishing boats. It interpreted the glow of portable generators as weapons fire. Instead of writing new code, they retrained the model with expanded examples of benign behaviour. The fix was trivial. The insight was transformative. If the navy had relied on hotfixes, it might have patched the symptom rather than the cause—turning a small bias into future catastrophe.

Rapid relearning creates uncomfortable questions of accountability. If a model is updated weekly, or daily, who certifies each update? Who signs off when a vendor deploys a silent patch? In software culture, continuous deployment is normal. In warfare, uncontrolled updates are dangerous. A bug in a video game causes annoyance; a bug in a targeting model causes funerals.

Some states resolve this with dual keys: engineers may propose updates, but commanders must approve them. Others use staged rollouts: the new model runs in shadow mode, analysing live data without authority to act. Analysts compare its judgments to the legacy model. Only after confidence is earned does the update go active.

These approaches mirror civilian safety engineering. But the stakes are higher, and the timelines shorter. A delayed patch may allow an adversary exploit to persist. A rushed patch may introduce new vulnerabilities. The governance tension is constant: too cautious, and the system is slow; too aggressive, and the system is reckless.

A more subtle challenge arises when updates change not just performance, but *behavioural incentives.* Suppose a model learns that certain buildings consistently harbour combatants. It becomes more willing to strike those buildings, increasing tactical advantage but also civilian risk. Every retrain embeds a valuc judgment: whose safety matters, how much uncertainty is tolerable, how aggressively the system should act.

In human warfare, these judgments are negotiated culturally—by ethics boards, commanders, and doctrine. In algorithmic warfare, they are encoded mathematically—by loss functions, confidence thresholds, and sampling strategies. After-action loops must therefore include human oversight not only of technical accuracy, but of moral drift.

Otherwise, models may become more lethal than intended—not because they disobeyed orders, but because they learned too well.

One of the strongest defences against catastrophic error is adversarial testing: engineers deliberately stress the model with edge cases. They feed it corrupted images, spoofed radar signals, synthetic decoys, and misleading patterns. The goal is to break it before reality does. These tests create training data for the next update. The weakest parts of the model become the strongest parts—if the lessons are learned.

Some militaries now maintain "red-models": AI agents whose sole purpose is to fool or jam the operational system. If the operational model falls for a deception, logs capture every detail, feeding post-incident learning. This turns adversarial pressure into a source of resilience. A model exposed to its own synthetic enemies is harder to surprise.

Yet this raises a philosophical tension. Models trained against clever fakes may start mistrusting real data. Overcorrection becomes paranoia. In human terms, the system becomes jumpy—triggered by shadows, overreacting to noise. After-action loops must therefore include damping: learning fast, but not too fast.

Governance is not glamorous. It lacks the drama of missiles and the brilliance of algorithms. But without governance, learning becomes chaos. States require audit trails showing when an incident occurred, how the system responded, who authorised the update, what changed, and whether the change improved outcomes. Without this, there is no accountability. And without accountability, there is no trust.

Some coalitions assign independent auditors—not lawyers, but technologists trained to dissect model updates. Their job is to catch silent regressions: improvements in one domain that damage performance in another. They are the modern equivalent of airworthiness inspectors, except the aircraft is logic, not metal.

As autonomous systems mature, after-action loops will define strategic edge. Nations that learn fastest will outmanoeuvre those that deploy the smartest code once and never revise it. The battlefield punishes static wisdom. It rewards adaptation—quiet, continuous, disciplined adaptation.

The haunting question, rarely spoken aloud, is whether governments are ready for a form of warfare that evolves faster than bureaucracy. In traditional procurement, systems change every decade. In algorithmic warfare, they change every week. If institutions cannot learn at that tempo, their machines will not save them.

The future will not belong to those with the largest models or the deadliest drones. It will belong to those who can admit mistakes, study them without shame, correct them without delay, and teach their machines to do the same.

# Chapter 4

# Cyber Sovereignty and the New Territory

On a winter morning in Frankfurt, a dispute erupted that never reached the front pages. No soldiers moved, no borders shifted, yet two governments confronted one another with the quiet intensity of a nuclear standoff. The conflict centred on a single data request: a European regulator demanded records stored on servers physically located in Germany but administered by an American cloud provider. The provider insisted it was bound by U.S. law; the regulator insisted German data, on German soil, must obey German sovereignty. Lawyers replaced generals. Subpoenas replaced artillery. The records remained locked behind a wall of encryption while diplomats scrambled to invent new language for a reality old treaties had never imagined.

This is the new geography of power: sovereignty expressed as tenancy, routing, and who controls the racks behind biometric doors. Territory without a coastline. Borders drawn in fibre. Data has become a citizen that lives in many states at once, and those states are beginning to demand allegiance.

It is tempting to think of cyberspace as weightless—ethereal packets drifting at light speed. Yet the internet is relentlessly physical: kilometres of submarine cable, blast-resistant data halls, chilled processors stacked by the thousands. Whoever controls this infrastructure controls the flows of finance, communication, intelligence, and now algorithmic warfare. The 20th century fought over shipping lanes; the 21st fights over cloud regions.

The first shock to traditional geopolitics is jurisdiction. A dataset in Dublin might be queried in Washington, analysed in Singapore, and backed up to Zurich. Which law governs? Which court prevails? Some states answer by extending jurisdiction across oceans, insisting that their companies comply regardless of geography. Others build national firewalls or demand that data never leave their borders. Both approaches reveal the same discomfort: the strategic terrain has shifted, but the legal map has not caught up.

This chapter traces that displacement of power—from land to infrastructure, from guns to permissions, from airspace to API keys. Clouds have become contested ground. Governments now negotiate tenancy the way they once negotiated basing rights. Routing decisions become sovereignty decisions. A country denied access to a cloud region may find its banks unable to clear transactions, its hospitals unable to share records, its satellites unable to receive telemetry. Blockades were once enforced by ships; now they can be enacted by quietly downgrading capacity.

Some states respond with ambition: *national stacks*. They build sovereign clouds, indigenous encryption standards, domestic semiconductor fabs, and model gardens—curated repositories of approved AI systems tested to local political and ethical norms. Sovereign stacks promise resilience: when sanctions strike or relations sour, services continue. But resilience has a price. Parallel ecosystems are expensive to build, slower to innovate, and often incompatible with global standards. A sovereign cloud may protect a nation from foreign influence while simultaneously isolating it technologically.

There is another tension—sovereign stacks give governments enormous leverage over their own citizens. If every service runs through a national data hall, surveillance becomes effortless. Dissidents do not need to be arrested; they can simply be throttled offline. The trade-off is stark: autonomy from foreign power versus dependence on domestic power. Some democracies attempt middle ground—hybrid architectures where sensitive government workloads sit on sovereign metal while commercial and scientific computing remains global. Others go further, pursuing regionalised compute zones: availability regions that never cross political boundaries, even when operated by multinational firms.

But even these compromise models invite questions of trust. If a state outsources infrastructure to a foreign vendor, who holds the keys? If a cloud provider can shut off access, does it quietly possess more power than parliament? Territorial control once meant tanks on a road. Now it may mean firmware updates on a server.

A quieter front in this struggle lies in standards. States have discovered that power can be exported not only through treaties or trade, but through norms. Safety benchmarks, model evaluation suites, and procurement guidelines act as invisible legislation. A country that defines what "secure" means for a neural network may find its standards adopted across alliances, supply chains, and eventually markets. Once everyone builds to your template, you no longer need to coerce; alignment becomes architecture.

This is not a new tactic—aviation and telecommunications were moulded by technical standards long before. But AI and cloud computing move far faster. A safety baseline drafted today might govern billions of inferences tomorrow. A certification scheme can determine who is trusted to host defence workloads and who is locked out. Nations compete to write the rules—not for prestige, but because rules shape the battlefield of the future. If your standards dominate, you do not simply win compliance; you win customers, mindshare, and geopolitical sympathy.

One vivid example is conformance testing: rigorous evaluation suites that determine whether an AI model meets safety, robustness, and provenance requirements. Alliances coalesce around these suites. Procurement follows them. Companies jostle to be certified. This is how policy becomes infrastructure—subtle, technical, and immensely consequential.

Sovereignty also depends on trust in the supply chain. A model may be world-class, but if its firmware is compromised, its compiler toolchain is tampered with, or its update channel is hijacked, every output becomes suspect. Adversaries no longer need to breach a data centre physically; they can poison the software supply chain, inserting backdoors invisible to human eyes and nearly invisible to automated scans. The most secure facility is meaningless if the code running inside it cannot be trusted.

This has forced a cultural shift. Defence ministries now demand chain-of-custody attestations: cryptographic proof that every component—from the underlying kernel to the trained weights—was built, shipped, and deployed without interference. Some insist on signed model artefacts, where updates can be traced and verified like ballistic fingerprints. Others require secure enclaves that can prove, mathematically, that no unauthorised code is executed during inference.

These measures sound dry, but they have strategic force. If states cannot trust one another's supply chains, they cannot cooperate. Joint operations falter. Intelligence fusion collapses. Diplomacy becomes paralysed by suspicion. The Cold War taught us to fear espionage; the cyber age teaches us to fear silent modification.

And then come the licences—the new levers of statecraft. A government can weaponise access not by banning hardware exports, but by restricting cloud usage terms. A hostile nation might find that its accounts are throttled, audited, or quietly revoked. Usage becomes a privilege, not a right. Export controls once targeted missiles and centrifuges; now they target pretrained models, high-bandwidth interconnects, and clusters large enough to train next-generation systems. Cloud providers become instruments of policy, whether they like it or not.

Control is rarely absolute. Nations experiment with graduated access tiers: partners receive full-service support, neutral states receive constrained performance, adversaries receive none. Even commercial customers are not exempt. Contract clauses allow states to demand audits or mandate kill-switch capabilities. The world's most powerful cloud operators sit in an awkward position—private firms that control strategic territory, bound to one jurisdiction yet serving many. Their lawyers now live the geopolitics once reserved for diplomats.

But leverage invites retaliation. A state excluded from a dominant cloud might retaliate by expropriating data centres on its soil or creating parallel platforms. Competition escalates. Standards diverge. Fragmentation becomes the price of autonomy.

All of this raises uncomfortable questions. If a country depends on foreign infrastructure for medicine, banking, and defence telemetry, is it truly sovereign? If shutting down a data region can collapse a power grid, does that region count as critical territory? And if clouds are territory, who has the right to patrol them, inspect them, or weaponise them?

Sovereignty used to be visible—flags, airbases, checkpoints. The new sovereignty is invisible: encryption protocols, routing policies, identity systems, uptime guarantees. Power has moved inward, into the semiconductor and the switch.

But something older echoes beneath this complexity. States have always sought control over the means of communication. Empires built roads and postal systems; victors seized telegraph lines; superpowers launched satellites. Today, control is more abstract but no less strategic. Nations claim digital territory not to collect rent, but to ensure continuity when the world grows unstable.

This chapter explores that transformation: clouds as contested ground, sovereign stacks as strategic insurance, standards as power projection, supply chains as battleground, and licences as levers of coercion. It is a story of states racing to rebuild sovereignty in a domain where borders blur and geography betrays them. It is also a story of fragility—of how quickly global interdependence can become a point of failure.

Some readers will find comfort in resilience: nations investing in reliability, citizens gaining protection from overreach. Others will see danger: a world fragmenting into incompatible camps, each cloud a fortress, each standard a declaration of alignment. Both views may be true.

What is certain is that the battles of cyber sovereignty are already underway. They do not roar; they hum. They are fought not on open plains but in server aisles lit by cold fluorescent light. And their outcomes will determine who governs the invisible infrastructure on which modern life—and modern conflict—now depends.

Turn the page. The borders you will encounter no longer run along rivers or mountain ridges. They run through fibres, chips, and code—territory at once intangible and fiercely, undeniably real.

## Clouds as contested ground

One night in São Paulo, police investigators sought access to a suspect's encrypted messages. The servers hosting the data sat in a gleaming data centre less than an hour's drive away. Yet every request bounced between legal departments on opposite sides of the Atlantic. Brazilian courts insisted the provider must comply with domestic warrants. The American company insisted the data was protected by U.S. law. Neither side budged. So a judge, in frustration, ordered the service throttled across the entire country, leaving millions of ordinary users caught in a geopolitical tug of war they never saw. The messages remained locked. No doors were kicked down. No vaults were blown open. The only battlefield was jurisdiction—competing laws wrapped around the same hard drives.

This episode captured an uncomfortable truth: the old idea that "territory" is defined by soil, borders, and buildings no longer holds. Power sits in racks, routers, and fibre. A state can have perfect physical sovereignty and still lack control over the digital arteries running beneath its cities. The paradox is sharp: data may be stored in one country, controlled by a firm headquartered in another, routed through a third, and cached in a fourth. Which flag governs? Which court speaks? Which government can compel compliance?

Few diplomats are ready for that answer, because it is no longer binary. Jurisdiction now pools in infrastructure—data centres, cloud regions, and backbone carriers. Tenancy is sovereignty's new anchor. If a government can terminate your compute, throttle your bandwidth, seize your encryption keys, or deny access to forensic logs, it wields coercive power without firing a shot. Conversely, if a foreign corporation owns the servers your hospitals store medical data on, sovereignty is shared, diluted, or—in moments of crisis—denied altogether.

The rise of global cloud providers created this tension not out of malice but efficiency. Centralised hyperscale centres are cheaper, faster, and more secure than fractured national infrastructure. Banks, health services, telecoms, and defence contractors all moved to the cloud for resilience. Yet resilience has a shadow: dependency. If the keys to your society's digital nervous system sit in a foreign data centre, sovereignty becomes conditional.

To understand why clouds are contested, one must recognise how physical they are. A modern data centre is a fortress: buried power lines, redundant generators, cooling towers, biometric checkpoints, armed guards. These facilities require billions in capital and sit at critical junctions of high-capacity fibre. Some are placed near rivers for cooling, others near financial hubs for latency, and many beside submarine cable landing stations. Geography shapes computation. National borders merely sit on top of it.

Routing adds another layer of control. Most internet traffic does not take a straight path; it hops through routers that decide which cables and exchanges will carry each packet. A state that influences routing can degrade, delay, or silently inspect traffic. Redirecting packets by a single autonomous system can move data through friendlier jurisdiction—or through intelligence adversaries. Routing is not a technical detail; it is a sovereignty lever. During tense diplomatic moments, some nations quietly reroute traffic away from foreign-controlled segments, just as navies redirect shipping away from contested maritime chokepoints.

The legal world has not caught up. Courts long assumed that jurisdiction followed geography: a police force obtains a warrant, seizes a server, and the matter ends. But servers are no longer static. Data burrows, replicates, shreds itself into encrypted shards, and sits scattered across availability zones chosen by algorithms. Seizing a server may seize nothing; the data you want lives elsewhere. Laws drafted for filing cabinets now confront distributed storage that does not care where its metal chassis sits. The result is diplomatic improvisation: bilateral agreements, compelled assistance, cross-border subpoenas, and political threats, none of which offer a stable equilibrium.

The real leverage lies with tenancy. Whoever controls access to cloud tenancy can cripple an organisation, a city, or a state. If a government orders a cloud provider to freeze a customer's account, the effect ripples instantly: payroll fails, email stops, satellites lose downlink capability. Nations have already learned this lesson. Some purchase strategic capacity in multiple clouds, spreading risk the way navies once dispersed fleets. Others demand data residency: critical systems may only run in domestic facilities, under domestic law, where domestic agents can audit logs and seize keys.

Lawful access regimes sit at the centre of this fight. Governments argue they cannot protect citizens if encrypted services resist warrants. Cloud providers counter that breaking encryption shatters trust for everyone, including dissidents, whistle-blowers, and ordinary democrats. The argument is not theoretical. In one well-known standoff, an international prosecutor secured legal authority to investigate a war crimes suspect's communications. The cloud vendor refused, asserting that foreign courts could not compel decryption. Allies who normally align on security found themselves whispering accusations: "You are shielding a criminal." "You are eroding global privacy." Neither side blinked. A server in the wrong region, under the wrong corporate policy, became an unmovable obstacle to justice.

The lesson is unsettling: laws may be local, but infrastructure is global. The gap between them is where power hides.

Cloud sovereignty cuts both ways. Some states exploit its reach to extend influence abroad. A government with jurisdiction over a company can require it to hand over data hosted in foreign countries. Allies accuse one another of extraterritorial overreach; adversaries accuse one another of espionage. A multinational provider sits at the centre, unable to satisfy all masters at once. To comply with one court is to betray another.

In response, new models emerge. Some clouds now offer "sovereign instances": deployments operated by a local entity under local oversight, even when built on global technology. Others create encrypted regions where no operator—not even the provider—can see the data or decrypt the logs. These are not mere engineering tricks; they are diplomatic stabilisers, attempts to square two incompatible truths: that modern infrastructure must be global to be efficient, and sovereign to be legitimate.

Routing sovereignty develops in parallel. During political crises, some states have demanded that domestic traffic stay on domestic fibres. They fear foreign interception or strategic chokeholds. Yet enforcing local routing is technically brittle—packets wander. The more aggressively a state tries to force compliance, the more it risks fracturing from the global internet, drifting towards a walled network like those of heavily controlled regimes. Nations weigh security against openness, autonomy against innovation.

And beneath the legal and technical argument lies a deeper philosophical question: who owns the cloud? Its cables are laid by corporations, its software run by private engineers, its power drawn from public grids, its tenants a mix of citizens and states. When a national archive or nuclear regulator stores its data on infrastructure owned by a foreign firm, sovereignty becomes a tapestry of contractual promises, not a matter of force.

This makes the stakes dangerously high. Imagine a confrontation between two nuclear powers. Instead of cutting submarine cables or bombing command centres, one power pressures a cloud provider to revoke access to critical services used by the other's civilian agencies. No shots fired; no treaties violated; yet public confidence collapses, hospitals fail, markets freeze, and leaders suspect sabotage. Does that count as an act of war? Does the cloud provider become a belligerent? Does the public ever learn the truth?

The opposite risk is equally troubling. When a cloud operator refuses lawful access to protect privacy, criminals may go undetected, intelligence agencies may fail to stop attacks, and democratic governments may appear powerless. Citizens want safety *and* liberty. Clouds have made that trade-off more opaque. Encryption and jurisdiction clash, and neither side feels secure.

Amid this uncertainty, states behave as they always have when a strategic domain becomes contested: they fortify. National cloud strategies multiply. Data localisation laws tighten. Geopolitical alliances write shared policies for forensic access, threat intelligence sharing, and fail-safe procedures. Some states subsidise domestic cloud infrastructure to reduce reliance on foreign giants. Others negotiate treaties for lawful access across borders, hoping to avoid the next diplomatic deadlock.

Yet every safeguard adds friction to a network built on fluidity. Walls rise. Interoperability suffers. The very openness that made the cloud valuable begins to wither.

Perhaps the most revealing moment occurs not when states quarrel, but when they cooperate. In joint cyber operations or multinational military coalitions, intelligence flows across secure rooms hosted in the cloud. Treaty partners gain shared dashboards, shared logs, shared AI models for cyber defence. But these systems only work if all parties trust the infrastructure. That trust is fragile. If one partner fears hidden legal hooks from another's government, the cooperation collapses. Clouds can unite—or stratify.

And so the contest continues. It is waged by regulators and diplomats, by engineers writing access control lists, by lawyers drafting service contracts, by intelligence agencies trying to peer through encryption. Every new region launched by a cloud provider is a geopolitical statement: "We are here, within your borders, under your laws—but our parent company lives elsewhere." Every new cable laid across an ocean is a declaration of intent: "This route will carry the world's data; we will maintain it."

The paradox remains unresolved. The more global the cloud becomes, the more fiercely states try to carve out sovereignty. The more sovereignty they demand, the more brittle global connectivity grows.

So the question hangs: will the cloud evolve into neutral ground—like international waters—or become a patchwork of fenced-off territories, each ruled by different statutes, different keys, different norms? If the next great crisis erupts not in trenches or airspace but in a data hall lit by the cold glow of server LEDs, who will have the final say?

The battle lines are already drawn. Not on maps, but on fibre routes. Not at checkpoints, but at API gateways. The contest has begun, and the cloud—sprawling, opaque, indispensable—has become the new high ground.

## National stacks, strategic forks

On a cold January morning, finance officials in a small European capital woke to find that their tax authority's analytics platform had gone silent. Every dashboard, every interface, every query: unresponsive. The cloud provider hosting the service insisted it was a "regional anomaly". But engineers suspected something else. Across the border, a larger neighbour had entered a diplomatic dispute with the platform's parent company. The outage was not a system failure; it was collateral. A state that owned none of the cables, none of the servers, and none of the software had suddenly lost a core public function, not through sabotage but through dependency. For those officials, it became a moment of clarity: sovereignty borrowed is sovereignty at risk. By the end of the year, parliament had approved the first sovereign cloud programme in the nation's history.

These debates were once confined to cybersecurity conferences and academic journals. Now they are mainstream politics. States are discovering that a digital life hosted elsewhere is a strategic liability, even when the provider is friendly, even when the terms are meticulously negotiated. The shift to sovereign clouds is not about nationalism or prestige. It is about insurance, autonomy, and bargaining power in moments of crisis.

A sovereign cloud is not a magical fortress in the sky. It is infrastructure—compute, storage, networking—physically located within a country, under its law and oversight, sometimes operated by domestic firms, sometimes by foreign companies under strict constraints. In practice, the model varies. France's approach differs from Singapore's; India's from Japan's. Yet the logic is shared: keep critical workloads, sensitive data, and essential AI services close enough to secure, audit, and compel.

The costs are heavy. Global cloud providers enjoy immense economies of scale: thousands of customers share the same data centres, cooling systems, and backbone lines. By building sovereign alternatives, countries trade cheaper services for harder guarantees. But many leaders believe the price is worth paying. In a crisis, a sovereign cloud remains reachable by domestic courts, domestic engineers, and—if necessary—domestic soldiers. No overseas subpoena or corporate decision can turn it off.

Strategic forks go beyond storage and servers. Increasingly, states are building "model gardens"—domestic AI ecosystems where models are trained, evaluated, and deployed under local rules. This is not merely a technical preference. It reflects cultural, political, and legal differences. A model trained on the behavioural patterns of one society may misfire in another. A policing algorithm honed on American crime data could be biased or useless in a West African city. A maritime interdiction model trained on Pacific shipping lanes might misinterpret traffic in the Baltic. Local context becomes a national asset.

These model gardens require vast computing power. So countries create regionalised compute zones: clusters of data centres dedicated to domestic AI training and inference. Governments subsidise them, just as they once subsidised railroads and power grids. Politicians speak of "technological independence" with the same solemnity their predecessors spoke of energy independence. Strategic forks are not accidents; they are deliberate.

Yet this autonomy has side effects. When nations build separate stacks—local clouds, local models, local standards—interoperability suffers. A health record system in one country may not talk to its neighbour's. A coalition military operation may struggle to integrate targeting data if each partner's AI follows different rules or confidence thresholds. Sovereignty strengthens the state but can weaken alliances. Finding balance is delicate, and no one has mastered it.

Some governments attempt hybrid approaches. They invite foreign cloud providers to build domestic regions, but only under strict conditions: keys must be managed by local entities; sensitive logs must never leave the country; machine learning workloads must be auditable by national security agencies. Corporate lawyers bristle at the complexity, yet providers comply. The market is enormous, and states are willing to pay for assurance.

Other nations take the harder path. They establish entirely domestic clouds, using local hardware where possible, relying on global vendors only for software components. These systems may be less efficient, less elegant, and more expensive. But they offer something priceless: control. When a hostile power threatens sanctions, when a multinational provider faces political pressure, when intelligence agencies suspect espionage, a locally owned stack cannot be switched off by a phone call from abroad.

Why has this moment arrived? Because the world learned a painful lesson from pandemic supply chains. Nations that offshored critical production found themselves begging for masks, ventilators, and medicines. The trauma lingers. Governments see digital infrastructure the same way they now see vaccines or semiconductors: too important to outsource entirely. A sovereign stack is a digital stockpile.

Yet even this is not enough. Cloud sovereignty solves location and compliance, but not intelligence. If a model garden relies on open-source frameworks riddled with vulnerabilities, or a supply chain infected with malicious firmware, the stack becomes a Trojan horse. States now talk of "secure provenance" for code and hardware, insisting on traceability from chip fabrication to model deployment. Domestic oversight extends deeper than data residency—it reaches the toolchains that build the software itself.

The practical benefits appear in quiet moments. When a cyberattack threatens a national bank, security agencies can coordinate with domestic cloud teams, isolate the breach, and recover systems without foreign approval. When a judicial warrant demands access to encrypted logs, domestic courts have enforceable authority. When diplomats negotiate intelligence-sharing agreements, they can promise partners that access will be governed by verifiable local controls, not by the whim of another nation's legal system.

But autonomy has costs. Domestic cloud regions are expensive to maintain. Talent is scarce. Economies of scale shrink. Updates arrive slower. Companies complain that sovereign instances lack the latest GPUs, the fastest networking, the newest optimisation libraries. Start-ups grumble that mandatory domestic hosting stifles innovation. Citizens worry that local oversight erodes privacy. Liberating oneself from foreign dependence can create new forms of dependence: on local politics, on local regulators, on the competence of domestic engineers.

Some argue that sovereign clouds are a step towards digital Balkanisation. In their view, each nation will build its own closed network, sealing citizens behind firewalls and degrading global connectivity. Others argue the opposite: sovereignty prevents emergency overreach. If data and models are scattered across the world with no clear jurisdiction, democracies risk paralysis. Sovereign clouds re-anchor accountability.

The truth lies somewhere between. Shared cyberspace demands shared rules, but no nation relinquishes security lightly. Strategic forks are attempts to navigate that tension. They acknowledge that the global cloud is a public utility controlled by private firms, and that states must carve their own safe lanes within it.

The stakes extend beyond economics. In future crises, a government may need to deploy AI models at scale—detecting misinformation, triaging medical supply chains, managing evacuations. If those models depend on foreign compute, sovereignty becomes theoretical. The real power lies with whoever controls the datacentre door.

And yet, isolation is not a sustainable future. Climate modelling, pandemic response, space traffic management, cyber defence—all require cooperation. Sovereign stacks must interlock, not splinter. They must allow national control *and* cross-border coordination. That is the architecture challenge of the next decade.

Perhaps the hardest question is this: what happens when the cloud itself becomes a bargaining chip? Imagine a trade dispute in which one nation restricts access to GPU clusters relied upon by another's hospitals or rail networks. Would that count as coercion? Retaliation? War?

National stacks promise safety, but safety is rarely costless. Strategic forks promise autonomy, but autonomy can fray the ties that keep the world intelligible and connected. The choice is not between global or sovereign, open or closed. It is about designing a system that can survive pressure—political, economic, and military—without collapsing.

The world is building these systems now. Slowly, unevenly, often painfully. Whether they become engines of resilience or instruments of fracture depends on decisions being made in quiet committees, procurement offices, and standards bodies. The map of cyberspace is redrawing itself, and the outlines of sovereignty are being carved into silicon, fibre, and code. The question is not whether nations will build their own stacks. It is whether those stacks can coexist when the next shock arrives.

## Standards as power

When a peacekeeping agency in West Africa went shopping for an AI-powered border monitoring system, it never imagined that the decisive factor would be a test suite written thousands of miles away in Brussels. The vendors brought glossy brochures, satellite demos, and even live drone feeds. But the procurement brief was blunt: only systems that passed a specific European conformance benchmark would be considered. Overnight, two-thirds of the contenders vanished from the shortlist. The agency had not adopted European law, and Brussels had no jurisdiction over its mission. Yet the standard travelled anyway. A checklist became geopolitics.

This is the quiet magic of standards: power without conquest, influence without territory. Nations can spend decades negotiating treaties only to discover that a single technical baseline—an encryption protocol, an emissions threshold, a safety benchmark for autonomous vehicles—reshapes markets far faster than diplomacy ever could. In the world of AI, standards are becoming the new instruments of statecraft. Not the grandstanding kind seen at summits or broadcast in parliaments, but the type embedded in procurement rules, testing labs, and software licences. They are subtle, bureaucratic, and profoundly consequential.

To understand why, we need to grasp a simple truth: governments cannot inspect algorithms the way they inspect lorries crossing a border. You can't peer inside a neural network and see its intent. You can't hold a model up to the light and spot the vulnerability. And even when states have the right to audit, they rarely have the tools. What they can do is demand proof of behaviour—under controlled conditions, reproducible tests, and worst-case stressors. That is where conformance suites come in.

A conformance suite is a battery of tests designed to answer a single question: does this system behave acceptably under specified conditions? The test may cover hallucination rates for large language models, targeting precision for defence analytics, or resilience to adversarial examples. If a vendor wants a government contract, it must pass. The suite leaves no room for charm, lobbying, or patriotic rhetoric. Performance speaks.

But the stronger effect lies not in who passes, but in who adapts. Developers change their architectures to satisfy the test. Data scientists retrain their models to clear the thresholds. Entire engineering cultures shift. Over time, a local rule becomes a global force, not because anyone imposed it, but because compliance is cheaper than overhaul. Standards migrate like weather fronts: invisible, inevitable, shaping what grows beneath them.

The proud example often cited is the General Data Protection Regulation. Critics derided it as cumbersome, costly, and provincial. Yet within a few years, companies in São Paulo, Seoul, and San Francisco were building to "GDPR-ready" specifications. Not because they suddenly fell in love with European jurisprudence, but because maintaining multiple privacy architectures was a nightmare. One global framework became the path of least resistance.

AI governance is heading the same way. Safety baselines—how a system handles sensitive data, how it logs decisions, how it responds under stress—are already spreading from a handful of regulatory centres. If a major trading bloc demands a certified audit trail or demonstrable anti-bias controls, the world's vendors will quietly converge on those norms. No battleships required.

And yet the trump card is not regulation, but procurement. When a government ties its spending to a standard, markets listen. Defence ministries, health systems, transport networks—these are clients with budgets measured in billions. If they insist on alignment with a particular conformance suite, makers of autonomous drones or medical triage systems have a stark choice: comply, or forfeit the sale. Many comply. Some complain. All adapt.

Of course, power through standards is not uncontested. It creates winners and losers. When a large country sets the benchmark, smaller players often feel coerced. A medical AI vendor in Nairobi might bristle at a standard written with European hospital infrastructure in mind. A manufacturer in Jakarta might resent having to certify its software according to tests developed by engineers in Tokyo. Even within alliances, the politics can turn sharp. To adopt another nation's standard is to accept its worldview—its risk tolerance, its ethical assumptions, its threat models.

These tensions are not hypothetical. When the United States began pushing for autonomous weapon systems to follow specific "meaningful human control" guidelines, some partners objected. They feared that the language was vague, that the metrics were ill-defined, and that adoption would disadvantage smaller defence firms unable to meet complex documentation requirements. The US insisted that the standard would save lives. The sceptics countered that it would concentrate power.

Behind those arguments lies a philosophical dispute: who gets to define safety? The country with the most advanced systems? The one with the most to lose? The group that acts first? Nations know that whoever writes the standard writes the future. And so the negotiations over conformance suites and baseline thresholds look increasingly like arms control talks—technical on the surface, strategic underneath.

For militaries, standards can be the difference between interoperability and chaos. If coalition members deploy autonomous reconnaissance drones from different vendors, following incompatible logging schemas and incompatible fail-safe modes, a battlefield becomes a laboratory. Shared standards bring consistency: a British decision log can speak to a Canadian forensics system; a French pause command can halt an American model grappling with uncertain targets. In some coalitions, adopting a common conformance suite has done more for safety than any diplomatic communiqué.

In civilian domains, the stakes are quieter but no less serious. Consider a city exploring AI-managed traffic flows. If it adopts proprietary standards from a single vendor, it may be locked in for a decade. But if it insists on open conformance benchmarks, competitors can enter with compatible systems. A single procurement decision shapes market structure. Europe discovered this long ago with GSM mobile standards: the rulebook created an ecosystem, not merely a product line.

As sovereign clouds proliferate and national stacks diverge, standards become the glue. Without them, an AI trained in one jurisdiction may misbehave in another. A safety threshold validated in Singapore may be meaningless in São Paulo. The goal is not uniformity—nations will pursue their own interests—but compatibility. Standards let ecosystems diverge without drifting into isolation.

Yet there is an uncomfortable irony: the more critical standards become, the more they resemble weapons. A country can write a testing norm so strict that foreign firms struggle to comply. A region can demand audit requirements that effectively ban models trained on opaque datasets. A bloc can impose export controls not against systems, but against conformance certifications, starving rivals of legitimacy. Power migrates from the product to the rulebook.

This raises a fraught question: who oversees the overseers? Most standard-setting bodies are dense networks of regulators, academics, engineers, and lobbyists. Their deliberations are arcane, their drafts technical, their influence vast. If the rules become geopolitical tools—if safety thresholds turn into trade barriers—trust erodes. Yet the alternative, a free-for-all without shared baselines, invites catastrophe.

The most thoughtful advocates argue for "minimum viable standards": benchmarks strict enough to prevent harm, but flexible enough to accommodate local needs. A conformance suite for facial recognition could prioritise bias mitigation without mandating a single architecture. A procurement rule for autonomous vehicles could require transparent logs without prescribing a vendor's proprietary telemetry format. Standards should shape behaviour, not freeze innovation.

But even these moderate positions hide dilemmas. Minimum viable for whom? What counts as bias? What is harm? Every threshold embeds a moral stance. Every metric implies a hierarchy of values. A probabilistic risk model used for border control might be unacceptable for healthcare. A safety floor acceptable in peacetime may be reckless in war. Standards give the illusion of neutrality, but neutrality is scarce in geopolitics.

There is one more twist. In the age of powerful AI, some states worry less about enforcing their standards and more about avoiding another's. They fear dependency on foreign baselines—particularly in defence-critical sectors. A drone manufacturer that tailors its software to satisfy overseas conformance tests may become beholden to judicial rulings in that jurisdiction. A cybersecurity firm that certifies under another country's audit scheme may find its update pipeline exposed. Sovereignty and compliance pull in opposite directions.

And yet, isolation is impractical. As models grow more complex, safety testing becomes too expensive for any one nation. The cost of certifying next-generation systems will be measured not in millions, but in billions. Shared standards spread the burden. They also create geopolitical goodwill:

a country that adopts another's rulebook signals alignment. Allies need not declare loyalty; they can encode it into benchmarks.

The resulting world will not look tidy. It will be stitched together by agreements, tensions, and accommodations. Some standards will win quietly by being practical. Others will dominate because powerful markets demand them. Some will coexist uneasily, like rival mobile protocols. Standards are rarely final; they are living documents, shaped by events.

Perhaps the clearest sign of their power is the political attention they now receive. Heads of government openly debate testing norms. Defence ministries fund conformance labs. Trade negotiators insert safety baselines into agreements once reserved for tariffs. Nations have discovered a form of leverage that does not require threats, just paperwork.

And that is the paradox: the future of AI governance will be written not just in laws or strategies, but in spreadsheets of test cases, in benchmark thresholds, in checkboxes on procurement forms. The world's next great alignment may not be a treaty. It may be a standard.

The question left hanging is whether these standards will make AI safer—or merely advance the interests of those who authored them. Power often hides in the fine print. Now, it also hides in the metrics.

## Supply chain trust

A military procurement officer once remarked, only half-joking, that the most dangerous adversary was not the enemy with the biggest missile, but the contractor with the smallest firmware patch. Everyone laughed, but the room was uneasy. They knew he was right. Modern power no longer relies solely on ships, aircraft, satellites, or even the models running inside them. It hinges on the invisible threads—compilers, dependency libraries, container registries, update servers, key-signing ceremonies—that bind an AI system together. Sabotage no longer needs explosives. It needs a pull request.

This is the unsettling reality of AI supply chains: the most sophisticated weapon in the world can be undone by a compromised dependency bundled by a junior developer, a tampered BIOS in a network card, or a malicious update slipped into a model checkpoint. Empires once guarded borders; now they must guard build pipelines. The danger is not hypothetical. Intelligence agencies maintain teams dedicated to hunting these weak seams, and rivals quietly invest in the art of digital contamination. A single poisoned component can turn a fleet of autonomous vehicles into bricks—or worse, puppets.

The problem begins with complexity. A modern AI system is not a monolith but an ecosystem. It is trained on datasets sourced from countless contributors, processed on geographically distributed accelerators, packaged using open-source libraries, deployed through container orchestration layers, patched via update channels, and monitored with third-party telemetry clients. Every layer adds capability, and every layer adds risk. It only takes one compromised cog to seize the gears.

Industry once assumed that signed binaries and encrypted channels would be enough. They discovered, painfully, that signing a malicious file produces a malicious file with a valid signature. Attackers do not need to break cryptography; they only need to compromise the step before the signature. A supply chain defence that focuses on tamper-proof delivery but ignores tamper-proof creation is comfort theatre.

Some nations have responded by demanding full chain-of-custody attestations. These attestations declare not merely that a file is intact, but where it came from, which compiler produced it, which libraries it linked, and who authorised the build. The process borrows from nuclear material tracking: every component has a lineage. If something goes wrong, investigators can follow the trail backwards through the build graph. Where the signature was added. Where the source was pulled. Where the patch was reviewed. Accountability by architecture.

It is not hard to imagine such attestations applied to model artefacts. A government might refuse to field an autonomous targeting system unless its model weights arrive embedded with cryptographic attestations: training dataset fingerprints, hash chains for each fine-tuning stage, provenance for code dependencies, secure enclave proofs for key generation. A model that cannot prove its lineage becomes a security risk by default. This flips the burden from auditors to vendors: prove it is clean, or it is treated as compromised.

The private sector has already tasted the consequences of failing to police the chain. Consider a case that quietly rattled a European robotics company. Its warehouse automation fleet began failing at random intervals. Robots halted mid-aisle and refused commands. Engineers tore into logs and found phantom processes respawning inside the control stack. The breach did not come from the robots themselves or from the cloud platform. It was traced to a third-party optimisation library updated through a package manager. The attacker had obtained access to the maintainer's account and inserted a dormant payload. The code sat undetected until a scheduled optimisation job triggered it. A minor dependency brought a multimillion-euro operation to its knees.

This is why cloud denial alone is no longer the attacker's favourite tool. The cleverer adversary contaminates the supply chain and allows the target to install the damage voluntarily. No firewall stops the enemy you invite inside.

Defenders know this, and their responses grow more disciplined. Some run "hermetic builds," where external network access is disabled during compilation. Others use deterministic build systems so that a binary can be independently verified to match its source. Nations with the most at stake—nuclear command systems, fleet coordination networks, integrated air defence—have begun treating supply chains like weapons-grade assets. Firmware updates require multi-party signatures. Compiler toolchains live in sealed enclaves. Update channels run through hardware security modules. If a single module fails attestation, the entire system halts.

These measures are expensive, but not as expensive as compromise.

And yet, there is a paradox: the more global the AI ecosystem becomes, the harder it is to validate. Open-source code is written by volunteers across jurisdictions. Hardware is manufactured in dozens of countries. Model developers rely on cloud platforms whose underlying drivers and kernels are maintained by teams they will never meet. No sovereign can fully inspect every line of every dependency. Even the best-funded intelligence services cannot guarantee perfect assurance.

This has led some to propose a different strategy: continuous scrutiny rather than static certification. Instead of assuming a component is safe because it was vetted once, treat every update as a potential threat. Monitor behaviour. Sandboxed model artefacts. Roll out updates gradually. Think of it less like construction and more like epidemiology: outbreaks must be contained, traced, eradicated.

But continuous scrutiny itself has limits. If a compromised update channel delivers new model weights that subtly bias a targeting system, detection may come too late. An adversary does not need to destroy—only nudge. A bias of one per cent in threat classification can tip decisions in contested airspace. Influence masquerades as malfunction.

This is why some defence organisations are experimenting with diverse toolchains. If three independent compilers produce the same binary, confidence rises. If three independent training pipelines produce weights that hash identically, tampering becomes harder. Diversity is a hedge against subversion. But it carries costs: parallel builds, parallel audits, parallel bureaucracy.

Supply chain trust also has diplomatic dimensions. When allies share AI systems, they implicitly trust each other's development pipelines. If one nation's vendor uses a compromised compiler, the damage spreads across the alliance. Coalition data rooms are particularly vulnerable: data from multiple states flows through shared infrastructure. A single poisoned dependency can compromise every partner.

To mitigate this, some alliances have begun exchanging attestations the way banks exchange compliance certificates. Before a model is shared, its provenance must be independently verifiable. Before a firmware patch is deployed, every signatory must agree that the update channel is secure. These rituals are cumbersome, but they prevent wider contagion.

A few nations have gone further, building "air-gapped sovereign build farms." These facilities never touch the public internet. They reproduce open-source dependencies from source using verified compilers. They compile models from scratch. They treat the global software ecosystem as contaminated until proven otherwise. This approach borders on paranoia, but the stakes justify it: better an expensive fortress than an elegant compromise.

Yet fortress logic has a price. It slows innovation. It isolates research. It discourages open-source collaboration. And it risks strategic fragility: a sovereign stack that cannot draw on global talent may fall behind rivals who embrace openness.

So the question becomes: how much trust is enough? Absolute assurance is impossible. Blind trust is reckless. The answer lies somewhere between—rooted in verifiable provenance, layered defences, and the humility to assume breach.

The world's most advanced militaries now treat model artefacts like munitions. They are signed, sealed, logged, and tracked. A targeting model pushed into a drone fleet may require approval from cryptographic officers. A patch that tweaks a perception subsystem might trigger a red-team exercise. Some systems even run dual-model redundancy: if two independently signed inference stacks disagree, an operation pauses. Safety by deadlock.

Civilian infrastructure will not be far behind. Cities deploying AI-managed grids or autonomous buses will demand proof that the code running in their streets has a traceable lineage. Hospitals relying on diagnosis models will require cryptographic attestations tied to regulatory audits. The world is moving towards an assumption: if an AI system cannot prove where it came from, it is unsafe to use.

But a more subtle frontier emerges. Supply chain attacks do not always aim for collapse. Sometimes they aim for influence. A backdoored compiler does not need to crash a system; it might simply model-drip private data to a foreign server. A poisoned training dataset does not need to sabotage performance; it might nudge policies, perceptions, or political decisions. The line between cyberwarfare and psychological operations blurs.

As these risks grow, supply chain trust becomes not just a technical requirement but a strategic one. Nations that cannot demonstrate provenance will be excluded from sensitive markets. Vendors without attestation systems will be locked out of defence procurement. Trust becomes a tariff.

The most unsettling question remains unanswered: what happens when the supply chain behind an AI system is too vast, too distributed, too opaque to audit? When even the defenders cannot verify every stage? When trust becomes probabilistic, not guaranteed?

Some believe decentralised attestations and reproducible builds will keep pace. Others doubt it. What is certain is that the most decisive battles in AI geopolitics may be fought not on digital front lines, but in build servers and signing rooms—won or lost with keys, not guns.

If power once flowed from territory, then today it flows from trust. But trust is brittle. And in a world where a line of code can be a weapon, the safest system may be the one that never assumes its own purity.

## Licences and levers

A curious contradiction defines modern geopolitics: the world's most powerful tools are freely downloaded. A language model capable of drafting legislation, designing molecules, or generating targeting plans may be accessible through the same pane of glass as a social media login. Power has never been so widely distributed, yet the levers that govern it lie in the least glamorous corners—terms of service, export licences, audit clauses, and usage logs. Empires once exercised control through territory; now they do it through paperwork.

The tension became visible when a sanctioned nation attempted to rent compute from an overseas cloud provider. The provider politely quoted policy: no service to blacklisted entities, no exceptions. Sanctions had been enforced not by warships or diplomats, but by a billing system. Underneath the corporate politeness sat hard power. Without access to high-end accelerators, advanced models could not be trained. The country's research labs stalled. Civilian universities protested. Engineers whispered about grey channels and proxy accounts. It was a reminder that cloud tenancy can function like maritime access in another century: when ports close, economies choke.

Export controls used to concern physical equipment: radar systems, missiles, cryptographic hardware. Today they govern model weights, training datasets, and cloud credits. Algorithms have become dual-use by default: the same model that churns through medical images can assist with missile guidance or biodefence planning. Yet preventing proliferation is not as straightforward as guarding a factory. Code moves invisibly. Researchers collaborate across borders. Open-source communities share innovations without passports.

To reconcile openness with security, governments experiment with **graduated access tiers**. High-risk capabilities—model weights that can design pathogens, optimise drone swarms, or break cryptographic primitives—are accessible only under audited licence. Lower-risk models remain open to the public. Some nations insist that companies maintain logs of sensitive queries and provide regulators with real-time oversight. Others require on-premise deployment, so that critical models never leave national infrastructure.

This logic sounds clinical until one remembers the stakes. A single unrestricted model could enable a small group to orchestrate large-scale harm. Yet overly restrictive regimes strangle innovation and push researchers into dark corners of the internet where there is no oversight, only anonymity. The question becomes not whether to regulate, but how to calibrate: enough control to mitigate catastrophe, not so much that progress evaporates.

The most powerful lever of all is cloud tenancy. Nations that cannot train frontier models domestically are forced to rent capacity. This gives host countries influence. A regulator can demand periodic audits, data access restrictions, and emergency shutdown triggers. If a tenant violates terms—working on prohibited weapons, exfiltrating controlled datasets, or ignoring safety requirements—the provider can revoke access within minutes. No blockades. No sabres. Just revoked credentials.

These levers are not hypothetical. Defence ministries increasingly require providers to supply kill-switch capabilities as part of national security contracts. Clouds are expected to identify unusual training runs, suspicious batch sizes, or unusual inference patterns. Anomalies trigger human review. If necessary, deployments are paused. What was once a neutral platform has become an instrument of statecraft.

Of course, these arrangements raise uncomfortable questions. Who decides what counts as misuse? What if a provider's home country demands shutdowns that conflict with the tenant's sovereignty? What if a democratic state and an authoritarian one both claim jurisdiction over a multinational training run? Cloud arbitration courts do not exist. Yet the disputes are already emerging.

Licences become strategically potent when tied to reciprocity. A nation that wants access to a partner's advanced models may be required to share its own evaluation results or transparency reports. Trust is traded for trust. States that refuse transparency find themselves locked out of international research groups, unable to procure high-end systems, and forced to build domestic substitutes at enormous cost. Isolation is technically possible, but strategically expensive.

Then comes proportionality. Not every violation merits total shutdown. Some can be handled with graduated penalties: reduced model capacity, limited batch sizes, geographic restrictions on inference, or the requirement to run under human supervision. The logic mirrors economic sanctions—pressure without escalation.

In practice, these measures require surveillance. Providers must watch what tenants are doing. Some countries demand encrypted enclaves that hide customer data from platform administrators; others insist on auditability as a condition for deployment. The tension is inescapable: privacy conflicts with oversight. Intelligence agencies will not outsource compute to a provider who cannot demonstrate clean audit trails. Civilian companies will not rent compute from a government that inspects every inference call. There is no perfect balance, only negotiated discomfort.

Export licences once arrived as paperwork stamped by customs officers. Now, they are enforced automatically by APIs. A model can be hard-coded to refuse queries from sanctioned IP ranges. A cloud region can whitelist who is allowed to run high-capacity training. Geographic geofencing and cryptographic attestation make compliance invisible: the user never sees the enforcement. It just works—or it does not.

But these systems carry risks of their own. Automated enforcement can be gamed. Proxy networks can disguise origin. Malicious actors can launch attacks from permissive jurisdictions. That reality has pushed regulators to require not just controls, but attribution. If a dangerous query is made, someone must be accountable. Logs must survive legal scrutiny. Evidence must be non-repudiable.

This leads to the rise of **auditable AI**. Sensitive models ship with secure logging modules. They record not only outputs but context: who asked for what, when, from where. Logs are tamper-proofed using hash chains or resilient enclaves. Investigators can reconstruct misuse with forensic precision. If a licensee goes rogue, a regulator does not need to guess—they have a trail.

Yet even here, the debate is uneasy. Civil libertarians warn that auditable AI risks becoming a mass-surveillance tool. Developers worry about liability. Companies fear losing trade secrets during audits. The same levers that prevent proliferation could erode privacy and concentrate power in the hands of a few dominant platforms.

Nations that cannot trust foreign clouds often turn inward. They build sovereign clouds, sovereign GPUs, sovereign model gardens. Domestic companies must host sensitive workloads locally and submit to government audit. This guarantees jurisdictional control, but carries a cost. Domestic infrastructure is more expensive. Domestic models lag behind those trained on global talent and data. The sovereign stack becomes a strategic insurance policy: valuable in crisis, costly in peace.

Some states hedge. They maintain limited sovereign capacity for defence, but allow commercial sectors to use global clouds under monitored licences. Others insist on bilateral agreements: data from allied states can be processed, but rivals are barred. Digital borders emerge, less visible than physical ones but no less real.

The most complicated frontier is reciprocity between non-equal partners. A small state might demand access to a frontier model from a superpower.

The superpower may grant it—but only under tight conditions: local monitoring agents, restricted parameters, capped throughput, continuous audits. Power is exercised through licences, not armies. Consent becomes coercion.

History rhymes. Maritime law once turned trading ports into leverage. Airspace treaties turned airports into chokepoints. Today, cloud regions and model licences are the new ports. States negotiate access, impose tariffs, demand inspections, and threaten embargoes. Geography persists, just disguised as infrastructure menus.

Some technologists dream of a future where models are open, borders irrelevant, and compute abundant everywhere. It is a noble vision, but geopolitics intrudes. Advanced AI systems can move markets, influence elections, guide missiles, or unlock biological secrets. No serious government will allow such tools to circulate freely. Even the most open societies will impose controls.

And yet, heavy-handed controls risk their own danger. If regulation becomes draconian, innovation flees to jurisdictions that promise fewer restrictions. If trusted platforms refuse to serve certain customers, underground markets spring up. Shadow clouds offer anonymous compute. Rogue states barter access to sanctioned actors. The cat-and-mouse cycle begins again.

So the world converges toward messy pragmatism: graduated access, auditable licences, proportional enforcement, reciprocal transparency. It is neither utopia nor dystopia. It is a negotiation.

The unanswered question lingers: when power flows through licences, who licences the licensors? When cloud providers become geopolitical gatekeepers, who sets the rules?

If the 20th century was defined by nuclear treaties written by diplomats, the 21st may be defined by access agreements drafted by product lawyers. A quiet transformation: war and peace negotiated in clickwrap.

# Chapter 5

# Alliances, Coalitions, and Interoperability

The first warning came not from enemy fire, but from a dashboard. A joint maritime task force was conducting a routine patrol when allied drones began flagging contradictory threats. One nation's fleet saw a merchant ship as benign. Another flagged it as a possible smuggler. Their sensors were staring at the same hull, yet their models disagreed. It was an uncomfortable moment: if allies cannot even agree on what they see, how can they act together?

Minutes later, a quieter discovery. Each navy held data the others did not—classified imagery, local human intelligence, historical shipping logs. If the information had been pooled, the picture would have sharpened. But sovereignty prevailed. Secrets stayed compartmentalised. Commanders faced the oldest dilemma in coalition warfare: shared risks, staggered trust.

This tension is no longer an inconvenience. It is a strategic fault line. As autonomous systems and predictive targeting become mainstream, alliances can no longer rely on manual deconfliction or polite diplomatic coordination. Machines must talk to machines. Dashboards must show not just a common operational picture, but a common logic. Coalition power depends less on shared flags than shared data formats, audit rights, and interoperable autonomy.

Alliances have always balanced cooperation and caution. During the Second World War, British and American cryptographers worked together, yet each maintained secure rooms the other could never enter. The same dynamic persists in the age of autonomous intelligence. Partners want shared situational awareness, but not full exposure. They crave joint action, not open books. The paradox is sharpened by speed: a drone swarm or cyber strike unfolds in milliseconds. Human diplomats cannot renegotiate trust mid-flight.

To function, alliances must accept partitioned transparency: enough shared insight to coordinate, enough secrecy to protect national equities. Some coalitions are experimenting with tiered visibility dashboards—interfaces that reveal different levels of granularity depending on clearance and provenance. One ally may see a vessel classified only as *suspicious*. Another, with deeper intelligence access, sees the underlying evidence. The coalition still acts together, but no state forfeits its sources.

Interoperability is not romantic; it is architectural. Autonomy must be engineered to work across political seams. Swarms from different nations require common timing protocols, shared message formats, and compatible fail-safe rules. Without this, joint operations fracture. A millisecond drift can cause autonomous aircraft to miscoordinate evasion. Hidden assumptions in one model—say, how to distinguish friend from foe—may clash with another's rules of engagement. When the machines negotiate faster than the humans, ambiguity becomes danger.

Traditional burden-sharing counted heads and hardware: how many troops, how many ships, how many aircraft. But in an age of AI-driven operations, value manifests differently. One ally may contribute satellite datasets; another provides test ranges where fleets can experiment safely; a third supplies compute capacity to retrain models after incidents. Data becomes ammunition. Sensor access becomes territory. Validation time becomes currency.

A few coalitions are experimenting with range-time credits—tokens earned by hosting exercises, contributing training data, or running evaluation suites. These credits can be exchanged for priority access to improved models or advanced autonomy modules. It is an economic metaphor applied to defence cooperation: effort in, capability out. Suddenly, small nations with limited hard power gain influence by offering unique testing environments or niche data. Coalitions become software ecosystems, not just joint command structures.

Yet even the most ambitious alliance can fall to bureaucratic inertia. Procurement has a habit of suffocating itself. If every line of code requires a multi-year review, there will be nothing left worth deploying. The challenge is to build agile frameworks that still meet public oversight. Some defence departments now adopt spiral development with stop-gates—rolling upgrades that ship incrementally, but pause at defined check-points for ethical and technical review. It looks more like modern software release management than military procurement, and that is precisely the point.

Trust remains the hinge. No ally will hand over frontier autonomy without confidence that it will not be misused or misappropriated. So coalitions build mechanisms of verification that stop short of full exposure. Red-team exchanges allow partners to stress-test each other's models without gaining access to source code. Cross-inspection weeks let engineers audit deployment pipelines jointly and go home assured, not enlightened. Randomised drills serve as an honesty tax—those who pass maintain access; those who fail are temporarily downgraded until they fix the gaps.

Some critics see paranoia. Others see prudence. In a multilateral world, every partner is a possible vector for compromise. A single infiltrated pipeline could leak sensitive autonomy to adversaries. Meanwhile, public scrutiny demands accountability: if something goes wrong in a joint operation, whose algorithm is responsible? Whose logs are authoritative? Whose oversight applies? Interoperability without governance is merely wishful thinking.

Still, alliances endure because they multiply power. No state can maintain complete coverage of every theatre, satellite orbit, or cyber corridor. Shared intelligence offers depth. Shared autonomy offers agility. And when machines operate in concert, coalitions extend from staff meetings to code repositories.

The diplomatic veneer hides a deeper reality: alliances are becoming software projects. Memoranda of understanding turn into API specifications. Status of forces agreements morph into audit protocols. Joint exercises double as data-collection campaigns. Commanders negotiate access keys alongside airspace corridors. The cloud region hosting a coalition targeting model becomes as strategically important as the physical base housing allied aircraft.

This transformation brings quiet opportunities. A small state with a world-class AI safety team may wield more influence in coalition design than a larger state with outdated platforms. A country with abundant test ranges becomes a node of experimentation. A member with strong export compliance can host sensitive modules others cannot. Power disperses across technical competence, not just military might.

The political cost, however, is that failure is suddenly mutual. If an allied model misclassifies a civilian vessel, the entire coalition carries reputational damage. If one partner's autonomy pipeline is compromised, attackers may exploit others through shared interfaces. Collective power means collective risk.

Which raises the uncomfortable question: how far does interoperability go? Do allies share not just data, but decision rights? Does a drone swarm accept command from a partner nation's officer? Do algorithms obey composite rules of engagement negotiated by committee? States built on sovereignty are now asked to trust software written by others, hosted by others, and perhaps influenced by adversaries.

That is the future alliances walk towards—interdependence coded into silicon.

The chapters ahead trace that journey. The common picture that is never fully shared; autonomous fleets that speak the same protocol but not the same politics; burden-sharing measured in terabytes and teraflops rather than battalions; procurement that must adapt or be bypassed; trust that is engineered, tested, and continually renegotiated. The page turns to a world where treaties are technical documents and solidarity is written in code.

The only certainty is that the alliances willing to build—and defend—true interoperability will shape the balance of power. The rest will watch and hope their sovereignty still matters.

## Common picture, different politics

The frigate's radar lit up first. Then the satellite feed confirmed an unknown vessel altering course towards restricted waters. Minutes later, an allied destroyer received the same information—except its dashboard labelled the ship *non-threatening*, a routine cargo hauler en route to a nearby port. Two screens, two flags, two versions of reality. The enemy had done nothing. The discrepancy came from the coalition itself.

For the officers staring at those displays, the problem was not just technical. Each nation held different intelligence about the ship's ownership, flag history, crew manifests, and past behaviour. Each nation had different laws governing how such information could be shared. The result was a paradox: a coalition possessed all the information required to produce a single, accurate picture, yet remained functionally blind because secrets stayed compartmentalised. The technology was interoperable. The politics were not.

This is the defining tension of modern coalitions. They fight together, patrol together, and rely on common AI-enabled systems to interpret the world—while refusing, for good reasons, to reveal everything they know. The battlefield has become a negotiation space, where allies calculate how much truth can be shared without compromising national advantage, legal obligations, or sources neither friend nor foe is allowed to see.

Shared situational awareness has always been the foundational promise of alliance. The phrase sounds straightforward—everyone sees the same picture. In practice, it is a minefield. The United States might monitor a region with space-based sensors; a European partner might have human assets on the ground; an Asian ally could contribute maritime drone surveillance. Individually, each insight is partial. Together, they form a mosaic.

But mosaics expose provenance. If one country reveals that a civilian tanker is operated by a shell company connected to sanctioned actors, it implicitly signals where that intelligence came from: financial surveillance, corporate infiltration, covert data access. Allies want to benefit from shared insights without exposing the machinery that produced them. National politics, domestic privacy laws, and intelligence agreements create red lines that even wartime pressure cannot erase.

The result: a coalition cannot simply create a single "truth" dashboard. It must create **tiered visibility dashboards**—interfaces that show the same targets, but with different justifications, confidence levels, and provenance masks. One nation might see that a suspected smuggler is dangerous due to "classified evidence". Another sees only that the vessel's pattern-of-life analysis is anomalous. Both receive enough signal to act, but not enough to reverse-engineer sensitive sources.

The architecture matters: who sees raw sensor data, who sees fused classifications, who sees the final decision recommendations. Some coalitions now treat situational awareness like a permissions hierarchy inside a multinational corporation—role-based access, compartmentalised feeds, and cryptographic assurance that the data cannot be misused or cloned. A lieutenant on a British carrier will not receive the same granularity as a liaison officer from a smaller partner navy, yet they may still collaborate in real time.

The deeper issue is that "common picture" does not always mean "common interpretation." Two nations might see identical video footage of a convoy. One, scarred by prior attacks, decides to classify it as a high-probability threat. Another, guided by political restraint, insists it is ambiguous. Algorithms reflect these biases. If one ally trains its models on data from a history of hostile border incursions, its autonomy will be more aggressive.

If another trains primarily on anti-piracy missions, its models will favour de-escalation.

This is why shared situational awareness is not just a technical puzzle—it is a philosophical one. Coalitions are mixtures of national doctrines, ethical codes, legal frameworks, and public expectations. When an AI system flags a vehicle as dangerous with 83% confidence, whose confidence metric is it? Whose threshold determines whether a drone tracks or ignores? The software might be common, but the politics baked into it are not.

Some alliances attempt to resolve this through **federated fusion**. Instead of pooling raw data, each nation runs its own models locally, then transmits only final classifications or alerts. The coalition receives a crowd-sourced consensus: five allies flag a threat, two express uncertainty, one abstains. Action can proceed even when secrets cannot be shared. Others pursue weighted voting, where states with stronger sensors or regional expertise wield more influence over the shared picture. Inevitably, this creates resentment. Who decides whose judgement counts most?

And yet, even partial sharing is better than isolated vision. The most advanced coalitions now build cryptographically secure enclaves where sensitive data can be analysed jointly without exposing underlying sources. Secure multiparty computation and homomorphic encryption allow models to ingest protected intelligence without revealing the data itself. The mathematics become diplomacy: trust drawn from algebra rather than promises.

The practical stakes are enormous. A misclassification in a joint air defence network can result in two allies firing on different targets—or worse, failing to fire entirely. Coalition commanders cannot wait hours while lawyers negotiate data releases. Real-time fusion requires architectures that encode political boundaries without paralysing action.

A recent experiment demonstrated what this might look like. A coalition naval exercise created three layers of intelligence sharing. At the base level, all nations shared raw radar tracks and automatic identification signals—nothing political, just physics. At the mid-level, they shared algorithmic classifications: suspicious, unknown, hostile. The confidence scores were visible, but not the underlying reasoning. At the top level, some nations shared human intelligence correlations with a smaller, vetted circle. The result was a functioning common picture where no state felt fully exposed.

Critics argue this is still insufficient. "If we cannot see why an ally's system raised a threat, how can we trust it?" is a familiar refrain. But perfect transparency is not on the table. Trust must be engineered in layers, checked by behaviour rather than omniscience. If an ally's system consistently proves accurate, confidence grows. If it produces false alarms, its influence can be downgraded quietly, without diplomatic incident.

Tiered dashboards create a political language: *We believe you enough to act with you, but not enough to know everything you know.* It sounds contradictory. In reality, it is a stable arrangement.

There is another, quieter function of partitioned sharing: error detection. When several national systems disagree, the coalition can identify whose model may be biased or outdated. Divergence is not a failure—it is a diagnostic. A single misaligned sensor might panic a lone nation. But if nine allies classify a vessel as harmless and one flags danger, command knows where to look for faults.

This turns diversity into resilience. Coalitions are not homogeneous. Their sensors differ, their models differ, their threat perceptions differ. Instead of forcing uniformity, modern architectures reveal disagreement without paralysing action. Commanders can treat dissent as data, not insubordination.

Yet there is a warning buried in this logic. If allies only converge when the stakes are low, and keep separate truths for everything else, the coalition will fracture under stress. Partitioned sharing must scale from peace-time exercises to crisis response. It cannot rely on human intermediaries alone. The autonomy that fuses sensor feeds today will eventually trigger targeting tomorrow. If allies cannot agree on what they see, their machines will argue silently, faster than diplomats can intervene.

At the human level, this tension mirrors the lived experience of cooperating professionals who never fully trust one another. Intelligence officers speak of sharing "just enough". Military lawyers negotiate what can be revealed without violating national law. Diplomats manage the bruised egos of partners who feel excluded. Machines do not erase these politics—they amplify them by shrinking the reaction window.

The coalition dashboards of the next decade will be political artefacts as much as technical ones. Every colour-coded icon—yellow for suspicious, red for hostile, grey for unknown—embeds a chain of national values, risk appetites, and historical scars. An American analyst, a German commander, and an Australian drone operator may stare at the same target, yet act with different instincts. Shared situational awareness is an aspiration, not a given.

And still, the alternative is strategic blindness. No single nation can maintain continuous surveillance across every maritime corridor, cyber route, and orbital trajectory. Alone, each suffers gaps. Together, they form a nervous system vast enough to matter. Partitioned sharing is the compromise that makes this possible.

Perhaps the most revealing question is not *what do we share?* but *what do we choose not to?* When the threat arrives without warning, secrecy becomes a luxury, and alliances discover whether their systems were built to serve politics or survive reality. Will the dashboards align when it counts, or will the common picture split into national fragments at the worst possible moment?

The answer will determine whether coalitions remain coherent forces, or merely comfortable fictions.

## Interoperable autonomy

The drones lifted from the carrier deck within seconds of one another, each the product of a different nation's engineers. Their aerodynamics, processors, and batteries bore the imprint of their respective defence industries. Some had been purchased; others were the result of years of sovereign research. Yet once airborne, they behaved as if they shared a single mind—circling, dispersing, reforming, handing targeting responsibility back and forth with no human command. At least, that was the promise. When one flock drifted out of sync by a mere two seconds, the entire formation's logic faltered. The swarm fractured. What looked like native cooperation had been a fragile choreography, held together by assumptions no one had noticed until the sky exposed them.

Interoperability used to mean ammunition that fit shared rifles, fuel that powered allied vehicles, or radios tuned to common frequencies. Today it means algorithms that must reason with each other cleanly enough to act faster than the humans they protect. A mixed fleet of autonomous systems—airborne scouts, surface drones, subsea gliders—does not simply pass messages. It shares tasks. It reallocates roles mid-mission. It must detect a threat, classify it, shadow it, and respond to it under an elastic chain of command spanning several governments. For thc first time, coalitions need machines that can *fight together before their operators even speak.*

The challenge is deceptively simple to phrase: autonomy from different nations must plug together as smoothly as multinational firefighters passing hoses during a blaze. In reality, hidden assumptions lurk everywhere. One system timestamps its coordinates using GPS time; another uses an internal oscillator that drifts by milliseconds each hour. A human pilot would never notice. A swarming algorithm will.

At the core of interoperable autonomy lies an architectural shift: **interface-first design**. Rather than forcing every ally to adopt the same platform, coalitions define universal ways for autonomous systems to communicate intent and exchange roles. What matters is not that drones are identical, but that they can understand each other's decisions. In effect, alliances are building a common language for machines at war.

A swarm is not a cloud of identical robots but a social ecosystem of agents, each with tasks, sensors, and local rules. Traditionally, swarms emerged from a single manufacturer's logic: one team wrote the perception, prediction, and control algorithms, ensuring perfect internal harmony. Coalitions overturn that assumption. A German targeting drone may jostle alongside a Japanese jammer, while a British logistic carrier navigates beneath. None has prior knowledge of the others' software. They must negotiate on contact.

Interface-first swarming does not mean sharing trade secrets. Nations keep their proprietary logic and classified models. Instead, they expose a narrow layer of interoperable signals: position, intent, priority, handover options, fallback modes. These signals act as diplomatic protocol for machines. Two drones can trade target assignments without revealing the sensors that motivated the switch. A fleet can elect a temporary leader without disclosing how it chose one. When connection degrades, a common set of failsafes ensures others do not panic.

The art is in the constraint. Too little information, and swarms collapse into chaos. Too much, and nations feel coerced into exposing intellectual property or sensitive capabilities. Coalitions must find the smallest set of signals that guarantees reliable joint action without compromising national secrets. This is not just coding—it is politics encoded in software.

Joint targeting magnifies these tensions. When two nations operate different autonomous systems over the same battlespace, who decides which platform tracks, which platform shadows, and which platform strikes? Humans once solved this with radios and command posts. Autonomy compresses that negotiation into milliseconds.

Imagine a convoy appearing at the edge of a shared surveillance grid. A French drone identifies it as a high-risk target; an American drone estimates low probability and recommends monitoring. Without harmonised interfaces, the two machines will pursue their own logic, doubling effort inefficiently or, worse, triggering contradictory actions. With a shared targeting interface, they can negotiate responsibilities in-flight: the French system shadows at altitude, the American one assigns a ground unit for closer inspection, both re-evaluate after thirty seconds. No human instruction required.

Yet hidden assumptions reappear. If one nation's autonomy prioritises civilian safety above mission urgency, while another's sacrifices caution for speed, identical alerts may diverge into incompatible behaviours. The coalition must either encode shared ethical parameters or allow tactical diversity. Either path exposes fragile alliances: shared ethics may feel like political overreach; tactical diversity risks friendly friction.

The emerging compromise is **negotiable autonomy**. Systems announce their intent using transparent, machine-readable logic—"tracking at distance", "holding engagement", "requesting confirmation". Allies then grant or restrict authority through digital rules of the road. No one nation yields full control, yet everyone gains the ability to coordinate.

Even when logic aligns, time betrays the coalition. Autonomous systems synchronise their behaviour through clocks and shared expectations of delay. A swarm that splits a search grid must coordinate updates every few seconds. If one set of drones drifts half a second behind, the swarm's internal map tears along invisible seams. Targets are missed. Paths overlap. Collisions become possible.

This is not theoretical. Timing drift already haunts multinational exercises. Satellite latency, encryption overheads, and variable cloud routing alter the tempo of message exchange. What appears instantaneous to one nation feels delayed to another. Human operators compensate intuitively. Machines do not. They compute. They assume. They act.

The remedy is not a single universal clock—too politically sensitive, too vulnerable to spoofing—but redundant timekeeping with graceful degradation. When synchronisation falters, autonomy falls back to safer modes: looser formations, local-decision rules, or temporary suspension of shared targeting. These graceful losses matter. A coalition that cannot degrade safely ought not to operate autonomy jointly at all.

Some defence scientists argue that full harmonisation of autonomy is unrealistic. Better, they say, to operate in "federated swarms": constellations of sub-swarms, each nationally coherent, cooperating via a narrower interface. Others fear this will replicate old mistakes—parallel command streams that talk too little, too late. The argument is philosophical as much as technical: should coalitions strive for unity or pluralism? Is perfect coordination worth the discomfort of shared control?

Beneath these debates runs a deeper truth: interoperability is not a question of technology. It is a question of trust. Machines that share tasks do so only because nations believe the resulting outcomes reflect their own interests. If one ally quietly upgrades its autonomy, making it more aggressive or more secretive, the entire coalition feels the tremor. Today, a radar upgrade is a national choice. Soon, a training-data update could alter how a swarm interprets civilian vehicles, fishing vessels, or ambiguous ground signatures. A minor revision in loss functions could shift a fleet from cautious escort to assertive interdiction. Would allies detect the change? Should they?

Coalitions are already experimenting with cryptographic attestation: each autonomous node proves it is running a certified version of its decision logic. Others test multinational red-teaming, where systems probe each other's assumptions in controlled environments. These solutions are partial. Trust, once lost, is not patched with a certificate.

There is also the human shadow. Military operators are more comfortable delegating authority to machines they believe they understand. Interoperable autonomy pushes them into unfamiliar territory—commanders authorise missions knowing that foreign algorithms will make life-and-death decisions before humans can intervene. Some nations respond by keeping a human on the loop for every autonomous action. Others allow autonomy to run without human oversight when communications degrade. These doctrinal splits are manageable when each nation operates alone. They become fraught when fleets mix.

Which raises a sharper question: what happens when interoperable autonomy fails? If two allied swarms collide—digitally or physically—who pays the diplomatic price? If a foreign model misclassifies a civilian vehicle and an allied drone responds, responsibility becomes a negotiation. Nations once feared friendly fire from misaligned radar codes. Tomorrow, they will fear friendly fire from misaligned ethics.

Every advance in interoperable autonomy therefore demands a parallel investment in governance. Shared logs. Shared audit trails. Shared post-incident learning. No coalition wants its soldiers explaining to the press that a foreign algorithm made a mistake and no one can prove why. Transparency is not a luxury. It is a shield against mistrust.

And yet the strategic payoff is immense. Interoperable autonomy allows coalitions to project power without co-locating every asset. A partner's submarines can coordinate with another's aerial sensors; one nation's satellite imagery can feed another's defensive swarm. Geography stops constraining collective response. Autonomy becomes the glue connecting distant forces into a single posture.

But powerful glue must be resilient. It must tolerate error. It must survive betrayal. If a hostile state compromises one nation's autonomy, the coalition must be able to detect, isolate, and neutralise it without falling apart. This requires not just technical firewalls, but diplomatic ones: agreements around quarantine, rollback, and verification.

The final paradox is stark. The more seamlessly machines cooperate, the less visible humans become in the loop. Trust migrates from people to protocols. Allies will increasingly judge each other not by how they talk in planning rooms, but by how their autonomous systems behave at speed. Mistakes that once took hours to unfold will occur in milliseconds. Diplomats will negotiate after the fact, not before.

Which leaves a lingering question. Coalitions have learned to share bases, carriers, pilots, and radar screens. But can they share decision-making machines—machines that interpret the world, choose tactics, and act before humans can object? Interoperable autonomy promises overwhelming combined strength. It also binds nations in ways they have never been bound before. The first true coalition swarm will not merely show that allied machines can see the world together. It will show whether allied nations are willing to let them.

## Burden-sharing redefined

For decades, alliances measured commitment in ships, battalions, and aircraft. A nation that brought fewer frigates to the task group, or fewer troops to the forward base, was seen as carrying less of the load. But imagine an exercise in which one country contributes only a handful of drones—yet supplies the training data that sharpens every other fleet's targeting model. Another hosts vast ranges where autonomous systems can fail safely and learn quickly. A third offers supercomputing bursts that let the coalition retrain overnight rather than next month. On paper, these nations look like minor players. In reality, they become force multipliers: not through mass, but through the invisible infrastructure that makes mass smart.

This is the quiet revolution of burden-sharing in the age of autonomy. Power is no longer measured solely by how many platforms a state deploys, but by how much intelligence, compute, and testing it injects into the common system. A small ally with modest armed forces may hold priceless leverage if it controls the dataset that teaches the coalition's swarms to navigate ice floes, coral reefs, or dense cities. A mountainous state that cannot field a blue-water navy might still provide high-altitude ranges where counter-drone tactics mature at record pace. The traditional ledger of "who sent what" is giving way to a new economy of contribution: data, compute, and test time.

This shift began quietly. When early autonomous exercises exposed divergent behaviours in multinational swarms, commanders discovered the cause was not faulty platforms—it was incompatible training. One nation's dataset contained months of maritime signatures; another's was biased towards desert convoys. When the fleets merged, the algorithms bickered over what they saw. To harmonise, the coalition needed pooled training data and shared validation. Suddenly, "burden-sharing" had an entirely new currency.

Think of a coalition's autonomy as a living organism. To grow, it needs nutrients. **Data** feeds perception: patterns of life, maritime corridors, civilian behaviours, wildlife signatures, weather anomalies. Some allies possess data no one else can gather—because of geography, jurisdiction, language, sensor architecture, or simple luck. The Arctic nation that logs sea-ice dynamics for fishing safety gives the coalition an edge in high-latitude patrols. The coastal state whose ports observe hundreds of vessels each week trains models to spot illicit transshipments elsewhere. In conventional warfare, such a state would appear peripheral. In autonomous warfare, it holds one of the rarest assets of all.

**Compute** accelerates adaptation. If machine-learning cycles take days, coalitions drift behind adversaries who retrain in hours. A state with sovereign supercomputers can offer compute bursts that compress learning into real time. This contribution does not show up in parade counts or defence budgets. But if those compute hours prevent a coalition swarm from misclassifying a humanitarian vessel as a hostile drone carrier, the strategic impact is enormous.

**Test ranges** unlock experimentation. Autonomous systems must fail visibly and often. Not all nations have the geography, safety regulation, or political cover to host live-fire tests of self-directing munitions, satellite-denied navigation, or electromagnetic spoofing. Those that do—deserts, high seas, remote tundra—become critical partners. They allow coalitions to validate behaviours that simulators cannot yet capture. A state with extensive unpopulated coastline may contribute more to autonomy readiness than a larger ally that declines to share its congested airspace. Traditional metrics cannot account for this, but outcomes can.

In short: burden-sharing now depends on who can help the coalition *learn*. Not merely fight.

This redefinition is not merely academic. It affects diplomacy, procurement, and public legitimacy. Nations that lack conventional firepower have historically feared appearing as passengers. Now they can credibly argue that their datasets, compute clusters, and ranges make them indispensable. But this, too, carries complexities. Who owns a coalition's refined model—the state that provided the data, or the state that provided the compute? What about the ally whose test range uncovered a model flaw that would have cost lives in combat? Old burden-sharing metrics never confronted intellectual property in killing machines.

A provocative solution is emerging: **tokenised validation credits**. When a state donates range time, labelled data, or compute bursts, it earns credits redeemable in coalition autonomy benefits—priority access to retrained models, early warning from fused intelligence, or rights to deploy coalition-tested swarming behaviours in its own theatre. This turns contribution into a quantifiable asset and removes the stigma of being "small". A tiny state with a world-leading cyber range can earn the same strategic credit as a larger state deploying brigade-strength forces.

But tokenisation also forces a debate: should military advantage become transactional within alliances? Shared security once rested on trust, not ledgers. A credit system could strengthen incentives—or sow resentment if one ally feels another is hoarding or gaming the system. Some fear that accounting for every hour of test-range time or every terabyte of training data risks commodifying solidarity. Others argue that without explicit credits, coalition autonomy will depend disproportionately on a handful of states, leaving contributions invisible and unrewarded. As autonomy grows central to deterrence, invisible contributors may demand visible influence.

The next frontier is **coalition validation labs**—joint facilities where allies test each other's autonomous systems under controlled sabotage. One nation hosts; others send hardware and software to be stressed by electromagnetic interference, deceptive signals, corrupted GPS, and swarm-on-swarm tactics. Every successful defence or unexpected failure generates new validation credits. A state too small to field a fleet can still break and improve the coalition's models. Contributions are measured in insights, not metal.

Such labs expose a philosophical tension: who bears the political risk when experiments go wrong? If a drone crashes on foreign soil during coalition testing, domestic audiences may recoil. That is why autonomous burden-sharing demands not only technical infrastructure but legal frameworks—liability waivers, insurance pools, revenue-sharing for damage. These once seemed absurdly bureaucratic for warfare. Now they are prerequisites for learning at scale.

An equally profound shift is occurring in defence procurement. Historically, alliances judged burden-sharing by percentage of GDP spent on defence. That metric made sense when expenditure correlated with deployable platforms. Today, a billion pounds spent on a frigate may deliver less coalition value than a hundred million spent building a high-fidelity simulator that allies share. A nation that invests in a secure cloud for multinational retraining may do more for joint readiness than one who buys another squadron of aircraft.

Yet public narratives lag behind this reality. Parliaments and pundits still equate spending with strength, platforms with prestige. Politicians reluctant to host controversial tests or share sensitive data prefer conventional procurement narratives. But adversaries exploit exactly that inertia. They know that coalitions built on legacy burdens will struggle to pivot when autonomy dictates new ones. Thus the hardest work of redefining burden-sharing may not be technological; it may be rhetorical.

This transformation also raises uncomfortable equity questions. If data becomes currency, states rich in surveillance infrastructure may wield disproportionate influence. If compute is a weapon, tech-advanced nations may dominate coalition AI regardless of troop numbers. Smaller states risk being valued only for what they can host—ranges, skies, electromagnetic quiet zones—rather than full strategic partners. Token systems alone cannot solve the politics of prestige.

So coalitions must go further. They must treat data, compute, and ranges as *shared capital*, jointly governed. If a state supplies a unique dataset, others could reciprocate by funding the sensors that maintain it. If one nation donates compute, others provide power or cooling or cyber-defence. If an ally opens its deserts to dangerous testing, partners should invest in safety infrastructure and local economic benefits. A mature burden-sharing regime rewards contribution, but also reinforces sovereignty.

The most compelling innovation, though, may be moral rather than mechanical. Alliances that once measured sacrifice by blood and treasure now recognise sacrifice in risk tolerance. A country hosting experimental autonomy—knowing a failed test could make headlines, spark backlash, or threaten its tourism or fisheries economy—is taking a political gamble for collective security. This deserves recognition, even reverence.

Yet as burden-sharing evolves, a dangerous question lingers beneath: what if one ally free-rides on coalition learning without contributing? In platform-centric warfare, freeloading was obvious. In autonomy-centric warfare, it is subtle. A nation might quietly harvest coalition-trained models while offering little data, compute, or testing in return. Traditional diplomatic pressure may not deter such behaviour; only transparent accounting of contributions and entitlements can.

Still, accounting is not enough. Coalitions must build a culture in which every nation—large or small—feels ownership of the collective intelligence that protects them. When a small state's coastal radar logs prevent a high-profile targeting mistake, that must be visible. When a minority partner hosts the test that reveals a safety flaw in a swarming algorithm, commanders must say so. Fairness is not a sentiment; it is a security measure. If under-recognised allies withdraw from the autonomy commons, the coalition loses its learning engine.

There is one final tension. As burden-sharing shifts towards digital assets and learning cycles, coalitions risk forgetting the human dimension. Alliances do not exist solely to integrate machines. They exist to protect people. If burden-sharing becomes too abstract—credits, tokens, data corridors—ordinary citizens may lose sight of why it matters. Democracies must keep the narrative grounded: a terabyte of training data is not a commodity. It is the difference between a drone navigating safely above a refugee boat or misclassifying it under hostile fog. A test-range hour is not bureaucracy. It is where machines learn restraint.

So the paradox remains vivid. Burden-sharing has never been easier to calculate—and never more crucial to perform with care. Alliances that succeed in this new economy will wield not just interoperable weapons, but interoperable wisdom. Yet the path forward depends on a delicate balance of incentives, transparency, and trust. Will coalitions build this new ledger together—or cling to the old one until adversaries render it obsolete?

## Procurement without paralysis

The cruel irony of modern defence procurement is that armed forces can spend a decade buying technology designed to win a war that ends in a month. During the long wait, requirements swell, committees multiply, contractors merge, and what was once cutting-edge quietly becomes obsolete. By the time a platform reaches the field, adversaries have already learned how to neutralise it. The world's fastest-moving threats are met with the world's slowest-moving bureaucracy. The question is no longer how to buy well, but how to buy fast without lowering the guardrails that protect public money, safety, and trust.

Several ministries have felt this pain in the most embarrassing way possible: unveiling "next-generation" drone systems that are outperformed by cheap commercial quadcopters with open-source autonomy. In some cases, prototypes sat in storage waiting for approvals while real battlefields evolved. Procurement officers know the stakes. Moving too slowly cedes tactical advantage. Moving too quickly invites scandal, waste, and potentially fatal flaws in testing. The challenge is not innovation—it is governance at speed.

A genuine breakthrough appeared in the form of *spiral development with stop-gates*. Instead of designing the perfect system upfront, states buy the minimum viable capability, field it early, gather real-world lessons, and iterate. But crucially, each spiral ends with rigorous oversight: independent safety boards, affordability checks, and audits on training data and testing protocols. Procurement becomes a cycle of "build → deploy → learn → approve → expand", not "design → delay → deliver → regret".

This model has already changed outcomes. In one joint programme, allies co-developed a maritime reconnaissance drone with the express aim of flying unstable prototypes. The first models could barely land without incident. Yet every crash was logged, simulated, and fed into the next spiral. By the third iteration, the airframe was robust enough for hostile weather, and the autonomy learned to classify fishing boats, container ships, and trawlers without supervision. Had the programme tried to perfect the system before first flight, it would still be in committee. Instead, it is operational.

Still, spiral development is not a free pass. Without strong oversight, iteration becomes drift—capabilities grow without clear objectives, and contractors burn money waiting for specifications that change monthly. This is why **stop-gates** matter. They freeze the spiral long enough to interrogate progress: Has safety improved? Are failure modes understood? Is the model verifiable and resilient to adversarial inputs? Does performance justify the next tranche of funding? No spiral proceeds on momentum alone.

Some defence ministries have gone further, creating **red-team procurement offices** whose job is to attack the programme before adversaries do. They attempt to spoof sensors, poison data, jam communications, and induce timing drift in swarming behaviour. If a contractor claims "resilience", the red-team demands proof. For the first time, procurement is not only about features—it is about survivability under stress.

Such scrutiny can be uncomfortable. Contractors dislike being told their latest model crashes under electromagnetic interference. Militaries dislike being told a platform needs a software rewrite mid-deployment. Politicians dislike headlines about "faulty" systems. Yet discomfort is the price of relevance. Systems that are never embarrassed on the test range usually suffer humiliation in combat.

The most powerful enabler of fast procurement is architectural humility: **interface-first design**. Instead of monolithic systems, states buy modular components—navigation, perception, targeting, comms—that can be swapped as models improve. If a small firm produces a breakthrough perception module, it can slot into the fleet without waiting for a full platform upgrade. If a cyber vulnerability is found, only the affected component is patched. Platforms become scaffolding for software evolution.

But modular procurement demands standardised APIs, shared safety metrics, and open testing protocols. This is where alliances often stumble. Each state prefers its own specifications, cybersecurity stack, encryption scheme, and certification pipeline. The result: beautiful prototypes that cannot integrate with coalition systems. The cure is politically sensitive but technologically simple: agree upfront on *minimum interoperable standards* and allow competition within them. A swarm does not care where each drone was made; it cares whether every drone speaks the same language.

Another obstacle lies not in technology, but culture. Many procurement agencies were built for the industrial era: ships, tanks, aircraft—assets measured in decades. They are ill-suited to machine-learning cycles that demand weekly updates. A model that performs well in January may degrade by July as adversaries alter tactics or visibility conditions change. For legacy procurement boards, constant change looks like instability. For modern warfighters, it is survival.

This requires a mindset shift: software is not a "feature" of a platform; it *is* the platform. Buying an autonomous system means committing to perpetual updates, red-teaming, and retraining. That is not wasteful—it is responsible. Oversight bodies must evolve accordingly, checking not only cost and schedule but data quality, test coverage, adversarial robustness, and ethical safeguards. Audit trails should include not only hardware inspections but end-to-end histories of model training runs, simulation provenance, and validation logs.

Some nations have begun to require **model attestations** as a condition of contracting: suppliers must prove the safety of their autonomy through reproducible testing, chain-of-custody on training data, and cryptographically signed updates. This transforms oversight from bureaucratic paperwork to engineering discipline.

A deeper tension remains between agility and fairness. Rapid procurement risks favouring firms already embedded in defence ecosystems, shutting out innovators who cannot navigate years of compliance and security screening. To counter this, some ministries now maintain *innovation sandboxes* where new entrants can demonstrate capabilities with clear legal immunity if their prototypes fail. If a start-up cannot crash a drone safely in a sandbox, it will never earn a production contract. But if it succeeds, it bypasses years of opaque gatekeeping.

In parallel, coalitions have begun experimenting with **joint procurement pools**. A small state may lack budget to buy full swarms but can contribute to a pooled contract that gives it access to shared platforms and models. This spreads risk, reduces duplication, and strengthens interoperability. It also forces larger allies to consider the needs of smaller partners—if the interface layer becomes proprietary, the coalition loses its edge.

Yet joint procurement carries political cost. If a shared platform crashes or causes collateral damage, which parliament answers for it? If shared autonomy violates one state's rules of engagement, does the fleet stop or split? Governance, not engineering, becomes the limiting factor.

The hardest question of all is ethical. Spiral development means fielding incomplete systems, allowing them to learn in the wild. Critics argue this treats civilians and soldiers as unwitting participants in experiments. Supporters counter that withholding a capable system until every defect is eliminated carries its own moral cost: unprotected forces, unnecessary casualties, and missed chances to deter aggression.

The compromise is transparency and constraint. Spirals begin in controlled environments—simulators, test ranges, remote theatres—before entering sensitive spaces. Stop-gates demand human review. Failures are disclosed, not buried. A system's autonomy expands only when safety evidence justifies it. Done right, procurement is not reckless acceleration; it is disciplined iteration.

All of this raises a larger philosophical point: procurement is strategy. Buying slowly is a strategic choice that favours predictability over adaptation. Buying quickly without oversight is a choice that favours innovation over accountability. Neither extreme works. The goal is balance—systems that evolve as fast as threats, with guardrails that preserve public trust.

Will governments embrace this candour? Will militaries tolerate short-term embarrassment for long-term superiority? Will contractors accept red-team scrutiny as a requirement, not an insult? Most importantly, will democracies learn to hold procurement honest without binding it in procedural knots?

The stakes are stark. Autonomy is rewriting the tempo of warfare. Whoever learns, fields, and fixes faster will win—not by building perfect machines, but by never letting them stop improving. The question is whether our institutions can learn as quickly as our technology.

## Trust and verification

Alliances are built on promises; deterrence is built on proof. In the age of autonomous systems, the difference matters. A state can declare that its targeting algorithms respect law, that its drones avoid civilian corridors, that its early-warning models cannot be spoofed by deepfake telemetry. But allies do not take each other at their word when lives and legitimacy are on the line. They ask to inspect, to test, to red-team. The result is unsettling and necessary: partners who trust each other enough to cooperate, but not enough to relax vigilance. It is diplomacy conducted with test harnesses, audit logs, and adversarial toolkits.

A recent multinational drill made this dynamic painfully visible. Several allied navies deployed autonomous patrol craft with supposedly interoperable deconfliction protocols. On paper, each fleet claimed rigorous testing. In the water, a simple spoofing packet caused half the vessels to believe a non-existent ship was on collision course. The drills were meant to demonstrate unity; instead, they revealed brittle code and overconfident certification. Yet no government condemned another. Engineers shared captures of corrupted telemetry, rebuilt stacks overnight, and patched the vulnerability by the end of the week. Not humiliation, but proof of adulthood: allies who can expose flaws without political theatre are allies who can survive real conflict.

That is the essence of trust in autonomous coalitions. It is not blind confidence. It is the mutual agreement to verify, challenge, and audit—even when it causes discomfort, even when it delays a press release. Trust without verification is naïveté. Verification without trust is sabotage. The art is to build both.

The first pillar is **audit exchange.** Nations increasingly run each other's code through controlled test suites before joint deployment. These audits do not require handing over proprietary source files—few firms or governments would tolerate that. Instead, they rely on *behavioural verification*: black-box testing that measures what the autonomy does under stress rather than how it was written. States supply encrypted binaries; allies provide testing harnesses that subject them to jamming, GPS drift, adversarial sensor input, hostile firmware signatures, and degraded comms. The result is a scored, time-stamped record of performance, failure modes, recovery behaviours, and edge-case anomalies.

This is why audit exchanges matter more than memoranda of trust. A nation may trust another's intentions but doubt its software supply chain. A perfect algorithm is worthless if its firmware updater can be compromised. Audit exchanges surface these weaknesses while there is still time to fix them. They create a shared language of risk: not diplomatic assurances, but reproducible evidence.

The political prize is flexibility. Once audit pipelines are established, states can deploy new models or patches with minimal negotiation. If France pushes a navigation hotfix to a shared maritime fleet, Germany can run the update through its audit suite overnight. If Japan discovers a sensor-fusion glitch, it can share the failing test as a self-contained scenario without revealing its proprietary simulator. Alliances become faster by becoming more transparent where it counts.

The second pillar is **red-teams**—not ceremonial groups that produce polite reports, but adversarial units empowered to break things. A red-team that pulls its punches is security theatre. Effective red-teams impersonate hostile actors: poisoning training data, forging ADS-B telemetry, injecting malware into update channels, simulating compromised ground stations, and pushing deception patterns that mirror real adversaries. Their task is not simply to find bugs, but to demonstrate how those bugs cascade into mission failure.

Some coalitions now rotate red-team leadership, giving each member—large or small—the chance to test the others. This creates an unusual balance: a small state with world-class cyber talent can challenge the systems of a superpower without risking diplomatic insult. Everyone wins. The powerful receive sharper feedback. The smaller earn legitimacy not by budget, but by skill.

Crucially, red-team campaigns must be unpredictable. If drills occur on a fixed schedule, engineers optimise for the test, not reality. That is why several alliances have adopted *randomised drills with no notice*. A fleet might wake one morning to find half its drones cannot authenticate with the mission server. Engineers scramble, telemetry streams fail over to backup channels, contingency plans activate. After two hours, the drill is declared. The humiliation is private, the lesson public.

This unpredictability builds resilience. Autonomy trained only for sunny days collapses when the weather changes. Organisations sheltered from surprise fail at the first sign of chaos. The point is not perfection—it is adaptation under stress.

The third pillar is **cross-inspection weeks**, a surprisingly humble innovation. Once or twice a year, engineers, lawyers, commanders, and safety officers gather in a neutral facility. Each nation presents its systems not with polished marketing decks, but with raw test logs, accident reports, system failures, and near-misses. Classified details remain sealed. But the structure, process, and corrective actions are on full display.

This ritual has three effects. First, it de-romanticises autonomy. When every participant sees that others experience crashes, misclassifications, corrupted firmware, and ambiguous ethical dilemmas, embarrassment gives way to candour. Second, it aligns expectations. No ally can credibly demand perfect systems when none exist. Third, it strengthens resolve. After a week of cross-inspection, partners come away with a shared conviction: vigilance is normal, humility is patriotic, safety is everyone's responsibility.

Some governments fear that admitting flaws will tarnish prestige. They prefer immaculate press releases to honest engineering. But secrecy creates fragility. The first time an ally learns about a vulnerability should not be during a crisis. The public never needs to know. Allies do.

There are hard limits, of course. Nations share what they must, not what they can. An air force may reveal the safety properties of its autonomous targeting but not the dataset that taught the model to rank decoy objects. A navy may demonstrate collision-avoidance behaviour without surrendering the encryption keys used for command. These boundaries are not signs of mistrust—they are signs of sovereignty.

The trick is creating **partitioned visibility**. Instead of demanding everything, allies demand proofs. Not "show me your model", but "prove that your model cannot target an object without two separate sensor confirmations". Not "give me your training data", but "prove that no personal data is present, and show the privacy attestations". Cryptographic commitments, signed telemetry, zero-knowledge proofs, and secure enclaves allow verification without exposure. It turns trust into mathematics rather than sentiment.

This is becoming a strategic advantage. Democracies that master transparent verification will build broader coalitions than autocracies that rely solely on secrecy. Smaller states will join frameworks that treat them as equal auditors rather than silent customers. Civil society will tolerate autonomy when accountability is demonstrable, not rhetorical.

Yet verification introduces a philosophical tension. How much transparency is too much? If every ally inspects every subsystem, innovation freezes under paperwork. If every red-team demands access, supply chains clog. If every update requires multinational certification, adversaries sprint ahead while coalitions mark forms. Verification can become a new form of paralysis.

Some alliances respond by creating **risk-tiered regimes**. High-risk capabilities—lethal autonomy, strategic ISR, counter-satellite systems—receive deep, intrusive auditing. Intermediate risks—logistics routing, convoy coordination—receive behavioural tests and red-team signatures. Low-risk capabilities—maintenance scheduling, weather prediction, non-lethal sensing—move on lighter tracks. This avoids bureaucratic gravity while keeping rigour where it matters.

Others use **reciprocity** as leverage. If a state wants access to coalition models, ranges, or datasets, it must reciprocate with equivalent transparency. If a state wants fast certification for its updates, it must contribute to the red-team roster or provide audit tooling. Sharing becomes a currency: those who verify earn trust; those who refuse become second-tier participants.

Still, some will try to game the system—delaying disclosures, sanitising logs, or negotiating exemptions. Alliances survive only if they enforce norms. A nation that repeatedly hides failures will find its platforms excluded from joint operations—not out of punishment, but prudence. In autonomous warfare, one weak link can compromise the whole chain.

Deep down, there is a human lesson. Engineers are trained to fix machines, not to bare their weaknesses to outsiders. Commanders are rewarded for confidence, not confession. Political leaders prefer triumphal speeches to technical autopsies. Yet the most secure alliances are those that normalise vulnerability. When failures can be discussed without shame, safety improves. When audits are routine, not accusatory, cooperation strengthens. When red-teams are celebrated for breaking things, systems become harder to break.

The future will only amplify this need. As fleets grow more autonomous and software defines more of warfighting, the most dangerous failures will be invisible until too late—silent sensor poisoning, data poisoning at supply-chain scale, firmware implants that sleep for years. Traditional treaties, built around hardware counts, cannot govern these risks. Verification must be continuous, not episodic. Trust must be earned, not assumed.

So the unresolved question lingers: will states embrace transparent scrutiny when it threatens their pride? Will they choose collective resilience over national vanity? Can trust survive the honesty that verification demands?

Alliances cannot rely on hope. They will discover, sooner or later, that the real measure of trust is not what partners say in summits, but what their systems reveal under stress. The coalitions that endure will be those willing to inspect each other's work, sharpen each other's edges, and run drills that expose every crack. Trust will not be a promise. It will be a practice.

# Chapter 6

# The Domestic Front: Industry, Labour, Legitimacy

On a grey Tuesday morning, in an anonymous low-rise office park outside a mid-sized European city, a dozen workers quietly decide whether a suspicious cluster of pixels is a fishing boat, a sandbar, or a camouflaged launch. They are not uniformed analysts in bunkers. They are contractors: former students, part-time gig workers, a retired marine biologist, a schoolteacher between terms. Their judgement will feed a model that guides maritime interdiction. One mislabelled frame could send an autonomous vessel towards a tourist ferry. Yet no politician will ever mention them. They are the invisible labour of national defence.

The new arms race lives in places like this. In server halls, annotation labs, simulation studios, ethical review boards, and union meetings. There are no patriotic posters on the walls, no marching bands, no medals. Just Jira tickets, subscription invoices, and incident logs. Power is shifting from defence primes with hangars and shipyards towards software-first firms whose biggest asset is an update pipeline. The supply chain no longer smells of oil and solvent. It smells of coffee and burned GPUs.

Governments sense the change. They once bought hardware that lasted decades. Now they subscribe to autonomy platforms that update weekly. The old procurement machinery is too slow, too rigid, too allergic to iteration. Yet the stakes are higher: failure is not a product recall; it is a violation of sovereignty or a breach of ethics seen around the world. The domestic front is no longer an afterthought—it is the arena where legitimacy is forged or squandered.

This chapter starts from a disquieting contradiction. Nations competing for strategic autonomy rely on industries that behave like consumer software companies. They want predictability, but pay for experimentation. They demand secrecy, but need the talent of civilians who will not sign up without transparency. Defence ministries still speak in the language of platforms and programmes, but their most critical suppliers are shipping code on Friday evenings and fixing bugs on Monday mornings. A single faulty model update can ripple across fleets spread over three oceans.

That shift upends contracting. Traditional primes promised physical sustainment: parts, maintenance crews, depot capacity. Today, sustainment is *subscription*: telemetry monitoring, safety patches, retraining cycles, and adversarial evaluation. The line between civilian and military customer blurs—sometimes the same vendor sells one algorithm to diagnose crop diseases and another to guide a loitering munition. Dual-use has stopped being a slogan. It is the operating model.

Yet capability without legitimacy is a time bomb. Citizens will tolerate defence budgets only if they believe systems are safe, governed, and morally constrained. Slogans and glossy brochures will fail. People want plain-language risk reports: did the drone corridor misclassify a delivery van? Did the maritime model generate false positives that wasted fuel and risked escalation? If the answer is yes, what changed? A democracy that cannot speak candidly about failure will be crushed by rumour and propaganda. The public does not demand perfection. It demands honesty.

Behind the technology is labour—messy, human, and indispensable. AI does not replace workers; it rearranges them. Autonomous targeting requires annotators to label sensor feeds, testers to break simulation builds, operators to verify launch authority, and field engineers to patch models in austere conditions. Unions of skill are emerging in strange places. A defence ministry might negotiate with a consortium of annotation cooperatives. A navy might sign agreements with gig-worker unions to ensure minimum standards for labelling that affects maritime safety.

The workforce needs more than certificates. They need ethical briefings: when does a model's blind spot become a moral hazard? When should a tester escalate a finding from an engineering lead to an inspector-general? Reservist tech cadres—data scientists who serve a few weeks a year—are becoming as vital as pilots. A nation without a pipeline for such talent is a nation with brittle autonomy.

This labour force is as much a political constituency as dockworkers were in the industrial era. Ignore them, and the system hollow outs. Empower them, and legitimacy deepens.

Economic geography is shifting too. The map of strategic autonomy looks less like missile silos and more like chip fabs, cloud availability zones, and research clusters. A government can deter adversaries by building a resilient network of sovereign data centres across allied regions. Conversely, a state that clusters all compute in one metro area invites a single point of failure—whether from cyberattack, earthquake, or political coercion.

Local communities feel the tension. A chip fab brings jobs, but demands water and power. A cloud zone revitalises a region, but raises land prices and energy bills. Incentives attract investment; resilience requires distribution. Voters will ask whether autonomy means opportunity or extraction. National strategy becomes regional politics—one zoning board meeting at a time.

Finally, legitimacy is institutional. Democracies build accountability architecture: ombuds to hear complaints from citizens and workers, inspectors to verify compliance with law, safety boards to investigate mishaps, and independent review panels to publish findings. These bodies keep the system humane. When an autonomous vehicle collides with civilian property, a transparent mishap review protects the public and teaches engineers. When a procurement goes wrong, an inspector-general's report prevents repetition. Without such architecture, autonomy becomes a priesthood. With it, autonomy is a public trust.

This chapter unpacks these domestic battlegrounds: industry that looks like software more than steel; labour that is technical, distributed, and ethically loaded; transparency that earns rather than demands consent; regional politics that decide where sovereignty lives; and accountability that keeps a nation worthy of its tools. The questions are uncomfortable. Can democracies adapt without losing their soul? Can the workforce be trained, respected, and heard? Can governments be honest without crippling public confidence? Can autonomy be fast, safe, and legitimate?

The answers will shape who wins the next arms race—not only abroad, but at home. The domestic front is not quieter than the battlefield; it is simply less visible. Yet it is here, in code audits and union halls and cloud tenders and public briefings, that strategic autonomy becomes real. Readers who care about power must care about what happens behind the curtain: the contracts, the workers, the inspectors, the communities. Turn the page. The battle has already begun.

## From defence primes to platforms

The contract was barely ten pages long, yet it governed a fleet of autonomous boats patrolling a tense stretch of coastline. There were no line-item lists of spare parts, no maintenance crews, no depot-level overhaul schedules. Instead, there were uptime guarantees, telemetry rights, patch cadences, and service-level penalties. The Navy did not *own* the autonomy stack on those vessels. It subscribed to it. When an unexpected swell confused the boats' vision models, the vendor pushed an overnight update from a data centre several hundred miles away. By dawn, the glitch was gone. In the cold light of morning, the admiralty realised something uncomfortable: the most critical capability it fielded was controlled not by a defence prime, but by a software platform with thousands of civilian customers.

The paradox is sharp. States want strategic autonomy. Yet their most advanced tools depend on companies whose flagship products are mould-detection models for farmers or logistics optimisers for supermarkets. Dual-use is no longer a category in a policy brief; it is the business model. A single firm may serve militaries, hospitals and haulage companies using the same architecture, differentiated mainly by fine-tuned weights and contractual terms. The boundary between national security and the commercial cloud has thinned to a membrane.

Behind the scenes, procurement officers accustomed to fifteen-year support horizons now negotiate subscription sustainment: a continuous pipeline of patches, adversarial testing, dataset refreshes, and red-team audits. In theory, this offers agility. In practice, it demands constant governance. If a vendor disables an update pipeline—whether for commercial leverage or geopolitical pressure—an entire class of platforms may revert to obsolete models overnight. For the first time, a defence ministry might lose capability not because a missile misfired, but because a SaaS licence expired.

The shift from hardware-centric defence primes to software-first platforms reflects deeper currents. Hardware wears out predictably. Software fails silently. A pair of frigates might be identical in build yet diverge entirely in behaviour because their autonomy stacks have taken different update paths. One may detect periscopes more reliably because its fleet's telemetry enriched its vendor's training set; the other may carry forward an undetected bug. Sustainment becomes statistical rather than mechanical.

This changes power dynamics. Traditional primes were deeply entangled with governments: multi-decade contracts, cabinet-level oversight, strict export controls. Today's platforms are global by design. Their infrastructure spans continents. Their engineering teams mix citizens of multiple nations. Their intellectual property lives in shared cloud repositories. They can shift workloads to friendlier jurisdictions within hours. When a government wants sovereign assurance—on access, on data residency, on supply chain integrity—it must bargain. Some states build national clouds and mandate in-country deployment. Others negotiate escrowed model weights or cryptographic attestation of every update. The defence-industrial base now speaks in APIs, not armour plate.

Yet platforms bring undeniable gains. When a fleet's sensors detect a new form of camouflage, a patch can roll out globally in a single release cycle. When adversaries spoof GPS, a vendor can integrate alternative positioning models and push the fix to every drone with a heartbeat connection. Classical procurement could never match that tempo. A decade-long programme would be overtaken by threat evolution before sea trials began. Software-first suppliers make autonomous systems living organisms—constantly adapting, constantly tested, constantly repaired.

The danger lies in complacency. Update pipelines that patch vulnerabilities can also introduce new ones. A model retrained against adversarial inputs may overfit or amplify bias. When sustainment is subscription, the state must not only fund capability; it must audit it. Many governments are only now realising they need software safety boards with authority to halt rollouts, demand red-team reports, or mandate fallback to a known-good model snapshot. Subcontracting that authority to vendors is not autonomy—it is dependency.

Dual-use cuts both ways. A company that sells predictive maintenance to airlines may, with a minor architectural modification, offer target recognition to a military. Both use time-series modelling and anomaly detection. But ethical obligations differ. Commercial fleets tolerate occasional false positives or downtime; militaries cannot. Vendors accustomed to agile experimentation find themselves confronted with rules of engagement, escalation risks, and political oversight. Some embrace the responsibility. Others underestimate it, discovering too late that their product has become a tool of force, scrutinised in parliament and press briefings.

This creates tension inside companies. Engineers who joined to build logistics optimisers may balk at supplying militaries. Shareholders may fear reputational fallout. Governments, desperate for capability, must navigate corporate values and public opinion. Transparency becomes currency: risk disclosures, independent audits, and incident reports assure not only regulators but employees. A platform without public legitimacy may lose its workforce faster than any export ban could constrain it.

For states, the challenge is to harness dual-use innovation without losing strategic control. Some adopt permissive frameworks: if a vendor meets safety baselines and residency rules, it may serve defence customers. Others demand sovereign variants: models trained within national borders, on government-curated datasets, with update channels controlled by in-country teams cleared for classified work. This reduces agility and increases cost, but buys political resilience. The calculus varies by threat perception and industrial capacity.

Contracting models are undergoing a quiet revolution. Instead of buying a finished platform, governments increasingly purchase access to a lifecycle. The contract does not end at delivery; it begins there. Subscription sustainment might include:

Continuous evaluation against red-team attacks:

- Mandatory rollback triggers if precision drops below thresholds
- Cryptographic attestations of every deployed model
- Access to vendor telemetry for incident reconstruction
- Obligations to retrain on state-provided datasets

These terms blur procurement and partnership. Vendors become stewards of capability, not mere suppliers. Governments become stakeholders in product roadmaps. Failure modes multiply: a contract dispute can freeze updates; a lawsuit can block deployment; a supply chain compromise in a third-party library can propagate across fleets.

Some states respond by nurturing domestic platforms—start-ups incubated with security clearances, sovereign data centres, and defence-focused engineering pipelines. The hope is to capture agility without forfeiting autonomy. But national champions struggle with scale. Training cutting-edge models demands vast compute and specialised talent. Competing with commercial giants is expensive. The trade-off is familiar: sovereignty versus cost, control versus innovation.

Other governments pursue hybrid models: civilian platforms for non-lethal tasks, sovereign platforms for sensitive missions. A navy might rely on a global vendor for fleet logistics while reserving domestic autonomy stacks for strike roles. This partitioned procurement reduces exposure but complicates interoperability. Mixed fleets must coordinate across heterogeneous APIs and update cadences. A patch applied to one platform may break compatibility with another.

A deeper philosophical question lurks beneath the surface: what does sovereignty mean when a state's coercive power depends on privately maintained code? There is precedent. Nations long relied on private shipbuilders and telecommunications firms. But those firms built infrastructure. Today's platforms operate infrastructure *and cognition.* They choose what a sensor sees, what a model infers, what a targeting algorithm prioritises. Delegation is no longer mechanical; it is epistemic.

In the past, the military owned its models—rudimentary, embedded in hardware, rarely updated. Now, the most valuable logic lives offsite, in repositories controlled by companies whose strategic interests may not align perfectly with the state's. Regulators are still groping for tools. Some propose mandatory escrow of critical model weights; others favour government-run test harnesses that certify each update. Both approaches imply a profound shift: governments must learn to govern code with the same seriousness they once governed gunpowder.

This is not only about risk. It is also about speed. War has always rewarded agility. The first states to embrace software-first sustainment will deploy systems that learn faster than their adversaries. Their drones will adapt to new jamming patterns within days; their autonomous patrols will refine anomaly detection from real-world feedback. Competitors stuck in hardware-era procurement cycles—ten years from concept to deployment—will field obsolete systems on arrival.

But the path to agility is narrow. A vendor can be acquired by a foreign conglomerate. A geopolitical crisis can trigger export controls. A patch meant to fix a vulnerability can introduce a catastrophic regression. The subscription model offers power at the cost of dependence. States must decide where to draw the line: which platforms require sovereign custody, which can be outsourced, which demand joint stewardship with allies.

The future of defence procurement will not be decided in shipyards, but in Git repositories and contract clauses. The centre of gravity shifts from manufacturing to maintenance, from hardware to lifecycle, from ownership to continuous control. A ministry that fails to adapt risks fielding "zombie" capabilities—models that still run but no longer learn, fleets that move but no longer understand.

And so a question lingers, unanswered: in a world where force depends on platforms, who truly commands—those who fire the weapons, or those who update the software behind them? States will need new doctrines, new partnerships, and new forms of accountability. The old primes are not gone, but they are no longer alone. The platform era has begun, and with it, a new map of power—one drawn not in steel, but in code.

## Workforce and unions of skill

The engineers arrived in borrowed uniforms, not because anyone expected them to salute, but because the airbase could not process civilian badges fast enough. A drone squadron had lost its autonomy stack after a corrupted update, and the only people who could diagnose the fault were software testers from a mid-sized tech firm in Manchester. They worked through the night in a tool-filled hangar designed for turbine overhauls, not machine learning pipelines. By dawn, the fleet was flying again. The officers were grateful. The engineers were exhausted. And everyone sensed a deeper truth: modern defence depends on people who were never trained by the military, never sworn in, and may never return.

If war once relied on welders, armourers, and radio operators, today's autonomy-first forces require annotators, data janitors, red-team modellers, ops engineers, and model validators. They are essential, yet structurally invisible. They do not march in parades. They do not appear on recruiting posters. And yet a thousand annotators labelling maritime anomalies can alter the outcome of a naval confrontation more than a thousand riflemen. The labour of modern conflict is digital, distributed, and often precarious.

This is an uncomfortable paradox. States talk about sovereign capability while outsourcing the cognitive scaffolding to temporary contractors paid by the hour. Governments invest in platforms but neglect the quiet workforce that teaches those platforms to see and decide. For decades, strategy focused on materiel. Now, the decisive frontier is skill. Not heroic skill—patient, exacting skill.

Training pipelines are the pressure point. Militaries can produce pilots and sailors; they struggle to produce incident responders who understand PyTorch logs, or systems engineers able to diagnose timing drift across a heterogeneous autonomous fleet. Commercial tech companies poach these workers with lavish salaries and flexible hours. Defence offers meaning and mission, but meaning is hard to quantise into a payslip.

Some states try to lure talent through national pride. Others rely on secrecy or security clearances as barriers to exit. Both approaches are unsustainable. The talent war rewards mobility, not loyalty. A skilled ops engineer with a newborn child may choose predictable commercial hours over the adrenaline of crisis deployments. The result is brittle dependence: a small cadre of overworked specialists maintaining fleets of increasingly complex machines.

A more promising path is the emergence of *unions of skill*—not unions in the labour-relations sense, but professional corps with shared identity, accreditation, and protective norms. Think of air traffic controllers: highly trained, rigorously certified, performing a mission-critical function without wearing a uniform. Similar models could apply to safety auditors, model testers, firmware security analysts. These workers need standing, career ladders, and public recognition. Otherwise, critical knowledge disperses after every contract, and the nation pays again to rediscover it.

The most forward-leaning militaries are creating reserve tech cadres: software engineers and data scientists who serve a few weeks each year, much like medical or logistics reserves. Their civilian employers keep them at the cutting edge; their reserve service keeps them aligned with national defence. When a crisis hits, these cadres can surge into operations centres, bringing skills the standing force could never maintain full-time. But reserve tech cadres demand careful design. If engineers feel they are pulled in only when disaster looms, the system becomes extractive. If service intrudes unpredictably on civilian careers, employers resist and workers lose autonomy. The relationship must feel like partnership, not conscription-by-another-name.

Annotators and testers offer a different dilemma. Their work is labour-intensive, often monotonous, and easy to outsource to low-cost markets. But if defence systems learn from cheap, loosely supervised annotation pools, they inherit biases, mistakes, and blind spots. A mislabelled periscope becomes a "fishing buoy." A civilian truck becomes a "soft target." These are not trivial accidents. They shape model priors and influence decisions at scale.

Ethical briefings are as critical as technical training. A commercial annotator labelling street scenes for self-driving cars may treat ambiguity as noise. A defence annotator labelling armed combatants cannot. They must understand rules of engagement, distinction, and proportionality. It is unreasonable to demand philosophical fluency from gig workers paid by the frame. That is why annotation for sensitive systems should be a profession, not piecework. Workers need context, oversight, and debriefs when edge cases cause moral strain. The state cannot outsource conscience.

Testing, too, demands professionalisation. Red-team modellers and adversarial testers must think like attackers, probing models for brittle reasoning, sensor spoofing, and unseen failure modes. They need the freedom to break things without fear of reprisal, and the authority to halt deployment when they uncover systemic flaws. The worst outcome is a theatre where everyone praises safety, but no one has the mandate to enforce it.

Ops engineers—those who keep autonomous systems alive in the field—sit at the fulcrum of risk. They bridge military operators and civilian codebases, translating sensor logs into patches, model regressions into mission constraints. A drone operator might see "unstable tracking"; an ops engineer sees "loss of temporal coherence in the motion estimation head." Without shared vocabulary, blame flies faster than data. When things go wrong, ops engineers often carry responsibility without agency.

To retain them, states must treat operational AI work like aviation: licensed, guild-like, with respected qualifications and clear liability frameworks. Aviation learned, after decades of catastrophe, to separate pilot error from maintenance error, and maintenance error from design flaws. Defence autonomy needs the same intellectual honesty. When a model misfires, the investigation should ask: was the annotation faulty, was the update unverified, was the ops engineer unsupported, was the interface misleading? Blame-free retrospectives, not scapegoats, build trust.

This leads to an uncomfortable truth. Many militaries still treat software sustainment as aftercare—something done once a year, far from the frontline. But modern autonomous systems need near-constant tending. They fail silently, degrade gradually, and recover unpredictably. A handful of highly skilled ops engineers can avert catastrophe. But those people burn out quickly if treated as invisible.

There is a philosophical layer beneath the workforce problem. Liberal democracies claim moral legitimacy because their use of force is accountable. If autonomous systems are to defend those values, the people who curate, test, and maintain them must embody those same values. Ethical briefings cannot be perfunctory. Annotators labelling bodies and combatants deserve psychological support. Ops engineers modifying safety parameters under pressure deserve clear guidelines on escalation risk.

Some propose creating ethical accreditation for defence AI professionals—much like medical ethics for surgeons or legal ethics for barristers. The idea is not to moralise engineering, but to acknowledge that decisions in code have lethal consequences. A technician deciding whether to deploy a patch with uncertain behaviour is, in effect, making a judgement about risk to life. These decisions should not be treated as technical trivia.

Recruitment strategies are starting to shift. Instead of trying to convert coders into soldiers, some forces are building civilian digital corps with rotational duty. Others are partnering with universities to create pipelines where students earn security clearances and serve internships in defence labs. The promise is compelling: hands-on experience, world-class compute, mission-driven work. But once again, retention depends on culture. If the environment is bureaucratic, hierarchical, and allergic to failure, talent drains away.

A small number of nations have begun experimenting with cross-service exchanges between defence and commercial tech. An engineer might spend six months inside a military innovation unit, then return to industry with deeper insight. These exchanges build trust and reduce the cultural gulf. They also seed informal networks for crisis response. When systems fail in wartime, the difference between hours and days may hinge on whether the right engineer knows whom to call.

Still, none of this solves the question of scale. A nation of millions needs, at most, tens of thousands of infantry. But it may need millions of labour-hours of annotation to keep autonomous systems current. Automation helps, but automated labeling still needs supervision. Synthetic data helps, but synthetic data can propagate unseen bias. The labour problem does not disappear; it mutates.

Some envision international labour-sharing: allied nations pooling secure annotation facilities and sharing standards. Others propose incentives for commercial vendors to contribute annotation and testing time as part of procurement agreements. A vendor selling an autonomy stack might be obliged to provide continuous validation, logging, and adversarial testing—not as optional extras, but contractual duties.

Yet labour is not only about skill; it is about dignity. The people who maintain autonomous systems are asked to shoulder responsibility for life-and-death behaviour, often under NDAs that bar them from public credit. A nation cannot expect loyalty from workers it refuses to acknowledge.

Public legitimacy requires honesty. Citizens deserve to know who keeps their defence systems safe—and those workers deserve recognition.

The next decade will test whether democratic states can build *unions of skill*—cohesive communities of annotators, testers, ops engineers, safety auditors, and reserve tech cadres—anchored by professional standards, ethical training, and meaningful career paths. If they fail, capability will hollow out from within. Machines may continue to fly and patrol, but the human scaffolding that keeps them safe will erode.

We are left with an open question. In a world of autonomous force, where quiet expertise holds the line, how will states honour the workers who never see a battlefield, yet shape its outcomes more than anyone in uniform? Until that question is answered, the workforce problem remains unsolved—and the legitimacy of autonomy remains incomplete.

## Public legitimacy

A self-driving patrol vehicle struck a barrier outside a coastal radar site. No one was injured, the damage was trivial, and the incident was rapidly contained. What mattered was everything that happened afterwards. Within hours, the defence ministry released a brief but frank statement: the model misclassified reflective signage; the fleet was paused; a software patch was being tested; and the investigation would publish a plain-language summary within seven days. Critics expected obfuscation. Instead, they received transparency. The public response was striking: mild concern, tempered by confidence that someone was taking responsibility.

Had the ministry said nothing—or worse, issued a swaggering slogan about "next-generation resilience"—trust would have fractured. In matters of autonomy, spin is corrosive. People fear what they do not understand, and autonomous systems can feel inscrutable even to experts. Legitimacy is not built by claiming infallibility; it is built by admitting fallibility and demonstrating control. Democracies cannot defend themselves with systems their citizens do not trust.

The instinct to hide mistakes is ancient. Militaries have always feared that acknowledging faults invites adversaries to probe weaknesses and allies to doubt competence. Yet silence does not calm nerves; it amplifies rumour. The more autonomous a system becomes, the more the public wants to know that humans remain accountable. When states avoid plain answers, citizens imagine dark ones.

Public legitimacy is now a strategic asset. Autonomous defence systems sit at the intersection of ethics, sovereignty, and technology. They make decisions that can cost lives. If people believe those decisions are ungoverned, arbitrary, or secretive, the backlash will not be gentle—it will be total. A single mishandled incident can collapse support for entire programmes. Nothing emboldens adversaries like domestic paralysis.

Many governments assume the public cannot understand technical detail. They underestimate citizens. People do not require a PhD in machine learning to grasp accountability. They want to know who checks the software, what happens when something goes wrong, and how mistakes are prevented from recurring. If a restaurant can publish allergen reports and hygiene scores, a defence ministry can publish risk summaries.

The lesson from aviation and nuclear energy is clear. Industry earned public confidence not through speeches, but through disclosure. Every crash is investigated. Every malfunction is documented. Findings are published. The reports are technical, but the conclusions are plain. Transparency does not eliminate fear, but it replaces paranoia with process.

Plain-language risk reports sound mundane. They are anything but. Their very existence signals maturity: the state knows its systems fail, monitors them constantly, and shares what it learns. Reports should answer simple questions. What failed? Why? What was changed? Which safeguards now exist? How will we know if they work? The public does not need source code. They need evidence that someone is watching the watchers.

Some officials worry that openness gives adversaries a roadmap. There is a boundary to draw—sweeping disclosures of tactical vulnerabilities are reckless. But transparency does not mean baring every wire. It means admitting that no system is perfect, and showing that oversight is real, not ornamental. Democracies defeated totalitarian claims of infallibility by embracing honesty, not matching arrogance.

One promising model is the *incident disclosure cadence.* Minor incidents are summarised monthly; moderate incidents trigger rapid bulletins; severe incidents demand full reports within fixed deadlines. This normalises disclosure. It signals that problems are expected, not catastrophic embarrassments. When silence is broken only by scandal, every mistake becomes a crisis. When disclosure is routine, mistakes are part of iterative improvement.

Transparency must extend beyond machine failures to human governance. Who audits autonomous systems? Who decides when they can fire, pursue, or escalate? Citizens want assurances that machines cannot run wild. They also want to know that operators, commanders, and engineers are accountable.

Some nations propose independent safety boards—civilian-led bodies empowered to inspect systems, demand logs, subpoena contractors, and publish findings. Others prefer military ombuds with specialist staff. The form matters less than the function: visible, credible oversight. If investigations remain internal, trust remains fragile. External scrutiny makes governments uncomfortable—and more trustworthy.

There is a deeper philosophical reason to embrace transparency. When a democracy delegates lethal force to autonomous systems, it makes an audacious claim: technology can serve justice. That claim is intolerable if shrouded in secrecy. Citizens delegate extraordinary power to their governments. In return, they expect candour. Public legitimacy is not earned with patriotic slogans about "smart defence" or "future warfighters." It is earned with humility.

Consider the civilian killed by an error in a targeting model. The state can deny responsibility, bury the logs, and praise the system's "unparalleled precision." Or the state can publish a clear account of what went wrong, compensate the family, and show how the system was fixed. One path protects pride. The other protects legitimacy.

There are counterarguments. Some officials fear that publishing incident reports will fuel anti-technology activism. Others claim the public cannot process probabilistic risk. But opacity does not prevent activism; it supercharges it. And ordinary people handle probability every day—insurance, medicine, weather, finance. They do not need certainty; they need honesty.

Plain-language reports can be concise, accurate, and humane. They should avoid techno-jargon. They should speak of causes and consequences as humans understand them: who might have been harmed, who was responsible, how risk has changed. They are a civic ritual, a reminder that the state answers to its citizens.

In time, disclosure norms can mature into legally mandated transparency. Aviation safety boards publish reports because they are required to. Nuclear facilities conduct drills because oversight is mandatory. Defence autonomy will eventually follow. Today's choice is whether that shift occurs voluntarily, as a mark of democratic strength, or only after scandal forces it.

The public has another demand: dignity. When systems malfunction, affected communities deserve more than statistics. They deserve explanations delivered in person, without euphemism. A model failure that damages property in a remote fishing village should not be summarised as a "minor anomaly." Trust erodes when language minimises experience. Democracies speak plainly not because it is comfortable, but because it is respectful.

Transparency does not solve everything. There will always be classified detail. There will always be strategic secrets. There will always be tension between openness and security. But the choice is not between total transparency and total darkness. The choice is between controlled disclosure and uncontrolled mistrust.

Some officials imagine that citizens will simply accept autonomy as inevitable. History suggests otherwise. Nuclear power faced protests, bans, moratoria—until transparency, regulation, and safety boards built confidence. Self-driving cars faced scepticism—until validators, crash reports, and testing logs became public. People must see the scaffolding that keeps systems safe.

A final, uncomfortable reality: if governments do not provide information, conspiracy fills the gap. Autonomy attracts myth. Rumours spread faster than official statements. If a drone crashes, someone online will claim sabotage, hacking, or secret weapons tests. Silence dignifies speculation. Clear reporting deflates it.

The open question is whether democracies will embrace transparency before they are forced to. When the first lethal autonomous incident occurs—and it will—the world will look not just at what happened, but how the state responds. Will leaders hide behind patriotic slogans and legal shields, or will they face the public with candour?

Public legitimacy is not an accessory to autonomous defence; it is its foundation. Without it, every system becomes politically radioactive. With it, citizens may accept the risks of modern deterrence, not because they are unafraid, but because they are respected.

The future hinges on a simple proposition: citizens can accept imperfection, but they will not forgive secrecy.

## Regional development politics

The mayor of a small coastal city stood in a converted warehouse, staring at a single cleanroom under construction. It was modest—barely the size of a supermarket—but to her it represented sovereignty. For years, her region had lost talent to megacities and foreign labs. Now, a chip packaging facility offered something rarer than jobs: relevance. Yet even as the first tools were installed, she knew the uncomfortable truth. If a single supplier faltered on the other side of the world, the line would stall. Silicon is local work built on global dependency.

That tension—between regional pride and global exposure—defines the geopolitics of high technology. Nations subsidise chip plants, incentivise data centres, and chase research clusters, not merely for economic gain but for strategic insulation. They want autonomy. They want security. They want the capacity to build, train, and operate the systems that will define modern defence. And they are learning that factories and cloud zones are no less political than warships and satellites.

A modern semiconductor fab costs more than an aircraft carrier, devours electricity, and demands water, rare gases, ultra-precise equipment, and engineers who know how to coax atoms into patterns measured in nanometres. No single region has every ingredient. That is why the world's silicon ecosystem became concentrated in a few places—brilliant, efficient, and fragile. A single drought, earthquake, or blockade can halt output felt across continents.

Governments have begun to respond with national and regional incentives: tax credits, infrastructure investments, guaranteed procurement, preferential loans. The ambition is noble—spread capability, reduce vulnerability, anchor talent. Yet incentives also invite distortion. When every country subsidises the same scarce expertise, prices rise, timelines slip, and smaller economies struggle to compete. The race to build resilience can undermine resilience: too many half-filled fabs, too few skilled technicians.

The politics deepen inside the walls. Chip plants require upstream ecosystems—photolithography, chemicals, packaging, design software—most of which remain global. A nation can pour billions into concrete, but without confidence in supply chains, a gleaming fab becomes an expensive symbol rather than a strategic asset. Officials discover that industrial sovereignty is not won by owning the building, but by securing every invisible input.

Cloud infrastructure carries a similar paradox. Defence agencies want sovereign data and hardened compute zones. They want to promise citizens that sensitive information never leaves domestic soil. So governments partner with hyperscalers to build "national cloud regions", wrapped in local compliance regimes and staffed by cleared engineers. The machines sit on home territory, yet the software, firmware, and orchestration tools often remain tied to global vendors.

This creates a strange blend of local control and external dependency. A security patch might originate in Seattle or Zurich. A routing optimisation might traverse foreign transit networks. A storage appliance might rely on firmware updated from an overseas repository. Regional cloud zones offer political comfort, but technical sovereignty remains conditional—negotiated through contracts rather than guaranteed through borders.

And yet, the alternative—building a national cloud stack entirely from scratch—is an illusion for most states. The world's best compute chips, model frameworks, and orchestration layers are developed collaboratively. True isolation means obsolescence. So governments settle for layered sovereignty: domestic hardware facilities, regional availability zones, local audit rights, and strict access controls, all sitting atop global software supply chains.

Research clusters add a human dimension to this geography of resilience. Laboratories thrive when engineers, mathematicians, ethicists, and operators share hallways, not just video calls. Breakthroughs are rarely sparked by lone geniuses; they emerge from dense networks of skilled people who trust each other. That is why nations court AI institutes with grants, visas, and academic freedom. They know that knowledge migrates with people. If talent concentrates elsewhere, capability follows.

Here, incentives collide with values. Researchers demand openness, international collaboration, and academic exchange. Defence ministries demand secrecy, classified datasets, and export controls. Governments attempt to square the circle: open research, except on sensitive models; shared publications, except when disclosure risks exploitation; free movement of scientists, except when alliances demand caution. The result is a patchwork of "controlled openness"—a new diplomatic dialect spoken in laboratories and export offices alike.

Some countries designate "sovereign research corridors"—places where industry, academia, and defence cooperate under shared governance. These clusters receive preferential funding and protected compute access, in exchange for security protocols and ethical oversight. The bet is that democratic values can coexist with strategic necessity. The risk is that too much control stifles innovation, driving talent away.

At the heart of regional development politics lies a question: should nations maximise efficiency or distribute risk? Efficient systems cluster. Resilient systems disperse. Efficiency rewards global hubs of excellence. Resilience hedges against disruption with duplication. The two logics are incompatible—and both are correct.

Take chip fabs. A single mega-facility offers scale, efficiency, and tight feedback loops between equipment and operators. But a single facility can be shut down by natural disaster, sabotage, or sanctions. So states consider spreading fabs across multiple cities or partner nations. The cost is enormous—more sites mean more engineers, more logistics chains, more redundancy. The reward is continuity if one node fails.

Cloud zones face similar choices. Concentrate compute in a handful of industrial parks, and power management is efficient; disperse them across regions, and latency, maintenance, and staffing become more complicated. Yet in a crisis—cyber attack, blackout, or physical sabotage—distributed zones keep systems alive. Defence planners increasingly value "graceful degradation": no single point of failure can cripple decision-making.

But dispersion brings politics. Every region wants the jobs. Every governor wants the ribbon-cuttings. Every locality argues that it deserves the next fab or the next cloud cluster. National strategy becomes regional lobbying. In some democracies, industrial policy can be hijacked by electoral calculus: the most electorally strategic region wins, even if another region is technically superior. When critical infrastructure becomes a political prize rather than a strategic asset, resilience suffers.

There is a deeper philosophical tension: development politics are shaped by memory. Nations that have lived through embargoes, sanctions, or supply shocks are quickest to invest in domestic capability. Others assume the global market will always provide. History suggests it will not. Demand for chips, compute hardware, and energy-hungry data centres is rising faster than supply chains can expand. The world is discovering that digital infrastructure is made of atoms, not abstractions.

Some governments seek not self-sufficiency, but interdependence with friends. They co-fund fabs with allies, share research networks, and negotiate reciprocal cloud failovers. These coalitions are messy, bureaucratic, and occasionally frustrating. But they distribute risk without descending into autarky. Shared infrastructure forces shared responsibility and shared restraint.

The alternative is technological nationalism—each nation with its own fabs, its own chips, its own models, its own clouds. It is theoretically resilient and practically ruinous. Costs explode. Innovation slows. Systems diverge, crippling interoperability. Democracies that cannot collaborate cede advantage to rivals who can.

Regional development politics, then, are less about digging foundations and more about choosing principles. What level of dependency is acceptable? Which allies are trusted with critical infrastructure? How much redundancy is worth the cost? And who pays for resilience—the taxpayer, the vendor, or the regions that benefit?

There are no perfect answers. But some policies point forward. Transparent incentive schemes tied to measurable outcomes. Local training pipelines funded alongside hardware. Environmental sustainability standards for power-hungry fabs and clouds. Export controls that protect security without suffocating collaboration. Shared test ranges and research grants that weave regions into networks, not silos.

And always, there is the public. Citizens see billions spent on chips and data centres and ask what value they receive. They deserve straight answers: jobs, security, research, innovation, protection against shocks. Without clear rationale, infrastructure becomes pork-barrel politics in new clothing.

The uncomfortable truth is that resilience costs money, time, and compromise. But the alternative—strategic fragility—is more expensive still. The next disruption, whether geopolitical or geological, will reveal which nations mistook subsidies for strategy and which built real capability.

As the mayor in the coastal factory understood, a cleanroom is never just a cleanroom. It is a bet on autonomy, identity, and the future. Whether those bets pay off will depend not only on engineering, but on the politics of place—and the wisdom to distinguish pride from prudence.

## Accountability architecture

On a grey morning at a naval test range, a drone failed to reacquire its target and banked abruptly toward a forbidden strip of coastline. The safety pilot pressed the abort command; nothing happened. The kill-switch froze. A junior engineer, noticing a buffer error cascading across the telemetry feed, cut power at the ground station. The aircraft slammed into shallow water, scattering carbon fibre and circuit boards. No one was hurt. The official report, issued four months later, named a hardware fault. Engineers privately knew better: the root cause was cultural. A contractor had rushed an update. A reviewer flagged concerns but kept quiet, fearing delay penalties. The safety pilot had not been trained on the new interface. When accountability is diffuse, responsibility evaporates.

In conventional weapon systems, mishaps are tragic but legible: a cracked weld, an untested battery, a human lapse. Autonomous systems blur the line between design, data, context, and intent. Was the drone's behaviour the product of faulty sensors, a mislabelled training set, or a latent consequence of an optimisation routine written three years earlier by someone who has since left for a startup in California? As defence shifts from hardware to software, accountability must shift with it. The old architecture—hierarchies, command chains, procurement reports—assumes human agency at every link. Today, the most consequential decisions may be emergent behaviours from millions of parameters, triggered in milliseconds. Oversight cannot be an afterthought; it must be engineered.

Modern safety regimes learn from the places where failure is unforgiving. Aviation pioneered black boxes and independent accident boards because denial is deadly at altitude. Nuclear energy developed layer upon layer of containment, inspection, and shutdown protocols because a single oversight can poison generations. The lesson is simple: complex systems require external scrutiny. It is too easy for pride, secrecy, or political pressure to warp judgement.

Autonomous defence demands the same architecture of candour. Not internal public relations teams polishing incident reports, but independent reviewers empowered to interrogate logs, source code, telemetry, and decision thresholds. Not boards that file recommendations into vaults, but bodies whose findings are published, scrutinised, and, at times, uncomfortable. Transparency is the price of trust. Militaries that refuse it will lose legitimacy at home, leverage abroad, and clarity within.

Some nations already maintain air accident investigation boards separate from the services. Extending that model to autonomous systems is logical. When a drone swarm misclassifies civilian boats, or an automated targeting system ignores a commander's override, investigations should not be led by the same offices that signed the procurement contracts. Independence prevents tribal loyalty from becoming institutional blindness. It also protects whistleblowers and junior engineers who know where the real skeletons lie: outdated datasets, unpatched firmware, managers who treat validation cycles as negotiable.

Critics warn that independent boards will slow innovation, leak secrets, or expose vulnerabilities to hostile actors. Yet secrecy is most corrosive when used to hide incompetence. During the Cold War, both sides kept catastrophic mishaps under wraps, believing that public knowledge would undermine morale. Instead, it undermined learning. Every classified failure repeated somewhere else. Pilots died. Errors compounded. When confidence becomes dogma, systems rot from within.

The balance is delicate: too much disclosure invites exploitation; too little invites decay. The best accountability structures use graded transparency. Sensitive technical details remain restricted. But the existence of incidents, the broad failures, and the corrective measures are shared publicly. Aviation and nuclear regulators have proven that openness need not compromise security. What it does compromise is complacency.

An effective accountability architecture has three pillars: ombuds for individuals, inspectors for systems, and safety boards for synthesis.

Ombuds functions matter because autonomous programmes are staffed by humans, and humans sometimes cut corners. Engineers face pressure to deliver features faster than safety testing can validate them. Data annotators are told to hit quotas even when edge cases are ambiguous. Operators, pressed by commanders, accept risk levels that would never pass an independent review. An empowered ombuds office gives these people somewhere to go—a confidential channel where concerns are logged, investigated, and addressed before they metastasise into failure.

Inspectors, by contrast, are structural. They audit code repositories, test ranges, incident logs, and patch cadences. They ask why a critical model has not been revalidated after a major firmware change, or why a training set still includes outdated threat recognition patterns. Think of them as routine hygiene: impartial, unglamorous, essential. Their power lies not in dramatic scandals but in the quiet prevention of disaster. When inspectors find nothing, that is evidence of a healthy culture, not a wasted effort.

Safety boards bring the two together. When something goes wrong—a misfire, a drift in target selection confidence, a kill-chain that escalates without human confirmation—they perform independent mishap reviews. These boards should include not just military officers, but ethicists, software engineers, legal experts, and civilian representatives. Their mandate is not blame but clarity. They trace the chain of causation: how a design decision, a contract clause, or a misaligned incentive created preconditions for error. When patterns emerge, boards issue systemic recommendations: mandatory red-teaming before deployment; minimum telemetry retention periods; bans on certain forms of opaque optimisation.

Red-team exercises are indispensable. A system that performs flawlessly in a vendor demo may unravel under adversarial probing. Red teams simulate hostile intent: spoofing sensors, injecting malformed data, exploiting edge cases. Their findings are rarely flattering. Good organisations celebrate that discomfort. Bad ones bury it. The difference is leadership. A commander who welcomes criticism saves lives. One who treats bugs as insubordination breeds silence.

Randomised drills reinforce this culture. Surprise audits of training data quality. Unannounced failover tests on cloud orchestration. Simulated GPS jamming or degraded communications. When operators know that scrutiny can come at any moment, discipline becomes habit. Autonomy does not excuse vigilance; it demands it. Continuous validation turns safety from an event into a mindset.

Cross-inspection weeks offer a powerful extension. Allies invite each other to inspect logs, simulators, and doctrine. One nation's red team evaluates another's targeting AI; the favour is returned months later. These exchanges build trust because they validate claims rather than repeat assurances. They also spread best practices. A small country with limited resources can benefit from the scrutiny of a larger partner, and the larger partner gains visibility into how its technology is actually used. Accountability becomes collaboration, not surveillance.

Some argue that fully independent oversight is unrealistic in wartime. They are right: when rounds are flying, boards do not convene. But systems are built long before conflict, and accountable architecture is part of that construction. A weapon designed with transparent logging, deterministic kill-switches, and human-readable decision traces will be easier to investigate and safer to operate. A weapon built as a black box, optimised only for speed, will be a liability when it malfunctions. War does not excuse poor design; it reveals it.

There is a philosophical dimension. Democracies justify force with legitimacy. They fight under the scrutiny of voters, allies, and history. Autonomous systems challenge this political contract. If machines make lethal decisions, citizens will demand to know how those decisions were reached. "Trust us" is not accountability. Neither is "the algorithm said so." A society that delegates force to machines without insisting on explanation erodes the moral basis of its own defence.

Accountability architecture is therefore civic infrastructure. Ombuds safeguard conscience. Inspectors safeguard diligence. Boards safeguard truth. Without them, public trust drains away. With them, autonomy becomes compatible with democracy.

The most serious risk is performative oversight: beautiful charters, glossy reports, no impact. Some agencies will create ombuds offices and starve them of funding. Some safety boards will be stacked with retired officers who never challenge procurement chiefs. Some inspectors will be instructed to avoid politically sensitive programmes. Hypocrisy is worse than absence; it teaches engineers that ethics are theatre.

Real accountability has teeth. It can pause deployments. It can cancel contracts. It can compel disclosure. It can protect dissent.

And it must evolve. As models self-update, as autonomous systems learn online, as swarms coordinate dynamically, oversight must be continuous, not episodic. Annual certifications mean little when software changes daily. The future will require real-time audit trails, immutable logs, continuous verification of safety constraints, and automated monitors that flag anomalies faster than human inspectors ever could.

These tools are emerging. Cryptographic attestations prove that deployed code matches audited code. Differential logs reveal when a model diverges from validated behaviour. Shadow models police live systems, comparing decisions against known safe baselines. Accountability architecture is no longer just paperwork; it is software.

The drone crash on the coast remained a minor headline. A few broken wings, a brief investigation, a line in a parliamentary report. But inside the programme, something shifted. Engineers demanded a proper mishap review. Operators refused to fly without retraining. A young staffer pushed for an independent audit. Months later, code pipelines were rebuilt, telemetry retention expanded, red-team drills mandated. Accountability did not come from orders. It came from culture—one that refused to accept silence as safety.

If autonomous defence is to endure, that culture must be engineered into the institutions that govern it. The next failure will be more serious. The stakes will grow. Automated systems will touch borders, infrastructure, and lives. Someone will ask who is responsible. The only honest answer begins with structure: ombuds who listen, inspectors who check, boards who investigate, and nations that prefer uncomfortable truth to convenient ignorance.

The price of accountability is effort, time, and humility. The cost of neglect is measured in lives and legitimacy. Which bill societies choose to pay will define not only the safety of their systems, but the character of their future.

# Chapter 7

# Adversarial Playbooks

Just after midnight, a research collective monitoring social networks noticed an anomaly. Thousands of new accounts, created within minutes, began posting messages that mimicked the tone of coastal emergency responders. The updates looked authentic: clipped sentences, GPS coordinates, urgent warnings about evacuation routes. Yet the storm on which they reported did not exist. Sirens wailed in two towns as residents, convinced a seawall had failed, fled their homes. By dawn, the posts vanished, the accounts dissolved, and the networks returned to normal. No buildings were damaged. The objective had been political, not physical: to test whether synthetic persuasion, delivered at scale, could manufacture panic faster than authorities could rebut it. It could.

This is the logic of the new adversary. They no longer need to breach a perimeter or fire a missile. They probe systems with queries that seem harmless, until the aggregate reveals sensitive capabilities. They poison datasets with thousands of carefully-crafted samples designed to shift model behaviour. They release swarms of mimics—benign lookalikes that confuse detectors and sap attention. Where conventional conflict was defined by force-on-force, algorithmic conflict is defined by ambiguity. The decisive battles are invisible until it is too late.

A quiet revolution is underway. States and non-state actors are assembling playbooks for the age of autonomous systems. Some resemble traditional espionage: reconnaissance, infiltration, denial. Others bend the logic of automation itself: feeding models with toxic data, stealing weights through gradient leakage, inverting systems to recover sensitive inputs. Adversaries do not need to break the machine; they merely need to nudge it, exploiting the brittle edges of optimisation. These tactics cost little and scale beautifully. A single clever exploit can ripple across fleets, platforms, and borders.

This chapter examines that shadow contest: how opponents surveil, subvert, and spoof the systems built to protect. The techniques vary, but their motivation is constant: erode trust in autonomous infrastructure. When a nation's defences depend on models, poisoning those models becomes a strategic weapon. When public communications rely on automated verification, synthetic personas become the perfect saboteurs. When supply chains hinge on telemetry and cloud orchestration, simulated outages can paralyse response. The terrain is digital, but the stakes are tangible: panicked civilians, blinded radars, corrupted targeting, markets on fire.

Probe, poison, and parody form the opening act. Probing looks innocuous—just queries, pings, and tests—but pattern analysis reveals architecture. If a classifier hesitates on certain images, that hesitation can be amplified. If a language model redacts one phrase but not another, that asymmetry hints at guardrails and gaps. Poisoning is subtler still. A hostile actor might upload millions of near-identical examples to open datasets. Each sample benign on its own, but in aggregate, sufficient to tilt decision boundaries. Parody completes the triad: create lookalike behaviour so convincing that filters cannot distinguish real from fake. Spam once meant nuisance. Now it is a strategic instrument.

Model theft and inversion escalate the stakes. Eight years ago, few believed a neural network could be stolen without touching the underlying code. Today, gradient-based inversion attacks quietly siphon sensitive parameters. A hospital's diagnostic model might be probed until private training data—rare tumours, children's ultrasounds—bleeds into outputs. A military targeting model might reveal its weight structure through carefully calibrated inputs, allowing an adversary to train decoys that look indistinguishable from valid targets. Watermarking, monitoring, and suspicious query detection are becoming part of national defence. Intelligence agencies no longer simply protect documents; they protect embeddings.

Then comes economic pressure. Not by embargoing oil or steel, but by sanctioning compute and toolchains. If an adversary cannot buy high-end accelerators, they buy cloud access under shell companies. Export-tightening triggers feedback loops: tightening supply chains, grey-market brokers, sovereign chip foundries in unexpected places. The armouries of this age include wafers, firmware, data centres, and compiler stacks. Dominance is measured in nanometres and nodes, not hulls and tonnage.

Denial and deception stretch old practices into terrifying scale. Botnets once spread malware; now they seed confusion. Synthetic personas, armed with generative text and deepfake voice models, can swarm a crisis zone with fabricated eyewitness accounts. The objective is not persuasion but overload: drown truth beneath orchestrated noise. At state level, these campaigns are cheaper than cyberattacks and sometimes more effective. Why hack a satellite feed when you can convince millions that its output is corrupted?

Yet defence is not hopeless. Counter-play is emerging. Resilience drills, borrowed from disaster management, now include simulated cloud region losses, corrupted telemetry streams, and model drift under pressure. Militaries run red-team tabletop games where operators must recognise poisoning in real time. Engineers practice chaos testing: disabling random nodes, degrading sensors, severing links, and forcing autonomy to fallback modes. These exercises reveal fragility long before adversaries exploit it.

There is a deeper pattern beneath this contest. Power in the age of algorithms accrues not only to those who build systems, but to those who can mislead them. The stronger a model, the more tempting the exploit; the more widely deployed, the greater the payoff. Nations that invest billions in autonomy must defend against adversaries who invest thousands in clever interference. It is an asymmetric race, and complacency favours the attacker.

The paradox is stark. Systems designed for speed, scale, and precision create incentives for covert disruption. Public confidence depends not on promises but on resilience under pressure. If a coastal town panics because a synthetic storm touches their phones, what happens when a synthetic missile alert arrives? If an autonomous interceptor confuses a decoy for a threat, who bears responsibility: the engineers, the commanders, or the adversary who poisoned the training pipeline?

These questions are uncomfortable, but unavoidable. And they are the reason adversarial playbooks matter. Understanding them is not a luxury; it is the foundation of defence. Nations that ignore the shadows invite catastrophe. Nations that study them will discover a subtler form of deterrence: systems that bend, adapt, and recover faster than attackers can break them.

This chapter is a map of that landscape. It traces the tactics of probing and poisoning, the high-stakes game of model theft, the economic chokeholds of compute sanctions, the psychological frontiers of synthetic deception, and the countermeasures that restore balance. It is a catalogue of ingenuity—malicious and defensive—and a reminder that competition in this century will be waged in code as much as in steel.

If the midnight storm was a rehearsal, the real tests are yet to come. Somewhere, an adversary is refining a new exploit. Somewhere else, a defender is running a resilience drill, hoping that when machines are deceived, humans will not be. The battle is ongoing, mostly unseen, and decisively human in its consequences.

Turn the page. The shadows deserve attention.

## Probe, poison, and parody

Hours before a ceasefire agreement was due to be announced, a foreign intelligence unit began firing thousands of harmless-looking queries at the defence ministry of a small coastal state. None of the requests breached a firewall or accessed a classified system. They did not need to. The attackers were listening to the rhythm of the replies: the milliseconds of latency here, the minor formatting quirks there, the error codes that only appeared when certain structured prompts were used. By dawn, analysts on the other side had built a detailed portrait of the ministry's automated monitoring stack—its filters, its guardrails, the categories that triggered human review. The probing was invisible, legal, and bloodless. It was also the first step in a campaign that would, days later, flood the same channels with exquisitely tailored misinformation.

This is the strategic beauty of adversarial probing. Nothing breaks; nothing even creaks. Machines simply answer questions. Yet those answers, when stitched together, reveal where the weak points lie. An autonomous border sensor that shaves a millisecond off response time when it spots a quadruped rather than a vehicle tells a disciplined adversary that the model includes an animal-detection subroutine. A medical triage chatbot that redacts "radiation" but not "gamma exposure" announces the shape of its safety filters. Systems betray their secrets through the way they say *no*.

Probing is reconnaissance in a digital terrain. Traditional espionage depended on human moles, surveillance, and intercepted telegrams; now a clever graduate student can learn how a governmental classifier behaves just by issuing a thousand innocuous prompts from a suburban café. The attacker does not need the code. They only need the *pattern*.

Once reconnaissance has mapped the contours of a model, poisoning begins. If probing is about listening, poisoning is about whispering—

quietly altering the data a system learns from. A century ago, an agent might sabotage a railway bridge. Today, they sabotage training sets. A hostile actor might upload thousands of user-generated images to a popular open dataset, each one containing a subtle artefact—say, a pixel arrangement that shifts a classifier's decision boundary. No single image looks suspicious; moderators approve them without hesitation. But as the dataset grows, the model trained on it begins to "learn" that the attacker's chosen trigger—perhaps a particular sticker or shape—should be interpreted as benign.

The genius of data poisoning lies in its deniability. There is no malware signature, no unauthorised access. The defender cannot patch out the corruption with a software update; the rot sits inside the statistical heart of the system. Worse, poisoned behaviour may only surface in rare conditions—high winds for a drone, dusk for a border camera, a specific accent for a voice authenticator. When systems operate autonomously and at scale, even a small tilt in judgement can ripple into catastrophe.

There are darker variants. Poisoning can aim not only to hide attackers but to reclassify civilians as threats. An adversary who subtly biases a humanitarian decision system might cause aid convoys to be flagged as hostile or deprioritised. In financial markets, poisoning models that assess creditworthiness can deny loans to entire demographics. In policing, corrupt training data can reinforce false positives for innocent patterns of behaviour. This is not science fiction; it is a contest over who defines the categories of trust.

The uncomfortable truth is that the more data-driven a society becomes, the more vulnerable its foundations are to covert statistical sabotage. A government that relies on autonomous detection to patrol its borders may be defending itself with an algorithm the enemy has already bent.

But poisoning is not the endgame. Parody is where espionage blends into theatre. An adversary does not need to break a system if they can flood it with realistic lookalikes. When a military drone swarm hunts for enemy vehicles, attackers can create inflatable decoys with heat signatures calibrated to mislead the sensors. When social platforms rely on machine learning to moderate content, attackers generate millions of benign posts that mimic harmful ones—teaching the system to fear its own shadow.

Parody exploits a familiar human weakness: the mind's difficulty separating signal from noise. Automated systems have the same problem, only worse. They are trained to find patterns and generalise from them. If adversaries flood a system with millions of "almost threats", the model may swing between paralysis and overreaction. A spam filter hammered with near-identical benign variants of a known attack may widen its allowance and let the real attack glide through. A radar-classifier bombarded by thousands of fabricated traces may fail to spot a single real missile.

One particularly elegant tactic is to establish "benign reputation" for malicious infrastructure. Botnets used for disinformation may spend weeks posting only harmless content—birthdays, recipes, sports highlights—behaving more politely than genuine humans. Once automated monitors have categorised them as low-risk, the accounts detonate, flooding crisis channels with coordinated lies. Filters hesitate; moderators doubt; truth is lost under the avalanche.

Parody also corrodes public trust. When deepfake videos of senior officials become indistinguishable from genuine press conferences, citizens may stop believing *anything*. In such an environment, reality is not just manipulated—it is contested. If the attacker can make truth uncertain, they win without firing a shot.

The defenders of open societies face a dilemma. Excessive suspicion turns every citizen into a suspect and corrodes civil liberties. Excessive trust makes systems brittle. So how do nations safeguard their autonomy without suffocating the freedoms that define them?

One answer lies in transparency—*real* transparency. Not slogans about resilience or political boasts about "military-grade AI", but plain-language disclosure of risks and mitigation. Citizens do not need to understand gradient inversion attacks or adversarial perturbations; they need to know that systems can fail and that their institutions are preparing for that possibility. Governments that admit uncertainty earn what propaganda cannot buy: credibility.

Another answer is diversity of data. Monocultures are fragile. If every classifier draws from the same open dataset, poisoning one source poisons everyone. Nations that cultivate multiple, independent data pipelines make poisoning harder and detection easier. Diversity is not just a scientific virtue; it is a strategic asset.

Still, the tension remains unresolved. Autonomous systems are brittle in ways that weapons and institutions have never been. A tank does not forget what an armoured vehicle looks like because an adversary uploaded 10,000 doctored images to a public repository. But a model might. The more we delegate judgement to machines, the more we create targets that can be subverted, spoofed, and misled.

Every conflict crafts its own grammar. In the age of AI, the grammar is probabilistic, statistical, and adversarial. Probing maps weaknesses without ever touching the source code. Poisoning rewrites behaviour from within. Parody overwhelms perception and corrodes confidence.

The question facing modern governments is stark: how do you defend a system that can be defeated without being attacked? Is deterrence possible when a hostile actor can flood you with harmless queries and learn your secrets from the rhythm of your replies? Can a democracy maintain legitimacy if citizens must verify whether every image, voice, and alert is real?

We have built machines that see more than any human and learn faster than any bureaucracy. But an adversary who understands their blind spots can turn that strength into weakness. Somewhere tonight, a hostile analyst is crafting new probes. Tomorrow, those probes will become poisons. Soon after, the poisons will mature into parodies so convincing they fool the sentinels we trusted to protect us.

The defenders will adapt. They will deploy meta-detectors, diversity pipelines, provenance standards, and anomaly monitoring. Yet the struggle remains fundamentally human: a contest of ingenuity, patience, and imagination.

There is no final victory in this domain—only staying one step ahead. The adversary's next move is unpredictable, but one thing is certain: the cost of being surprised is rising.

## Model theft and inversion

Late one night in a small security lab, a researcher stared at a screen in disbelief. An "anonymous client"—a polite front for a foreign procurement office—had spent days querying a proprietary language model with thousands of meticulously structured prompts. Nothing outwardly malicious, nothing that would trigger an intrusion alert. Yet when the researcher trained a small, cheap neural network only on the observed outputs, it began producing eerily similar responses to the original model. Same quirks. Same blind spots. Same stylistic fingerprints. The client had not hacked the model. They had *stolen* it, piece by statistical piece, through the front door.

This is the unnerving paradox of modern machine learning: a model can be replicated without ever touching its source code. In cyber-security, the alarm bells ring when someone breaks in. In the age of AI, the threat arrives as a whisper—harmless queries that slowly pull a model's internal logic out into the open. If probing is reconnaissance, replication is the heist. With enough carefully chosen questions, a rival can clone years of training, millions of pounds of compute, and the intellectual labour of entire research teams.

Two decades ago, intellectual property theft meant smuggled schematics or an insider with a memory stick. Today, the blueprint *lives in the behaviour itself.* Ask the model enough questions about enough edge cases, and its decision boundaries begin to reveal themselves—how it classifies toxic speech, how it ranks risks, how it weighs instructions against safety policies. Attackers perform what the field calls "model extraction": query a system, store the outputs, then fit a new network that mimics the original at a fraction of the cost.

The most patient attackers do not rush. They start with broad prompts, narrowing with each iteration. They measure latency—because delay patterns reveal internal complexity. They submit adversarial examples, mapping the tipping points where the system switches from refusal to compliance. They adjust temperature, sentence length, and input format to triangulate which families of architectures the defender is running. A sophisticated attacker treats every response as a breadcrumb.

Once the boundaries are visible, the second act begins: inversion. Here the adversary does not merely recreate the model's behaviour—they infer the data inside it. In image recognition, inversion attacks can reconstruct training images from gradients. In large language models, inversion can recover fragments of text the system was exposed to: medical records, proprietary documents, sensitive customer data. No breach, no stolen database—just mathematics turning a model inside out.

In 2020, researchers demonstrated that by observing gradients exchanged in federated learning, they could reconstruct images of training participants, including faces, with alarming clarity. The participants never shared their photos—only gradient updates meant to preserve privacy. The system obediently protected raw data while accidentally leaking its ghost.

And that is the deepest flaw of inversion: systems that are designed to *never reveal their training data* can be coaxed into revealing it anyway, simply because the model has incorporated that data into its internal representations. What an AI learns, it can unknowingly regurgitate. For attackers, this is espionage with legal cover. They never "access" anything directly; they simply observe what the system outputs in response to benign prompts.

This is where watermarking enters the conversation—not decorative marks on a PDF, but mathematical fingerprints woven into the model's behaviour. A watermark might be a hidden pattern in output token frequencies, detectable only with a secret key. Or it might be a behavioural quirk—when given a specific rare prompt, the model produces a tell-tale sequence. The point is simple: if a rival deploys a stolen model, the original creator should be able to prove it.

Watermarks change the stakes. They turn theft from a covert advantage into a legal liability. They also act as early warning systems: when attackers probe too deeply or generate outputs that statistically align with extraction attempts, monitoring tools can raise alarms. A model does not need to *know* it is being copied; telemetry around unusual query patterns can tell the story.

Defenders have begun to track these patterns meticulously. Most legitimate users vary their prompts. Extractors do not—they send structured grids of inputs, sweeping the model's behaviour like a camera lens scanning a crime scene. Queries arrive in regular increments, with systematic variation: slight changes to punctuation, synonyms, random seeds. No one writes or talks like that naturally. When a model sees the linguistic equivalent of a LIDAR scan, defenders should take notice.

Yet monitoring has a dark edge. If detection is too aggressive, legitimate researchers are caught in the net. If it is too lax, state actors can walk away with technology paid for by taxpayers. Every defence introduces new tensions: security versus accessibility, verification versus privacy. In democratic societies, the balance is fragile.

The gravest risk is not that a foreign competitor copies an AI model. It is what they do *after*. Cloned models may be altered to remove safety guardrails, producing incitement, malware, or disinformation at scale. A stolen model becomes a weaponised mirror: familiar enough to mimic benign speech, yet free of ethical constraints. In information warfare, mimicry is devastating. When a stolen model speaks in the same tone and cadence as a trusted commercial system, detection becomes a game of shadows.

Consider a language model used by a humanitarian agency to route emergency aid. A rogue copy could issue fabricated instructions or forged authorisations that look legitimate to automated pipelines. Consider a military model used to assess radar signatures. A stolen version could be subtly adjusted to ignore a specific class of object—say, a fleet of modified drones. The theft is not just economic; it is strategic.

Some governments have begun to treat high-end AI weights like enriched uranium: too powerful to export freely. Licences restrict who can deploy them and under what conditions. Cloud providers enforce geographic constraints, ensuring that protected models only run in specific jurisdictions. Auditors scan logs for extraction-like patterns, much as banks watch for money laundering. Intelligence agencies run deception campaigns of their own—planting decoy models to waste an adversary's time.

Still, stolen models continue to surface in unexpected places: in academic papers from abroad, in bootleg code repositories, in sudden leaps of progress from regimes that previously struggled to train at scale. Theft is not hypothetical; it is already part of the global AI economy.

Defence strategists sometimes comfort themselves with a simple argument: "Even if they steal the weights, they cannot steal the training pipeline." But that comfort is fragile. Pipelines can be replicated. Data can be scraped. Toolchains can be copied. And when the architecture itself is public, theft becomes optimisation: steal the model, compress it, fine-tune it, deploy it. The clone may even outperform the original.

So what can be done?

One answer is provenance—precise, cryptographically anchored proof of where model weights came from, how they were trained, and who handled them. Just as the diamond industry tracks stones to prevent conflict mining, nations may track models to prevent duplication and misuse. Another answer is periodic behavioural attestation: require models operating in sensitive sectors to respond to secret diagnostic prompts, verifying that they still align with ethical baselines and have not been silently swapped with a stolen or modified variant.

A third defence is architectural hardening: compartmentalise components so that an extractor must replicate multiple interlocking pieces rather than a single monolith. This is expensive and complex—but so is losing control of a strategic model.

The most radical idea is *deliberate unpredictability*: introducing controlled randomness so that identical prompts do not always produce identical gradients. Extraction thrives on stability; defenders can fight back by adding noise just below the threshold of human perception. Of course, randomness in high-stakes systems is dangerous. A missile-warning classifier cannot afford artistic freedom. But in conversational models and simulation engines, small perturbations can frustrate attackers without harming real users.

None of these solutions are perfect. They are fragments of a defensive posture still taking shape.

There is a philosophical issue beneath the technical one. When a machine learns from public data and interacts with the public, can its behaviour truly be considered private? If someone can reproduce the same learning process—or simply reverse-engineer it—are they guilty of theft or merely of competence? In other fields, we draw sharp lines. Copy a drug formula, and you have committed industrial espionage. Reproduce it through independent research, and the law applauds you. AI blurs the boundary: the creation and the reproduction look almost identical.

Yet the stakes demand clarity. A state that cannot protect its strategic models will lose its informational sovereignty. A company that cannot defend its intellectual property will struggle to justify investment. A democratic society that cannot distinguish real speech from synthetic mimicry will find truth eroding beneath its feet.

Model theft is espionage without entry. Inversion is surveillance without access. Together, they form a quiet arms race—one where the most damaging attack leaves no fingerprints.

So the question that hangs over every AI lab, every defence cloud, every commercial platform is this: how do you protect something that leaks its secrets every time it speaks?

There is no final answer, only a horizon. Watermarking will improve. Monitoring will grow sharper. Legal regimes will tighten. But adversaries will keep innovating—asking better questions, shaping subtler probes, building smarter clones. In the future, we may not fear the model that fails. We may fear the model that succeeds too well—because success itself becomes the path to theft.

Somewhere tonight, someone is extracting a model. They will not break a lock or hack a server. They will simply ask, politely, again and again, until the system betrays itself.

The defenders can only hope they are listening.

## Economic pressure tactics

A curious pattern surfaced after a sudden spike in AI model performance inside a sanctioned state: researchers had not published breakthrough algorithms, acquired new talent, or revealed any dazzling scientific leap. Instead, satellite imagery showed a convoy of refrigerated lorries crossing a border at night, each filled not with food or weapons, but with high-end GPUs—millions of pounds' worth of compute smuggled like narcotics. For two years, export controls had choked that country's access to advanced chips. Still, the models kept improving. Somewhere, someone was paying the black-market premium for compute. The world's newest contraband was measured not in kilos, but in teraflops.

In the age of AI, economic power is not just measured in currency or commodities; it is embedded in access to compute, tooling, and supply chains. Traditional sanctions aim at banks or oil. Modern sanctions choke off accelerators, advanced lithography, rare-earth processing, and cloud access. The irony is brutal: the most peaceful tool of statecraft—economic pressure—may shape the military balance just as decisively as missiles or treaties. A nation that cannot train large models cannot compete in AI-enabled warfare. A nation that cannot fabricate high-performance chips becomes dependent, vulnerable, and slow.

Economic pressure tactics are not abstract strategy. They are daily logistical fights for hardware, tooling, and time. When one country tightens chip exports, another stockpiles. When cloud regions are geofenced, entrepreneurs turn to foreign resellers. When sanctions bite, contraband compute emerges: GPUs hidden in crates of medical equipment, shell companies bidding for cloud credits, academic "collaboration" fronts laundering access to restricted clusters.

Trend analysis shows that illicit AI supply chains now resemble narcotics networks of the late 20th century. There are smugglers, brokers, laundering operations, encrypted communication channels, and financial middlemen who obscure transfers. The difference is moral ambiguity. A state seeking chips is not buying vice—it is buying computation. Insisting on legality feels neat; reality is messier.

And yet, governments persist because the strategic logic is compelling. Control the flow of compute, and you limit the speed of an adversary's military AI. Control the tooling—EDA software, lithography machines, high-bandwidth memory—and you remove the ability to move up the value chain. Sanctions turn progress into maintenance, innovation into survival.

But there is a deeper shift underway: from sanctions as blunt embargoes to sanctions as **feedback systems**. Rather than waiting for illicit procurements, exporters now monitor anomalous demand from distributors, track unusual shipping patterns, and deploy machine-learning detectors to flag suspicious cloud usage. Sanctions no longer end at the border; they live in dashboards and monitoring feeds.

Consider "export-tightening feedback." When intelligence agencies detect a sanctioned regime acquiring accelerators through a third country, they tighten restrictions on that intermediary. If resellers reappear under new names, licensing regimes expand. If cloud credits are laundered through academic programmes, those programmes face scrutiny and identity verification. The result is a ratchet: every circumvention triggers the next layer of control.

This feedback loop is powerful, but dangerous. It risks collateral damage—innocent researchers denied tools, small businesses throttled by bureaucracy, global innovation slowed by opaque processes. Democracies must justify such pressure with transparency and predictable rules, or they risk driving neutral states into the arms of rivals offering "no-questions-asked" computing.

Critics argue that economic pressure cannot prevent AI proliferation any more than encryption bans prevented secure communications. Compute can be smuggled; models can be copied; open-source weights can leap borders in seconds. The counterargument is strategic delay: slowing a rival's progress by five years may be decisive. It took Israel years to develop indigenous lithography after export controls tightened. Iran still struggles to scale deep learning workloads, handicapped by ageing hardware. Sanctions may never be perfect, but they can change the pace and shape of power.

A second criticism is escalation. When Country A cuts off chips, Country B responds by restricting rare-earth exports. When one bloc threatens cloud sanctions, another proposes sovereign compute alliances. A world where AI is the decisive military technology becomes a world where economic interdependence is weaponised. Some see inevitability: better to compete economically than kinetically. Others fear a slow slide into techno-nationalism, where knowledge and compute are hoarded like oil fields.

There is also a philosophical tension: knowledge has historically been the most difficult thing to police. A scientist can memorise ideas. A researcher can carry training techniques in their head. Blueprints can be hidden in DNA sequences, QR codes, or innocuous text. When the same open-source frameworks, compilers, and libraries sit on laptops from São Paulo to Singapore, can export restrictions meaningfully constrain capability?

Here the target shifts not from knowledge to *execution*. You can know how to train a frontier model, but without tens of thousands of advanced GPUs operating in low-latency clusters with high-bandwidth memory, your knowledge remains theory. Sanctions do not stop learning; they slow scaling. In AI, scaling is the currency of dominance.

This leaves sanctioned states in a frantic scramble for substitutes. We have seen attempts to build indigenous fabs, hammered together with imported machinery and outdated nodes. We have seen hybrid solutions: clusters of consumer gaming GPUs, stitched together with clever parallelisation hacks. Some of these efforts are heroic; many are brittle. When every GPU is precious, experimentation shrinks. Safety research shrivels. Rigorous red-teaming becomes a luxury. The result is a Darwinian pressure: systems that work only just well enough, but without the robust guardrails of mature ecosystems.

Economic pressure is not only about hardware. Tooling—compilers, kernel libraries, EDA suites—can be more critical than chips themselves. Lithography machines built by ASML embody decades of engineering knowledge that simply cannot be replicated quickly. CUDA, PyTorch, and cuDNN embody optimisation work that armies of engineers have refined. Restrict these tools, and even with chips, training slows to a crawl.

Some states try to replace restricted tooling with open-source equivalents. Success varies. For basic research, open-source is a blessing. For frontier performance, the absence of proprietary acceleration libraries becomes a handbrake. Progress becomes incremental, not exponential. In a race, the gap compounds.

But pressure cuts two ways. Overuse of sanctions incentivises others to build sovereign stacks: national chips, national fabs, national AI frameworks. If those ecosystems mature, the sanctioning states lose leverage. There is an almost Newtonian symmetry to it: the harder economic pressure is applied, the more countervailing sovereignty is sought.

Even where sanctions succeed, they create strategic blind spots. A sanctioned nation forced to innovate under constraints may discover novel architectures or training regimes that require less compute. Sparse models, mixture-of-experts routing, distributed training across heterogeneous consumer hardware—what begins as necessity becomes advantage. History is littered with cases where embargoes catalysed acceleration rather than decline. Some defence officials quietly worry that starving adversaries of GPUs simply pushes them to invent disruptive alternatives.

Meanwhile, the global South watches carefully. Many governments are wary of a world where access to computation becomes conditional on geopolitical loyalty. Developing nations ask: will we be allowed to run our own models, or will frontier AI remain the domain of a club? Sanctions might contain proliferators, but they can also create resentment and fragmentation. The line between strategic necessity and technological colonialism is thin, and not everyone agrees where it lies.

Still, the fundamental point remains: the power to sanction compute is the new power to sanction steel, oil, or currency. It is soft control over the hard machinery of war. A denial of chips is a denial of autonomy—autonomy of weapons, industry, and information. In conflicts where code fights code, silicon is the high ground.

And so a strange future looms. A war may not begin with missiles. It may begin with cloud suspensions. A nation on the brink of aggression finds its training pipelines abruptly throttled. Its export customers lose access to optimisation libraries. Its semiconductor equipment shipments halt at a port. The message: stop now, or fall behind irreversibly.

Will it work? Sometimes. But there is a risk: a cornered state may lash out, betting that a conventional conflict is preferable to slow technological suffocation. Economic pressure is a scalpel, not a hammer. Used wisely, it can de-escalate. Used bluntly, it can provoke.

The stark truth is that compute sanctions will not disappear. They are now embedded in the geopolitical toolkit, a financial and technological chokehold that can be tightened with a keystroke. The only open question is how the world will respond: fragmentation into rival tech blocs, or negotiated regimes that balance security with scientific openness.

Somewhere tonight, a cluster of GPUs is being loaded into a shipping container under false labels. Somewhere else, a cloud provider's anomaly detector is flagging suspicious request patterns. The silent contest continues.

And beneath it all, an uneasy question lingers: if power flows through silicon, who gets to decide who may compute, and who must stand still?

## Denial and deception at scale

When a coastal nation suffered a sudden blackout after a tropical storm, its authorities rushed emergency responders to the hardest-hit districts. Yet traffic cameras revealed an eerie quiet: no crowds, no blocked roads, no visible damage. The storm had indeed passed—but the crisis was manufactured. A swarm of fake distress reports, autogenerated videos, and synthetic social-media posts had drowned the country's information channels. Ambulances were diverted to places where nothing had happened. Hospitals cancelled scheduled surgeries to make room for non-existent casualties. What looked like humanitarian chaos was in fact a denial attack, waged not against power stations or water grids, but against attention itself.

That episode signalled a shift. The old logic of cyber warfare was blunt: crash servers, encrypt drives, jam signals. The new logic is subtler and crueller. You don't always need to knock out communications; you can simply bury them. If authorities cannot distinguish the real from the fake, the effect is the same as shutting the network down. The battlefield is perception. The weapon is scale.

Denial and deception have always been part of statecraft, but they were once artisanal. A forged letter here, a radio spoof there. What has changed is the industrialisation of disinformation. AI makes fabrication cheap and distribution frictionless. A single operator can now summon a million synthetic voices, each feigning authenticity, each tuned to exploit linguistic nuance, cultural reference, or platform algorithm.

Spam—once a nuisance—has become a scaffold for strategic operations. It is the chaff of the digital world: low-cost, high-volume noise that buries signal. When floods of autogenerated emails, comments, or messages hit emergency call centres, transport networks, or public-health systems, the effect is operational paralysis. Even if 99 per cent of the activity is obviously fraudulent, the remaining 1 per cent can waste thousands of human hours. In crisis response, that delay kills.

Botnets have evolved accordingly. There was a time when compromised machines merely sent junk mail or mined cryptocurrencies. Today, they can pose as citizens, amplify political narratives, overwhelm reporting channels, or imitate the behavioural patterns of ordinary users. Some are controlled by states; others by criminal syndicates who rent their services to the highest bidder. Attribution becomes a foggy exercise: is this campaign ideological, commercial, or a decoy designed to look like one while masking another?

The most unnerving development is the synthetic persona—AI-driven "people" who live full digital lives. They post at plausible hours, hold opinions consistent with their supposed backgrounds, and build relationships with unsuspecting users. A few are clumsy puppets; others are disturbingly lifelike. In long campaigns, these personas are cultivated like crops, nurtured quietly until the harvest: a moment of political crisis, a disputed election, a border incident. Then they strike, coordinating messaging swarms that shift public sentiment just enough to muddy consensus.

A crisis messaging swarm is a brutal demonstration of how scale changes psychology. Imagine an earthquake strikes a region already suffering from political tension. Within minutes, thousands of local users receive messages urging them to flee to particular shelters—shelters located near choke points or infrastructure assets. Others receive the opposite message: stay home, roads are blocked. Some are told military forces are responding heroically; others see synthetic images of soldiers looting. No single lie is decisive. But the inconsistency corrodes trust, and trust is the glue of crisis response. When no one knows whose information to believe, every decision slows. A relief effort punctured by doubt is a relief effort that begins late and saves fewer lives.

This is not merely propaganda. It is the weaponisation of confusion. Traditional censorship silences dissent. Modern denial and deception overwhelm the senses until truth becomes statistically invisible. Humans do not have infinite cognitive bandwidth, nor do institutions. Flood a society with enough noise and it cannot hear itself think.

There is a deeper philosophical discomfort here. Democracies rely on the presumption that citizens share a minimum common reality—facts about weather, hospitals, borders, ballots. When synthetic personas and automated campaigns erode that foundation, the harm is not just operational; it is civilisational. An election where people cannot trust official communications is not simply flawed. It is paralysed.

And yet, defenders face a cruel paradox. The more aggressively they filter synthetic activity, the higher the risk of silencing genuine speech. Platforms that purge bot-like behaviour inevitably sweep up activists, minority languages, or niche communities that happen to exhibit abnormal posting patterns. Real people are wrongly erased; synthetic identities slip through. The defensive posture becomes a moral maze.

Technical countermeasures help but never fully solve the problem. Pattern detectors flag coordinated swarms, but attackers continually adapt cadence, tone, and linguistic variety. Metadata filtering catches puppet networks until they migrate to privacy-preserving channels. Some platforms experiment with cryptographic attestations for content provenance, embedding signatures to prove that a message originated from a verified device. Promising, but brittle: not every citizen will—or should—use such tooling. And adoption at global scale is slow, especially in low-income regions where connectivity itself is precarious.

Governments have begun their own experiments: digital ombuds for crisis communications, public-sector rapid-response debunking teams, and transparent dashboards that show when false narratives are detected. These tools help restore signal, but they require trust—and trust is precisely what adversaries are trying to destroy. If the public doubts official channels, debunking becomes just another claim in the cacophony.

The most successful defensive strategies combine technological filtering with social resilience. Some cities run drills where citizens receive mixed messages and must rely on official verification protocols. Schools teach media literacy not as a moral handbook, but as a practical survival skill. Civil society groups build peer-verification networks—neighbours confirming reports through local channels. It is imperfect, slow, and deeply human. Yet it reminds us: in crises, communities can route around noise in ways machines cannot.

The stakes escalate when militaries are targeted. A botnet that overwhelms logistics databases or air-defence alerts in the opening hours of conflict can be as effective as a kinetic strike. If commanders spend crucial minutes sorting genuine warnings from synthetic ones, deterrence falters. The fog of war, once a metaphor, becomes algorithmically enforced.

Some defence planners fear a future of "decoy wars", where synthetic personas create the illusion of unrest in one region while distracting security forces from a real incursion elsewhere. Others worry about global contagion: a misinformation swarm so large it destabilises multiple nations at once. When adversaries can hire deception as a service, the barrier to entry drops. A mid-sized state, or even a well-funded non-state actor, can manufacture political chaos hundreds of miles away.

This new territory forces an awkward question: what counts as an act of aggression? If a foreign power floods your emergency lines with false reports, is that cybercrime, sabotage, or an attack on critical infrastructure? If synthetic personas erode trust in official health information during a pandemic, who bears responsibility? International law has barely begun to systematise these harms.

But perhaps the most disquieting problem is psychological collision. Humans evolved to sense deception through facial cues, tone of voice, and social familiarity. Online environments strip these away. When thousands of plausible strangers say the same false thing, it is hard to resist—even when you know the game. People do not simply believe lies because they are naïve. They believe because lies arrive wrapped in the appearance of consensus.

The answer is not despair. It is clarity. States, platforms, and communities can invest in verification tools, provenance standards, and crisis-time transparency protocols. Red-team exercises can simulate information floods, forcing responders to identify weak links before they matter. And public communication can be frank: not everything you read is real, and that is not your fault. But the challenge is cultural, not only technical. A society that expects noise is less easily manipulated by it.

Still, the uneasy truth remains: denial and deception at scale are no longer fringe tools. They are strategic instruments wielded by states and mercenaries alike. The next geopolitical flashpoint may not start with missiles or drones. It may start with a million messages, a thousand synthetic faces, and a single fabricated emergency that no one can quite disprove in time.

And so the lingering question, the one that keeps civil servants and commanders awake at night, is painfully simple: if the world's communication channels can be drowned by machines, how do societies stay coherent long enough to act?

## Counter-play: resilience drills

The air was still when the alarm sounded. Screens across the command floor bloomed with red notices: satellite downlink failures, corrupted telemetry, stalled logistics queues. Officers snapped into emergency procedures, dispatching repair teams and recalculating routes. Only then did the message appear on the central display, short and brutal: *This is a drill. Systems were intentionally broken.* Half the room went silent; the other half muttered disbelief. Months of planning, huge budgets, superb engineering—and yet it took just seconds of simulated failure to jam the arteries of an entire command chain.

That is the painful power of resilience drills. You do not learn how a system fails by theorising. You learn by breaking it and watching who bleeds first.

States and militaries—like corporations and hospitals—have spent decades designing systems for efficiency, not adversity. They optimise supply lines, centralise data, automate procedures. It works beautifully in peacetime. Then something snaps. A cloud region goes dark. A routing table collapses. A hostile actor poisons an update pipeline. Even without an attacker, entropy alone can cause enough mischief. And yet, astonishingly, many critical institutions still treat failure as an aberration rather than an inevitability.

Resilience drills are the antidote to that delusion. They force leaders to inhabit uncomfortable spaces where redundancy, decentralisation, and improvisation matter more than glossy dashboards. When a logistics AI cannot plan because its training data is corrupted, who steps in? When a swarm of drones loses satellite guidance, what failsafe kicks in? These are questions best answered in practice, not in memos.

Tabletop exercises are the gentlest entry point. Officials gather around a giant map; facilitators serve up hypothetical disasters: a border incursion paired with a cyberattack on medical infrastructure; a contested election amid disinformation floods; a supply chain choke as cloud compute is sanctioned. Participants must make decisions under imperfect information, negotiating with allies and civilians, balancing military urgency with democratic restraint. It is theatre with teeth. Failures here are cheap and illuminating. They expose blind spots: missing protocols, overconfident doctrine, brittle dependencies on single vendors or single datasets.

But tabletop games, for all their value, are abstractions. Chaos testing is worse—and therefore better. Borrowed from high-availability engineering practices, it involves intentional, real-time disruption of live systems to validate resilience. A famous precedent from the technology sector involved randomly killing servers in production to ensure automated failover actually worked. Defence ministries have begun borrowing this logic. Imagine a procurement office that periodically revokes access to a key catalogue, demanding teams source components through secondary suppliers. Or an air-force network that, without notice, simulates satellite degradation to test whether autonomous fallback behaviours are reliable. Chaos is not accidental. It is scheduled.

Consider simulated cloud region loss. Defence systems increasingly rest on commercial compute. If an adversary—or a mundane technical incident—cripples a region, everything from payroll to battlefield analytics can freeze. Drills that yank the plug reveal ugly realities: authentication keys expired months ago; data replication was misconfigured; human operators forgot manual override procedures. There is no shame in discovering these problems—shame lies in discovering them during a crisis.

The logic of resilience drills is not only technical. It is social. During a simulated outage, do teams communicate clearly or descend into parallel monologues? Does authority concentrate on the loudest voice or the most informed one? Are junior engineers empowered to bypass rigid processes when time is scarce? These questions matter because failures rarely respect hierarchy. The person who spots the problem first is often not the one wearing the rank.

Some commanders resist drills for a predictable reason: fear of embarrassment. Public agencies dread headlines about flunked simulations. Elected leaders worry that exposing fragility will erode confidence. Yet secrecy is the enemy of progress. Aviation learned this long ago; every near-miss became a lesson, not a scandal. In defence, humility must replace bravado. It is better to suffer humiliation in training than calamity in war.

In countries serious about resilience, drills are ritualised. There are seasonal chaos tests for core networks, randomised red-team intrusions, and mandatory crisis rotations where civilian ministries must swap data channels. Some run "silent city" exercises: a simulated blackout where hospitals, banks, and emergency responders operate on backup power and degraded communications. Citizens are warned but not spoon-fed guidance. The drill tests not only infrastructure, but societal reflexes—how communities self-organise when central command is muted.

The results are humbling. In one exercise, a major city's digital ID system went offline for six hours. Supermarkets could not verify payments. Pharmacies could not check prescriptions. People queued with cash that tills could not register. The failure was not catastrophic; it was revealing. Every contingency plan had assumed stable cloud connectivity. None anticipated the mundane chaos of outdated paper processes.

There is a deeper philosophical reason resilience drills matter. Complex systems seduce us into believing we control them. Dashboards and metrics give the illusion of certainty. But systems do not fail gracefully. They surprise. They amplify human error. They buckle at unexpected nodes. Drills cultivate a culture of doubt—not paralysis, but informed scepticism. They teach teams to ask: *What if we are wrong? What if our assumptions fail? What if our backup is broken and we didn't notice?*

That mindset is lethal to complacency and priceless in crisis.

Critics argue that chaos testing is expensive and disruptive. Why deliberately sabotage functioning systems? The answer is stark: your adversaries will do it for you. Better to learn under controlled conditions than on the worst day of your nation's life. A simulated outage that uncovers a silent dependency on a foreign-managed certificate service might save billions in future disruption. A tabletop scenario that exposes misaligned rules of engagement between agencies might prevent escalation in real conflict.

Moreover, drills foster interoperability. When allied militaries share exercise designs or run joint chaos tests, they uncover mismatched interfaces, divergent doctrines, and incompatible data formats. Fixing those frictions before conflict is the difference between a cohesive coalition and a disjointed one. A drone fleet that cannot share situational maps because of inconsistent metadata standards is a liability. Drills force the issue.

Yet the most consequential form of resilience is emotional. Humans respond poorly to uncertainty. Panic, blame, and tunnel-vision decision-making can turn small failures into cascading disasters. Drills teach restraint. They normalise disruption. Teams learn that outages are not existential, that workarounds exist, that improvisation is a skill, not a shameful breach of protocol. When the real crisis arrives, their pulse stays lower. They focus.

And still, a tension lingers. How much disruption is enough? What if a drill itself causes genuine harm—lost revenue, public panic, diplomatic fallout? There are no perfect answers. A state that never tests is fragile. A state that tests recklessly loses credibility. The art lies in tuning the difficulty: harsh enough to reveal truth, careful enough to avoid collateral damage.

The final twist is sobering. As AI systems take on greater autonomy, drills must evolve. It will not be enough to simulate broken wires and dead servers. Future resilience exercises will need to test how machine decision-making falters under degraded data, corrupted inputs, or adversarial deception. We will need drills that pit AI against chaos—and measure whether humans can still intervene when the automation goes astray.

The uncomfortable reality is this: resilience is not a destination but a discipline. Systems rot when untested. Organisations stagnate when unchallenged. And adversaries adapt faster than bureaucracies. The states that endure will be those that treat failure as a laboratory, not a scandal.

So the open question—the one leaders cannot ignore—is simple, relentless, and slightly haunting: if tomorrow's peace depends on surviving tomorrow's failures, who is brave enough to break their own systems today?

# Chapter 8

# Ethics Under Fire

A dusty operations room on the edge of a conflict zone. A screen flickers, showing a convoy creeping along a ridge. Somewhere in that column is a weapons truck. Somewhere else are conscripts who would rather be anywhere else. The targeting AI presents its confidence scores, hazard projections, and predicted collateral risk. The junior officer watching the feed knows the rules of engagement to the letter. Yet her stomach tightens. Numbers do not feel like certainty. Lives do not feel like statistics. Somewhere in this scenario, if she gets it wrong, there will be funerals—perhaps of enemies, perhaps of children, perhaps of her own conscience.

This is the unspoken heart of modern military ethics: decisions are faster, data is richer, and responsibility is still unbearably human.

Autonomous and semi-autonomous systems promise precision: fewer misidentifications, cleaner engagements, reduced fog of war. Yet precision is not innocence. A machine that is 98 per cent confident might still be lethally wrong. A dataset that works perfectly in one town might quietly misclassify another population because their clothing, accents, or vehicles differ. In these gaps lies a simple truth: ethics does not vanish when machines arrive. It mutates. It demands new forms of vigilance, new mechanisms of accountability, and new expressions of dignity that are more than slogans.

This chapter is not about handwringing lectures. It is about practical ethics under genuine pressure—when time is short, when information is messy, when politicians demand results, and when soldiers must sleep at night. The questions here are uncomfortable and necessary: How do we define a lawful target when machine perception is probabilistic? How do we protect civilians when a model's training data was never meant to represent the people now living under its gaze? And what happens to the humans in the loop—those who make the final call—when their moral burden becomes a daily, digital weight?

The first thread runs through targeting. Traditional doctrine teaches proportionality and distinction: strike only when benefits outweigh harm, and only against lawful combatants. It sounds clean. In practice, it is murky, subjective, and situational. When autonomy enters, the temptation is to offload morality into code. Set a threshold. If civilian risk is below X, if object classification confidence exceeds Y, proceed. Yet every threshold is a value judgement disguised as a number. A no-strike list is not just a database—it is a claim about whose lives matter, whose property is sacred, whose culture must endure.

Some militaries now test their autonomous targeting systems with plain-language safety rules: structures marked as schools are untouchable; gatherings in religious spaces require direct human override; ambulances remain protected regardless of livery. The best systems can enforce these rules even when under deception. But a rule is only as durable as the data behind it. If the training set barely includes rural clinics or temporary shelters, the algorithm's certainty may evaporate. Ethical targeting is not moral poetry—it is engineering detail, lived restraint, and the humility to say "no strike" even when the operation is costly.

Then there is bias and harm. Engineers know that datasets reflect their origins. If the majority of training imagery was collected in specific regions, seasons, or cultural contexts, the resulting models will quietly inherit those patterns. In civilian life, this leads to mislabelled photos or clumsy customer service chatbots. In conflict, it leads to lethal misjudgement. Bias in warfare is not a philosophical puzzle; it is operational risk and moral injury. When these systems fail, redress must be real: technical review boards, public reporting of mishaps, compensation paths for harmed families, and clear avenues for revisiting deployments. Nothing corrodes legitimacy faster than a system that harms civilians and then hides behind secrecy.

Ethics is also about the people who operate these machines. A remote pilot may never hear the explosion. A satellite analyst may never see the consequences on the ground. Yet moral injury does not need proximity. Humans in semi-autonomous operations experience a strange burden: they are responsible, but the machine shaped the choice. When they approve a strike based on system recommendations, they carry the outcome. When they veto a strike and a later attack kills their comrades, they carry that too. Some forces now rotate crews more frequently, mandate decompression periods, and embed counsellors in operational units. Not because soldiers are weak, but because the ethical load has become heavier in ways their predecessors could not imagine.

At the societal level, legitimacy matters. Democracies do not wage secret wars with secret machines and expect trust to endure. Citizens deserve more than polished slogans about "smart weapons" and "surgical precision". They deserve plain-language explanations of risks, oversight, safeguards, error rates, and near-miss incidents. Annual posture statements, parliamentary briefings, and public-facing safety reports are not luxuries—they are democratic armour. Silence breeds conspiracy; transparency builds consent.

The legal dimension offers no easy refuge. International humanitarian law predates facial recognition, drone swarms, and algorithmic targeting. Yet its core doctrines—humanity, distinction, proportionality, necessity—still hold. The challenge is interpretation. What counts as "foreseeable" civilian harm when machine predictions drive planning? How do we preserve accountability when a model generates recommendations but a human signs the order? The answer lies in traceability: logs of training data, audit trails of decisions, retention windows long enough to allow independent investigation. Law without evidence is theatre. Evidence without access is propaganda. Meaningful accountability requires both.

We cannot pretend that perfect ethics exist. War is tragedy by definition. But there are better and worse ways to fight. Systems can be designed to default toward restraint. Operators can be trained to question the confidence scores flashed before them. Parliaments can demand proof of compliance, not marketing claims. Civilians can insist on knowing when machines are deputised to judge life and death. These are not utopian standards. They are the minimum required for legitimacy in a world watching every mistake in real time.

The tension that runs through this chapter is stark: speed versus conscience, autonomy versus accountability, secrecy versus trust. If militaries embrace automation to avoid casualties and reduce fog, they must also embrace new responsibilities, deeper transparency, and harsher self-scrutiny. The public will forgive imperfection; it will not forgive denial.

So the provocation to carry into the pages ahead is blunt and unavoidable: when the next conflict demands split-second decisions by learning machines and tired humans, will we have built systems worthy of both our security and our conscience—or will we discover, far too late, that ethics was retrofitted to war rather than built into it?

## Targeting thresholds and dignity

A quadcopter spirals above a village road at dusk. Its thermal camera shows a truck idling near a school. Inside the command post thousands of miles away, targeting software overlays predictions: probability of munitions aboard, likelihood of civilian presence, expected blast radius. A junior officer, trained in both statistics and humanitarian law, watches the confidence bars turn from amber to green. The system indicates a lawful strike. It cannot see the children playing in the courtyard beyond the camera's cropped frame. She can. The only sound in the room is the hum of servers. The law says she may fire. Dignity says she must wait.

This is the modern paradox of military targeting: precision has reduced the fog of war, yet heightened the moral stakes. Machines deliver probabilities, not truths. And even a lawful strike can be unjust in the eyes of those who bury the dead. For decades, militaries spoke of "minimising collateral damage" as if harm could be balanced on a ledger. Autonomy does not change that calculus—it makes it sharper. It demands rules that are coded, not merely recited; thresholds that are visible, not implied. But every threshold, every constraint, rests upon a deeper question: how do we treat human dignity in the split-second world of algorithmic war?

To define proportionality is to admit ambiguity. Commanders must judge whether anticipated military advantage outweighs expected civilian harm. That judgement once relied on experience—seasoned officers who knew the terrain, the culture, the likely consequences. Autonomous systems cannot draw on wisdom. They compare features, not histories. And so militaries now rely on numerical constraints: confidence levels for target classification, probability bounds for collateral effects, and minimum distances from protected sites. These are rational tools. They are also fragile.

Consider a semi-autonomous artillery system tasked with neutralising mobile missile units. It has been trained on thousands of images, including decoys, farm trucks, and humanitarian vehicles. When it identifies a suspected launcher, the operator sees a probability: perhaps 92 per cent. At what figure does lawful become acceptable? Ninety? Eighty-five? A number too low invites error; a number too high delays strikes until too late. Engineers speak of thresholds as if they emerge from mathematics. In truth, they are policy choices wearing scientific clothes.

No-strike lists exemplify this tension. Historically, these were hand-scribbled grids on plastic-covered maps: hospitals, schools, aid convoys. They depended on human memory and visible markings. Now, advanced systems ingest geospatial datasets that evolve hourly. A school can be protected in code; a temporary shelter, less so. Uploading new protected coordinates requires constant maintenance, especially in fluid urban conflicts. When autonomy is involved, a system must know not only where not to shoot, but how to recognise deception: adversaries who paint red crosses on weapons depots or drive ambulances packed with explosives. Protection and exploitation live uncomfortably close.

Some militaries have begun stress-testing their targeting algorithms with deliberate edge cases. They feed in imagery of markets during festivals, roads clogged with refugees, convoys interspersed with civilian vehicles. They ask the machine to prove restraint. It is a humbling exercise. Algorithms trained on neat datasets stumble in the mess of real life. Village clinics built from shipping containers are mislabelled as warehouses. Children running across a road confuse motion detectors designed to estimate hostile manoeuvres. Engineers discover that a safe test environment is not a safe battlefield.

The answer is not to abandon autonomy, but to widen responsibility. A practical ethics of targeting demands three elements: transparency, scepticism, and the authority to refuse. Transparency means that operators see not only the recommended strike, but why. Which features drove classification? Which assumptions shaped collateral estimates? When software becomes a black box, ethics dissolves into faith. Scepticism means that operators are trained to challenge the machine—not to rubber-stamp it. If a village looks different from the training data—different roof styles, different vehicles—the operator must treat every model output as provisional. And authority to refuse means genuine power: careers must not be ruined for saying "hold".

These principles are not theoretical. They are grounded in lived experience. During counterinsurgency operations in dense urban terrain, one Western force quietly implemented a "reverse threshold": if the civilian risk surpassed a certain bound, the system would default to *no strike* unless a human explicitly overrode. It slowed operations. It also saved lives. Commanders noticed something else: when the public learned of this constraint, trust increased. Local leaders began sharing intelligence instead of hiding from drones. Restraint became strategy.

Behind these rules sits an older, deeper idea: dignity. Not as an abstract virtue, but as a limit. Civilians are not acceptable loss; cultural sites are not expendable scenery. International humanitarian law protects them not out of softness, but because war without constraint corrodes the victor as surely as it destroys the vanquished. Yet dignity cannot be written into code with a poetic flourish. It must be operationalised.

One approach is what some call proximity tests. If a target is within a radius of a protected site, the system is barred from autonomous engagement. Another approach embeds civility directly into model training: include thousands of permutations of schools, clinics, shelters, ambulances—daylight, night, dust storms, festival crowds—so that the machine recognises not only the pristine logo of aid agencies, but the improvised tents where displaced families take refuge. This is engineering as ethics.

Still, thresholds are bets, not certainties. A responsible system never claims infallibility. That is why auditability matters. Every model inference should leave a trail: what data was used, what parameters mattered, what alternative actions were considered. When civilians are harmed—and harm will occur—those logs allow independent review boards to determine whether the strike was lawful, mistaken, or negligent. They also allow compensation, apology, and learning. Nothing restores dignity after death, but public reckoning acknowledges humanity.

The uncomfortable truth is that autonomy intensifies accountability. When a human pilot errs, we speak of fog and fear. When software errs, we ask why the code was not safer. It is tempting to demand perfect machines before deployment. That day will never arrive. The real question is whether the systems act more responsibly than the humans they support. Precision does not absolve; it obliges.

Just war theory once lived in thick books and general staff colleges. Now it lives inside firmware, user interfaces, and operational dashboards. Engineers, ethicists, lawyers, and soldiers must share one language. When they do not, thresholds become arbitrary, and dignity becomes a slogan.

Some fear that too many constraints will paralyse militaries. Others fear the opposite: that automation will normalise killing by spreadsheet. Between these poles sits a fragile, necessary discipline—the discipline of restraint under pressure. When a drone hovers over a crowded street and the algorithm flashes green, the noblest act may be patience.

And so the question that shadows every threshold is simple and urgent: when calculation says "fire", will there still be room for conscience to say "no"?

## Bias, harm, and redress

A convoy of aid workers pulls into a dusty town at dawn. Their lorries carry food and antibiotics, marked clearly with the blue-and-white emblem recognised across conflicts. Yet an autonomous checkpoint system flags one vehicle as suspicious. The pattern-matching model has learned—incorrectly—that trucks of this make and colour often transport contraband. Moments later, armed guards pull the driver out at gunpoint. The error is corrected within minutes, but the humiliation lingers. The villagers watch. Trust evaporates. A minor algorithmic misjudgement becomes a strategic wound.

Bias in military AI is not an academic abstraction. It is humiliation at a checkpoint, suspicion cast on the wrong families, surveillance trained more aggressively on some neighbourhoods than others. When algorithms learn from skewed data—imagery over-indexed on one region, speech samples dominated by one dialect—they inherit those asymmetries and project them back onto the world. In civilian life, such systems can deny loans or mishandle job applications. Under conflict, they can escalate tension, trigger pre-emptive force, and fracture fragile ceasefires.

Engineers often claim that data is neutral. It is not. Training sets reflect the world as it has been recorded, not as it is. Footage of insurgent fighters may be plentiful from one valley but rare from the next, simply because one unit had better cameras. Satellite imagery may capture urban warfare in crisp resolution but treat rural districts as blurred afterthoughts. Models trained on this imbalance learn to "see" more threats where sensors have been pointed longest. Bias becomes geography disguised as objectivity.

A well-documented pattern in counterterrorism analytics is the feedback loop: an area identified as high risk receives more surveillance, which produces more detections, which justifies yet more surveillance. The model appears accurate because it continuously confirms its own priors. Meanwhile, equally dangerous regions with less historical data remain unseen. This is bias operationalised as tunnel vision.

Autonomous targeting is more than probability thresholds and precision strikes. It is pattern recognition at scale: distinguishing farmer from fighter, convoy from cartel, radio chatter from encrypted signal. When the training corpus contains more images of combatants from one ethnic group than another, or more speech samples from certain dialects, the system quietly, relentlessly, misclassifies. Bias becomes harm. Harm becomes policy. And policy acquires the unearned aura of algorithmic neutrality.

Some militaries have begun conducting "dataset audits"—structured reviews of where their training data came from, who labelled it, what cultures, dialects, and terrains it covers. The findings are uncomfortable. In one case, thousands of images of humanitarian workers were unintentionally used as negative examples of combatants, simply because they appeared in the background of battlefield photography. In another, speech recognition for radio intercepts failed to understand a minority language, leading command to assume silence where there was noise.

These are not mere oversights. They are signals that operational success depends on representativeness. A model that fails to recognise a rural clinic because its architecture differs from the concrete hospitals in the training set is not just inaccurate—it is dangerous.

Harm flows not only from misclassification but from the perception of injustice. A community that believes it was targeted because of its ethnicity or faith will view every future operation through a lens of grievance. Adversaries exploit these perceptions, spreading footage of mistaken raids as proof of discrimination. Bias becomes propaganda fodder. And propaganda, in conflict, can be deadlier than any drone.

The hard question is what to do when bias causes real harm: a wrongful arrest, a misdirected strike, a community traumatised by false suspicion. Traditional military culture responds with terse statements—"procedures were followed", "investigation ongoing", "no misconduct found". That may satisfy lawyers; it does not satisfy families. Nor does it prevent recurrence.

Redress demands structure. Independent review boards—armed with technical expertise, access to logs, and authority to recommend restitution—are a start. When civilians are harmed by algorithmic error, these boards can adjudicate compensation, public apology, procedural change. Crucially, they provide a forum where grievance is heard rather than buried. In some peacekeeping missions, community liaisons now sit on such panels, translating both language and expectations.

Transparency also matters. If a targeting model mislabels a structure and a strike goes ahead, a public statement explaining the error may seem risky. But secrecy breeds conspiracy. Honest accounting builds legitimacy. During one operation, a coalition published quarterly reports detailing incidents caused by automation defects: false positives at checkpoints, failed recognition of medical convoys, mistaken flagging of journalists' drones. Critics scoffed that such openness exposed weakness. Locals saw it differently. They described it as respect.

The philosophical debate is blunt: can an algorithmic system truly avoid bias, or will it always reflect the prejudices of the world that trained it? Some argue that perfection is impossible; therefore, machine judgement in war is unethical. Others reply that humans are biased too—perhaps more so. The better comparison is not machine versus ideal, but machine versus human under fire, in fear, at midnight.

Yet even if algorithms outperform humans on average, averages mask the outliers. A model that is 99 per cent accurate may still repeatedly misclassify members of a marginalised group, simply because the training data lacked their faces, speech, or cultural markers. For them, the promise of algorithmic fairness sounds hollow. This is why redress is not a luxury; it is a necessity. Justice delayed becomes grievance entrenched.

Engineers sometimes propose "debiasing" techniques: algorithmic reweighting, synthetic data augmentation, adversarial training. These help. But they are guardrails, not guarantees. Without continuous monitoring—logs that flag disproportionate false positives in particular regions or demographics—bias resurfaces. And without channels for affected communities to challenge outcomes, harm festers.

Conversation often returns to accountability. When an autonomous system triggers a wrongful raid, who answers? The commander who deployed it? The data scientists who trained it? The procurement officers who bought it? Traditional command structures were not built for distributed responsibility. Yet distributed responsibility is the reality of digital war.

Some countries have begun drafting legal frameworks that treat algorithmic harm as a distinct category—neither pure accident nor deliberate misconduct. These frameworks demand proof of reasonable mitigation: dataset audits, human oversight, bias testing before deployment. If these practices were absent, the state owes restitution. It is an imperfect system, but it is better than silence.

There is also a moral dimension: recognising the dignity of those harmed. Compensation without acknowledgement feels like pay-off. Acknowledgement without change feels like condescension. Both matter. Communities remember who listens.

Consider a different kind of redress: learning. Every mistaken identification, every wrongful arrest, every civilian death should become training data for improvement. That requires what militaries hate—admitting error. But when errors are hidden, models remain blind. When errors are studied, systems become safer.

This principle has precedent. Aviation safety improved not through secrecy, but through mandatory reporting and independent accident boards. Pilots who make honest mistakes are protected from punishment if they self-report; the price of silence is catastrophe. Autonomous military systems need a similar culture: blame less, learn more.

There is a lingering fear that acknowledging bias hands ammunition to adversaries. Perhaps. But refusing to acknowledge it hands ammunition to history. War fought by machines must still be governed by human conscience. If autonomy becomes a shield for injustice, it will provoke resistance, radicalisation, and collapse the very legitimacy that makes conflict resolution possible.

So the uncomfortable question remains: when algorithms injure the innocent, will militaries build the courage to say, publicly and plainly, *we got it wrong*—and will that admission be followed by restitution, reform, and renewed restraint?

## Operator moral injury

The monitor shows a target moving through a dusty street. A child walks beside him, clutching a plastic bag. The autonomous system highlights the adult in amber: probabilistic threat, 73 per cent. The operator hesitates. They can override, escalate, or let the system decide. Adrenaline surges; the clock is not kind. A minute later, the screen fades to grey. The event has passed. The child lives. The operator closes the session and drives home, where dinner is waiting and the neighbours know nothing.

This is the quiet strangeness of modern warfare: the people with the power to end lives leave the battlefield by car. They sleep in their own beds after a day of remote operations, wrestling with the same questions that once haunted soldiers in trenches and cockpits—only now the aftermath is silent, invisible, and isolating. The idea that distance protects the psyche is a comfortable fiction. Moral injury does not require blood on one's hands; it can be delivered through pixels and probability scores.

Semi-autonomous conflict introduces a new category of psychological stress. Operators do not always pull the trigger themselves, yet they witness what their systems do. They review logs of missions, often knowing that decisions made with imperfect information determined the fate of strangers. They sign off on interventions that algorithms recommend.

When things go wrong, they bear responsibility without the traditional rituals of soldiering: no comrades in the mud beside them, no chaplains, no ceremonies of grief.

In interviews across several militaries, operators describe a common sensation: *permanent proximity.* They are not on the battlefield, yet never entirely away from it. Their screens show faces, bodies, heat signatures, and sometimes the aftermath. They cycle between intense focus and mundane normality—commuting, shopping, family life—without the psychological decompression that traditional deployments enforce. The mind struggles to reconcile both worlds.

The paradox is stark. Remote operators often suffer stress levels comparable to forward-deployed troops. They live with guilt for actions taken and for actions not taken. They experience vicarious trauma from reviewing footage. And unlike units in combat zones, they rarely speak openly about it. The stigma is subtle: *You were never in danger, so how could you be hurt?*

Yet the injury is moral, not physical. It comes from witnessing harm that feels avoidable, from issuing commands that take effect continents away, from trusting systems that sometimes misjudge. When semi-autonomous operations go well, the operator is background noise. When they go badly, the operator becomes the focal point of inquiry, often alone.

Automation changes the emotional burden. In many control rooms, operators supervise fleets of semiautonomous systems rather than micromanaging every action. The machine does the tracking, recognition, and prediction. Humans remain "on the loop," responsible for monitoring and intervening in edge cases. But when something terrible happens, the distinction between "oversight" and "decision" becomes morally foggy. If the operator could have overridden the algorithm and did not, is that omission a choice? If the system made an error the operator did not detect, is that negligence?

Consider a real dilemma: a pattern-recognition model flags a vehicle as hostile based on heat distribution and route patterns. The operator glances at the feed. The image is grainy, the window small, the time short. They trust the system and authorise the block. Moments later, the occupants emerge confused, not dangerous. Nobody dies, but the operator sees the mother shielding her children, then replaying in their mind the scenario where a strike had been recommended instead. It is a brush with catastrophe, visible only to those in the room.

Traditional military training prepares soldiers for the personal risk of battle. It does not prepare them to harm others while remaining physically safe, nor to carry that guilt into the mundane world. Some operators describe feeling like ghosts—present everywhere, responsible nowhere. Others feel like executioners. Some detach emotionally, but detachment can become its own injury.

Moral injury is not identical to post-traumatic stress. It is the ache of violating one's own ethical code, or of participating in an act that feels wrong even when it was lawful. An autonomous system might be calibrated to minimise harm, but when harm occurs, the human mind rarely accepts probability as absolution. A 2 per cent chance of civilian presence is still someone's life. A mislabelled object is still a mistake that cannot be undone.

Semi-autonomous operations also blur authorship. A pilot who drops a bomb lives with the decision; an operator who permits an algorithm to do so lives with a more disorienting burden. Who *caused* the harm? The coder? The commander? The model? The operator? This ambiguity is psychologically corrosive. Humans are wired to make sense of responsibility; when responsibility feels diffused, guilt becomes difficult to place—and difficult to relieve.

Some nations secretly rotate operators to prevent exhaustion. Others impose maximum daily screen time or mandatory debriefs. A few experiment with "mission decompression"—structured psychological cooldown after difficult engagements, even when no one fired a shot. These measures are early, uneven, and often optional. The stigma persists: admitting distress can jeopardise career pathways, and many operators already feel their work is not recognised as "real combat."

Duty cycles matter. In aviation, pilots have mandated rest periods because fatigue kills. In semi-autonomous command centres, operators often work extended shifts, reviewing feeds for hours until their judgment blurs. Cognitive fatigue breeds moral fatigue. In one documented incident, an operator approved a machine's classification of an object as a hostile vehicle. When investigators asked why, he replied, "Because the last twenty were." He was not reckless; he was exhausted.

Ethical design requires scheduling that respects psychological limits. Not every operator should be cleared for continuous high-stakes evaluation. Rotations that encourage recovery—physical, mental, emotional—reduce error and preserve dignity. Yet many defence bureaucracies still see these roles as desk jobs, no different from analysing spreadsheets. They are not.

Decompression is not indulgence; it is operational hygiene. After intense missions, operators need space to talk, process, or simply sit outside without screens. Peer groups help, but only when systems protect confidentiality and careers. Some units now run facilitated reflection sessions: not therapy, but open conversation. The results are striking. Operators describe relief at acknowledging the weight they carry. Commanders discover blind spots in training and doctrine.

Technology vendors often claim their products will "remove humans from harm." They rarely consider the harm done to humans who remain in the loop. The psychological load is part of the hidden cost of autonomy. It does not appear in procurement spreadsheets, but it shows up in turnover, depression, insomnia, and in the quiet resignation of operators who cannot keep watching.

Moral injury also has a societal echo. When operators go home, they do not become citizens untouched by war. They carry knowledge the public does not see. Yet public debate about autonomous weapons often ignores their mental health entirely, as if the entire ethical burden will soon be outsourced to code. That fantasy is dangerous. For the foreseeable future, human oversight remains essential. And where there is oversight, there is conscience.

Some countries have established confidential hotlines for remote personnel to report distress or ethical concerns, akin to whistleblower protections. These are fragile but necessary. Operators who believe a system is misbehaving need avenues to halt deployment without retaliation. Otherwise the pressure to "just approve" corrodes ethical judgment.

The question is not whether autonomy will change the psychology of war. It already has. The deeper question is how militaries will protect those tasked with supervising it. Will they treat moral injury as a rare side effect, or as a predictable outcome requiring systematic mitigation?

There is a darker possibility: as autonomy increases, institutions may treat operators as disposable buffers—present only to absorb legal and moral liability when things go wrong. That cynicism will corrode trust from within. Skilled operators will leave. The ones who remain will be numb or reckless. Systems built on conscience will run on autopilot.

There is another path. It begins with honesty: acknowledging that remote war wounds the mind. It continues with structure: duty cycles governed by neuroscience, decompression protocols, confidential counselling, rotation out of high-intensity roles, and cultures that treat emotional health as part of readiness, not weakness. It requires commanders to recognise that "no physical danger" does not mean "no trauma."

And it ends—if it ends well—with dignity. Operators who oversee lethal systems deserve the same psychological support as soldiers on the ground. Their injuries are quieter, but no less real. The silent harm of modern war will not heal through denial. It will heal only if nations choose to care for the minds they rely upon.

So the unresolved question lingers: if the future battlespace is remote and algorithmic, will the human beings who supervise it be shielded, or forgotten?

## Civic consent

The first autonomous patrol vessel slipped into the harbour at dawn, white hull unblemished, antennas angled to the sky. There were no sailors on deck, no brass band to greet its return, only a technician with a tablet confirming that the machine had completed its circuit. The voyage had been legal, authorised, and fully logged. Yet when citizens saw the newsflash—*uncrewed warship conducts patrol*—the unease was immediate. People wondered who had approved it, what rules governed it, and what it might do next time. The patrol had been safe. The communication around it had not.

Modern defence establishments speak often about safeguarding national security. They speak far less about safeguarding democratic legitimacy. Autonomous and semi-autonomous systems intensify this tension. The more complex the technology, the more political leaders are tempted to hide behind technical language and classified briefings. Yet secrecy, however well-intentioned, erodes trust. Civic consent is not a box to be ticked; it is the foundation on which democratic force rests. When the public no longer understands—or believes—it is being told the truth, the mandate to wield lethal power collapses.

The paradox is stark. Democracies field increasingly sophisticated systems that can make or shape decisions at machine speed, but democratic legitimacy operates at human speed. Surprise deployments, unexplained incidents, and evasive answers create a quiet but corrosive doubt: who ensures these systems reflect public values rather than institutional convenience? Silence invites suspicion; transparency disarms it.

For decades, defence communication followed a familiar script: technical complexity as shield, national security as excuse. That world is changing. Citizens are better informed, better connected, and less forgiving of opaque power. The burden of proof now lies with governments to demonstrate both competence and conscience. Civic consent does not require broadcasting operational secrets. It requires clarity: what these systems do, what they are allowed to do, what they are *not* allowed to do, and who is accountable when they fail.

Public briefings can be honest without being reckless. Most democratic states already issue statements about troop deployments or international exercises. Extending that practice to autonomous deployments is not radical; it is responsible governance. Annual posture statements that explain the scale of autonomous capability, the ethical safeguards in place, and the number of incidents reviewed are a start. They show that military power remains answerable to civilian authority, not to the inscrutable logic of procurement offices or classified contracts.

Some nations have begun to experiment. They produce plain-language summaries of mishaps, publish casualty reporting standards, and describe the oversight mechanisms that constrain machine decision-making. When something goes wrong, they acknowledge it swiftly, rather than retreat behind the fortress walls of "ongoing investigation." These gestures are more powerful than press releases about cutting-edge sensors or new airframes. They reaffirm that the state trusts its citizens with uncomfortable facts.

The deeper purpose of civic consent is not public relations. It is constitutional. Democracies grant armed forces a monopoly on lawful violence because they accept that coercion is sometimes necessary to defend the whole. But that consent is conditional. It rests on the belief that force is governed by human judgment aligned with shared values. Autonomy complicates the picture. If a machine can recommend or initiate a strike, where is the human judgment? If decisions are informed by opaque models, where is the shared value?

Without public oversight, autonomy risks becoming a priesthood—obscure experts interpreting inscrutable algorithms on behalf of a confused laity. That is a dangerous model for democratic power. Citizens should not need a doctorate in machine learning to understand why their government can, in principle, let a system track targets or disrupt communications. They need assurance that elected representatives ask hard questions, and that independent auditors are allowed to verify answers.

Parliamentary oversight offers this backbone. Briefings that occur only behind closed doors create the illusion of scrutiny without the substance. Committees must be empowered to demand operational audits, question commanders, and inspect training data and model governance. A public summary of those hearings—stripped of names but rich in standards—signals accountability without compromising security. Democracies weaken themselves when they hide more than they must.

Transparency also strengthens deterrence. Adversaries watch how democracies manage their weapons. When they see clear procedures, disclosed incident reviews, and public discipline after wrongful use, they realise that democratic restraint is a feature, not a fragility. It signals seriousness. It shows that autonomy is not a loophole to escape responsibility. In contrast, opacity signals nervousness. Powers that hide their mistakes teach others to assume they have something to hide.

Critics argue that public disclosure might reveal vulnerabilities. The fear is understandable but exaggerated. Commercial aviation publishes safety bulletins after accidents without revealing classified avionics. Hospitals share infection data without disclosing patient identities. Banks report cyber breaches without exposing every control. Mature systems recognise that transparency and security reinforce each other. The same logic applies here. Autonomy is too significant a shift in the conduct of force to be shrouded in technical mystique.

There is also a moral dimension. When autonomous systems misidentify a target, glitch during an operation, or cause unintended harm, victims and families deserve a path to acknowledgement. Secrecy deepens their grief. Clear reporting mechanisms—both domestic and international—help repair legitimacy. They demonstrate that the state accepts responsibility, not merely risk management. Civilian harm tracking has existed in counterterrorism operations for years. Automated or semi-automated operations should not be exempt.

Public consent is not just about mistakes. It is about preparation. Annual posture statements and public briefings clarify strategy: what threats autonomy is meant to deter, what rules govern engagement, how human oversight works. Citizens understand trade-offs better than elites assume. Most people know that modern conflict is messy. What they resent is being treated like subjects rather than stakeholders.

There is another reason to take civic consent seriously: technology moves faster than morality, but legitimacy cannot be rushed. If governments fail to explain, citizens will fill the silence with speculation. Conspiracy grows in secrecy's vacuum. Social media already magnifies distrust; the notion of silent machines acting on secret orders is fertile ground for misinformation. Clear communication inoculates against fantasy.

Democratic militaries sometimes fear that transparency will provoke anti-military backlash. More often, it prevents it. Public debate does not weaken national defence; it roots it in shared values. Democracies win long wars not merely through firepower but through legitimacy. Citizens support institutions they believe are honest. They abandon those that appear arrogant or inscrutable.

Some of the most respected armed forces in the world maintain open relationships with the public: publishing operational codes, setting out ethical frameworks, and acknowledging constraints. They recognise that consent is not static. It must be renewed, argued for, and earned. Autonomous forces demand the same renewal.

There is a subtle threat beneath all of this. If governments treat autonomous defence as too complex for public discussion, they risk hollowing the very basis of democratic force. Power becomes technocratic rather than accountable. The nation fights through machines, controlled by specialists, justified by secrecy. That model is efficient—but only until the public rebels. Legitimacy is slower than autonomy but stronger when earned.

The future battlefields will be saturated with sensors, data, and autonomous agents. But the authority to unleash them must still come from citizens, expressed through transparent governance. Civic consent is not fragile. It is resilient when nourished. Democracies do not need slogans about "trust us." They need evidence: oversight, reports, and the candid admission that no system is infallible.

So the unresolved question remains: will democratic governments choose openness and earn durable consent, or will they cling to secrecy until mistrust becomes irreversible? The answer will determine not only how autonomous systems are deployed, but whether the public continues to grant its armed forces the moral mandate to act in their name.

## International humanitarian law, reinterpreted

The first autonomous artillery round that landed in a residential street did not break international law. The battery had targeted a military convoy. The convoy had taken shelter between apartment blocks, one lorry parked beneath a balcony. The machine identified the vehicle, calculated the probability of civilian presence, and initiated fire. When the dust settled, two civilians were injured and a child was cut by flying glass. The state issued a statement: the system behaved as designed. Yet the families asked a simpler question—*who decided*?

The paradox of modern conflict is not that international humanitarian law (IHL) has become obsolete, but that it suddenly matters more. Automation does not dissolve responsibility; it amplifies the need for clarity. The enduring principles—distinction, proportionality, precaution, humanity, military necessity—were forged in a world of human perception and human pace. Now, decisions can unfold at the speed of distributed computation, with sensor fusion guiding actions across air, sea, cyberspace, and urban terrain. The law was written in sentences; the battlefield now speaks in probabilities.

The most dangerous misconception is that autonomy requires a new legal system. It does not. What it requires is reinterpretation: a translation of timeless principles into technical design. Distinction is still distinction. A child is still a child, a hospital still a hospital. But when machines assist in selection, the test shifts from *Can a person tell the difference?* to *Can a system reliably encode the difference, and can a human operator foresee when it might fail?*

This notion of foreseeability is the hinge. Commanders have always been expected to anticipate collateral harm. With autonomous systems, anticipation becomes partly statistical. If a model has a known failure mode—say, misidentifying ambulances at night—then deploying it in low-light conditions may breach precaution. The rule does not change; the standard of knowledge does. A force cannot hide behind mystery. It must show that it *knew* its tools, that it tested them, and that it held back when confidence collapsed.

In practice, this demands rigorous logging. When an incident occurs, investigators must be able to reconstruct what a model saw, what threshold triggered action, which human authorised escalation, and whether the system behaved within its demonstrated limits. Without traceability, accountability collapses. The old legal question—*Why did the commander act?*—transforms into *Why did the commander trust the system, and what evidence supported that trust?*

Traceability becomes a legal safeguard rather than a bureaucratic chore. Logs, model versions, and command authorisations form the backbone of post-incident review. A state that cannot produce them is a state that cannot prove compliance. This is why serious programmes already mandate retention windows: months or years of telemetry, decision thresholds, override events, and training data lineage. If international law rests on responsibility, autonomous warfare cannot rely on guesswork. It must be auditable.

Critics worry that logs can be forged or suppressed. They are correct to be wary. But digital chains of custody, hashing, and independent oversight bodies strengthen integrity. Some nations are experimenting with cryptographic attestation: systems that sign their decision pathways so that commanders cannot later deny what actually happened. This sounds technical, but it is simply a digital form of the handwritten war diary—a record that can be inspected by courts, allies, and even adversaries in negotiations.

The real shift is cultural. In the past, a commander might invoke good faith. Tomorrow, they will be expected to invoke data.

Proportionality is another principle that survives, though its application changes texture. A human commander weighs likely civilian harm against military advantage. Autonomous decision aids calculate expected harm, sometimes with chilling precision: predicted blast radius, civilian density estimates, structure fragility. Yet proportionality is not a mathematical equation; it is a value judgment. Machines can inform judgement but cannot define it.

This is where the principle of human control remains indispensable—not as sentiment, but as law. States that delegate lethal authority without mechanisms for oversight risk breaching proportionality simply by default. If a system acts faster than a human can intervene, then the state must prove that pre-set thresholds embodied the proportionality test. Claims of "the algorithm decided" will not survive legal scrutiny.

The fear that autonomy erodes humanity often misses this nuance. Machines do not remove compassion; poorly governed systems remove accountability. Properly governed systems can encode caution: reject uncertain identifications, de-escalate when sensors degrade, and request human confirmation in ambiguous environments. These are not moral fantasies; they are design features.

Precaution, too, evolves. In traditional doctrine, precaution meant checking the target, warning civilians, or choosing weapons that minimise collateral harm. In autonomous operations, precaution begins before deployment. It includes training data audits to prevent systematic misidentification, model evaluation in environments resembling the battlefield, and scenario testing for failure cases. If a system has only been tested on clear satellite imagery, using it in fog-heavy mountain valleys may violate precaution, even if no law explicitly mentions fog or valleys.

Failure to test becomes a failure of law. The principle demands foresight. Autonomy demands even more.

This is where international humanitarian law becomes unexpectedly practical: it rewards engineering discipline. A state that can show its models underwent red-team testing, bias evaluation, and civilian harm simulations is not merely showing technical excellence. It is demonstrating legal compliance. The best engineers are becoming custodians of legal principles, whether they choose to or not.

What of distinction—the bedrock rule requiring separation of civilians and combatants? Autonomy does not change its moral force, but it complicates its implementation. Sensors can be spoofed. Identifiers can be forged. Civilian behaviour may resemble hostile movement, especially in crowded cities. If a system misidentifies a journalist's camera as a weapon once, is it error? If it happens repeatedly, is it negligence?

The answer lies again in foreseeability. If a model is brittle, operators must know where. They must restrict its use accordingly. No-state can deploy a system in environments where it is known to fail and then claim compliance because the code contained no malicious intent. Good faith is insufficient. Good engineering becomes a legal obligation.

Some militaries are building "no-strike" databases that hardcode protected sites: schools, hospitals, cultural landmarks. When autonomy is involved, these lists cannot be mere text files. They must be geofenced, versioned, and actively checked against every targeting request. A strike that bypasses the list becomes a traceable violation, not an unfortunate oversight. Once again, the law asks: could a responsible actor have prevented this? If the answer is yes, no technology excuses the failure.

The principle of humanity—the prohibition of unnecessary suffering—might seem simple. Yet autonomy forces new questions. What counts as unnecessary in a world where a machine can track a single vehicle for hours without fatigue? If a slower shot would expose soldiers to risk, does a machine-fired faster shot count as "necessary"? Autonomy shifts tactical options. The law must reinterpret necessity in the light of new capabilities, not old habits.

Then there is military necessity itself. Autonomy promises efficiency: fewer troops at risk, faster neutralisation, reduced collateral damage through precision. But necessity cannot be used as a blanket licence. If a system can disable an enemy engine rather than destroy the vehicle, necessity might require de-escalation. If behaviour can be stopped by jamming, hacking, or sensor blinding, destruction may no longer be legally available as the first response. Autonomy offers alternatives; the law may demand them.

All of this requires traceability. A machine battlefield without records is a legal void. Nations that store telemetry for hours will find themselves accused of hiding the truth. Nations that store it for years may resent the burden, but they will possess something more valuable than convenience: demonstrable compliance. Log retention is to autonomous conflict what body cameras are to policing—not a guarantee of virtue, but a safeguard against denial.

Some states will resist. They will claim strategic secrecy, technological sovereignty, or operational urgency. Yet history shows that armies which reject transparency often find themselves distrusted abroad and disgraced at home. International humanitarian law is not a punishment; it is a shield. It protects civilians, yes—but it also protects the integrity of the forces that obey it.

The reinterpretation of IHL is therefore less about rewriting rules than about expanding competence. Commanders must understand probability, not merely maps. Lawyers must understand models, not merely manuals. Engineers must understand legal obligations, not merely specifications.

The battlefield will demand polyglots—leaders who can translate between law and code, ethics and telemetry.

The unresolved tension is stark. Can states build systems that act at machine speed while preserving accountability at human speed? Can logs, oversight, and operational restraint keep pace with self-directing sensors and distributed swarms? Will the temptation to circumvent public scrutiny overwhelm the discipline that humanitarian law requires?

International humanitarian law has endured because it adapts without surrendering its core. The machines are new. The principles are not. What changes now is whether nations treat those principles as burdens—or as the democratic scaffolding that allows lethal power to remain legitimate in a world of automated force.

# Chapter 9

# Treaties, Norms, and the Possible

A diplomat once joked that negotiating technology treaties is like "trying to nail fog to a moving wall". Everyone agrees the fog is real, everyone knows the wall keeps shifting, and yet there is political theatre in pretending that resolution lies one meeting away. The joke was meant to be cynical. It is oddly hopeful instead. Fog does not vanish because it is hard to grasp; walls do not stand still because the world wants simplicity. States find ways to fix handholds in messy reality. They always have.

The history of arms control is full of imperfect successes. Chemical weapons were never fully abolished, yet the taboo against their use is now so powerful that even rogue states frame violations as accidents. Nuclear material is still trafficked, and yet the Non-Proliferation Treaty has prevented a world of fifty nuclear-armed nations. Treaties fail often in detail and triumph unexpectedly in culture. Formal agreements matter less than the shared assumptions they create.

AI will be no different. Those who dream of sweeping bans are destined to collide with geopolitics. Those who insist nothing can be done are wrong as well. The future belongs to a third path: slim baselines, shared technical expectations, mild but meaningful verification, and commitments that travel even across rival blocs. The story of treaties in AI will not be grand or glamorous. It will be incremental, administrative, and astonishingly consequential.

Calls for outright prohibition appear whenever a technology feels frightening. They contain moral clarity and political comfort: draw a line, outlaw the line, punish the transgressor. It sounds elegant. It also dissolves in contact with reality. No major power will unilaterally abandon machine intelligence in national defence. No alliance will sacrifice strategic parity while adversaries accelerate research. Bans feel principled until they meet national interest. Then they fade.

Baselines, however, travel. A state can refuse to renounce autonomy while agreeing that models must be tested before deployment. It can reject disarmament while accepting the need for incident reporting. It can keep its secrets while committing to basic safety evaluations. These are not grand gestures. They are small, hard commitments, the kind that survive domestic politics and geopolitical tension. The nuclear age learned this lesson early: verification is rarely perfect, but confidence-building is powerful.

A baseline is not a promise of virtue. It is a promise of procedure. Test before deploy. Retain logs for investigation. Maintain human override. Share incident taxonomies so that when a rival's system misfires, the world recognises the vocabulary of failure. These norms do not prevent competition; they prevent catastrophe disguised as competition.

The most radical idea in modern arms control is deceptively simple: confidence-building measures for code. Missiles were once tracked by satellites; weapons silos were inspected by foreign officers. Code has no silo. It lives in data centres and firmware, in weights and biases impossible to list in a treaty annex. Yet all is not lost. Software can be signalled.

States can commit to notifying each other before live deployment of a new autonomous weapon class. They can share safety test results without revealing architecture. They can designate no-go targets for any system that acts with machine-speed—hospitals, humanitarian convoys, nuclear facilities—then publish proof that these are hard-coded into their decision thresholds. Hotlines can trigger machine-level failsafes: a call from one state signalling accidental escalation could automatically suspend high-risk autonomy modes until humans re-authorise them.

It sounds fanciful only to those who forget history. The Cold War maintained hotlines capable of stopping nuclear launch sequences within seconds. Why should states trust code less than they trusted missiles?

Transparency does not require surrender. A shared incident taxonomy offers a lingua franca of malfunction: "classification ambiguity at threshold", "sensor spoofing false positive", "reinforcement loop escalation". States need not reveal their blueprints; they need only reveal the kinds of mistakes they fear most. Once vocabulary is shared, responsibility becomes mutual.

Verification is the perennial challenge. Inspectors cannot demand source code. Engineers will not allow foreign auditors to paw through proprietary models. The secret of arms control has always been the same: you do not verify intent, you verify behaviour.

Challenge trials offer one path. A state claims its system never fires without two confirming sensors; a neutral body supplies test data designed to confuse one sensor. If the system hesitates, the claim stands. If it fires, the claim falls. No source code required. Behaviour does not lie.

Provenance is another tool. If weights are trained on controlled datasets, cryptographic signatures can prove lineage without exposing content. Manufacturers already do this for intellectual property cases. The same mechanism can serve treaty compliance. Verifiers need not inspect the mind of the machine; they need only confirm the pedigree of its making.

This is the logic of arms control reborn for software. No x-rays for warheads; no white-glove inspections for code. Just behaviour under agreed tests, outcomes recorded, and consequences clear.

Some will call this naïve. They forget that arms control has never depended on perfection. It depends on friction. The purpose of verification is not to catch every violation; it is to make cheating harder, slower, and more diplomatically expensive. Perfection is theatre. Friction saves lives.

Regional regimes are inevitable. Universal compacts are rare even for mature weapons. More likely is a lattice of overlapping norms. Some nations will sign procurement-aligned pledges—contracts requiring that any autonomous system meets minimum testing standards, supports audit logs, and contains hard-coded no-strike classifications. Others will form inspection clubs, agreeing to share safety evaluations the way financial regulators share banking stress tests.

Clubs create leverage. If a coalition of states representing half the world's defence procurement demands baseline compliance, manufacturers will follow. Those who refuse will find export markets shrinking. Norms travel along supply chains faster than they travel along diplomatic cables.

But clubs invite suspicion. Non-members will worry about exclusion, about "technological cartels" that freeze their strategic growth. The answer, paradoxically, is openness: allow observer status, publish incident reports, create pathways for accession. Even rival blocs can adopt similar baselines while disagreeing on geopolitics. During the Cold War, both superpowers independently followed safety protocols that were never formally coordinated. Norms can converge without friendship.

The hard lesson is that universality is not the starting point. It is the destination. Regional regimes seed global norms by demonstrating that cooperation is possible at all.

Incrementalism is the only working strategy. Grand treaties emerge only after small norms become boring. The path begins with transparency: annual posture statements, public briefings, even redacted safety reports. Next comes testing: adoption of shared evaluation frameworks, cross-lab competitions to detect vulnerabilities, publication of anonymised failure cases. Thresholds follow: commitments to human authorisation for specific classes of lethal action, safeguards for protected sites, automatic abort criteria during sensor degradation.

Coalition pilot compacts will lead the way. A handful of states, willing to demonstrate restraint without sacrificing capability, will adopt shared standards. They will run joint challenge trials. They will publish joint incident logs. And when a minor mishap inevitably occurs, the world will see what accountability looks like in practice.

This is how norms form: not through speeches, but through administration. Once procedures exist, critics lose ground. Once incident reviews are routine, deniability collapses. Transparency, testing, thresholds—each step a constraint that does not impede power, only sharpens its responsibility.

Sceptics ask whether any of this matters in a world of rivalry. History answers them. The most hostile nations have accepted arms control when they recognised that mutual catastrophe lay one false move away. AI is no different. Autonomy introduces speed, ambiguity, and the risk of accidental escalation through algorithmic error. Even adversaries understand that miscalculation is a greater threat than malice.

A state can race to lead while still agreeing not to let its machines shoot first in the dark.

The deeper truth is that treaties and norms do not exist to make states virtuous. They exist to make states predictable. Predictability is the bedrock of deterrence. Without it, every radar blip is a potential war. When machines act faster than diplomats, norms become survival tools.

The coming decades will not produce a shining global charter that solves autonomy. They will produce footnotes, annexes, procurement rules, and technical standards. They will produce dull administrative miracles that keep crises from becoming wars. The work will be boring, until the day it averts disaster. Then it will be remembered as genius.

The possible is narrow, but it is real. Baselines can travel. Confidence can be built. Verification can rely on behaviour, not secrets. Clubs can open their doors. Compacts can be sequenced. The fog will never vanish, but nations can nail enough of it to the moving wall to prevent catastrophe.

The reader knows what comes next in this chapter: the details of those baselines, the scaffolding of trust, the mechanisms that turn good intentions into enforceable practice. The world will not wait for ideals. It will settle for mechanisms that work—and mechanisms, as history shows, are how peace is kept when perfect cooperation remains out of reach.

## From bans to baselines

The most desperate negotiations in history have shared the same uncomfortable ritual. Someone proposes a ban—total, sweeping, absolute. Heads nod, cameras flash, speeches are drafted. Then the details arrive. What counts as a weapon? What counts as dual-use? How do you verify compliance without giving away secrets? Within weeks the grand prohibition shrinks to footnotes, caveats and exceptions. It is tempting to call this failure. It is, more often, the beginning of progress.

AI autonomy has already entered this familiar theatre. Activist groups demand outright bans on autonomous weapons. Defence ministries reply with polished ambiguity. Diplomats try to find moral clarity in a fog of machine logic, dual-use components, and strategic fear. Every side can quote history and ethics. Every side insists it is acting responsibly. And every side knows that total prohibition will fail at the first collision with geopolitical reality.

Yet something quieter is happening beneath the speeches. The world is not drifting towards an unregulated arms race. It is drifting towards baselines: minimal, enforceable, technically grounded rules that travel between rivals because they cost little and prevent catastrophe. Bans are moral proclamations. Baselines are engineering choices.

To understand why bans struggle, one must start with the fundamental mismatch between law and innovation. Prohibition works only when the forbidden object is both visible and unambiguously evil. Landmines were slow to remove from battlefields, but at least they were discrete weapons. Chemical agents could be catalogued, traced and detected. Even nuclear warheads, at colossal diplomatic cost, could be inspected with seals, satellites and x-rays.

AI systems do not sit obediently in crates. They live in software updates, firmware patches, cloud deployments and a thousand dual-use models that change weekly. A ban cannot simply say "no lethal autonomy": what qualifies? A missile defence interceptor identifying targets at speed—is that autonomy or classification? A loitering drone that navigates autonomously but fires only with human confirmation—is that banned or permitted? One ambiguous definition becomes a loophole; two become an invitation to cheat; three become an unratified treaty.

The second problem is trust. A ban requires transparency. Transparency requires disclosure. No serious defence laboratory will hand over its source code to foreign inspectors. The paradox is obvious: the more advanced a system becomes, the less likely a state is to reveal its internals. Even allies hesitate. The result is deadlock—moral certainty colliding with national secrecy.

And yet, the story does not end there. Because while bans stall, baselines quietly advance.

A baseline is a minimum procedure, not a moral declaration. Test before deploy. Retain logs for accountability. Maintain human override for defined classes of action. Report incidents above a threshold. None of these commitments require disarmament. None demand that a great power reveal its architectural secrets. They solve a simpler, more urgent problem: avoiding catastrophe by accident.

Test-before-deploy is perhaps the most illustrative example. It does not ask a state to restrain its ambitions. It asks only that a new autonomous targeting model run through audit simulations before entering a live theatre. The simulation parameters can be shared without revealing architecture. The failure cases can be published without compromising classified capabilities. Crucially, test-before-deploy helps everyone: the state that fields the system, the rivals watching nervously, and the civilians who live beneath the flight paths.

This is how baselines travel. Not because nations suddenly agree, but because they quietly discover that responsible procedures are cheaper than diplomatic fires.

History supports this pattern. The taboo on chemical weapons did not take hold because every state suddenly became humane. It took hold because commanders realised that gas was unreliable, hard to control, and politically ruinous. The Non-Proliferation Treaty did not end nuclear ambition. It created paperwork, monitoring, and inspections that slowed proliferation enough for deterrence to work. In both cases, the world did not get morality; it got administration—and administration worked.

The AI equivalent will be more technical, less theatrical. A ban is a speech. A baseline is a checklist.

Consider autonomous sensor fusion—multiple AI subsystems that classify, track and assess targets. A ban could outlaw this entirely, but any state fearing hypersonic missiles will ignore it. A baseline, however, can require that autonomous fusion systems refuse to fire based on a single ambiguous sensor. Two independent confirmations, logged and auditable, create a safety floor without revealing the system's inner logic. Rivals can verify behaviour through challenge trials, not code access. The state keeps its competitive advantage; the world reduces the risk of algorithmic misfire.

Baselines do not remove competition. They prevent competition from careening into tragedy.

There is also a political truth rarely admitted aloud. Governments love to signal virtue while quietly preserving capability. Baselines enable this double act. A minister can announce that the nation recognises the "grave moral weight" of artificial autonomy while signing a policy that merely standardises audit logs and review thresholds. Critics call this incrementalism. Engineers call it progress.

The critics are not entirely wrong. Baselines are modest. They avoid the grand gesture. They refuse to draw bright moral lines. And for those who believe autonomy should never cross the threshold into lethal decision-making, baselines can feel like compromise.

But baselines do something bans never manage: they scale. They can be embedded in procurement contracts, export licences, military doctrine and industry standards. They can survive election cycles. They can be copied by rivals without diplomatic ceremony. They can be enforced by software itself—a system that will not arm until test certificates are present.

Every regulation that endures began this way: first as a technical inconvenience, then as habit, then as norm.

The most revealing case study is incident reporting. A ban on autonomous strikes sounds principled until a state claims that its system is only "decision-assisting", not "decision-making". But incident reporting bypasses that argument. It simply requires that any malfunction, misclassification or unintended engagement be logged, audited and—above a threshold—shared with oversight bodies.

A state can deny that it used autonomy. It cannot deny that an incident occurred.

This is why transparency, not prohibition, becomes the backbone of safety. Logs speak when architectures are silent. Procedural norms outlast diplomatic language. A ban can be signed today and violated tomorrow. A baseline, once woven into technical processes, is harder to escape.

There is a deeper philosophical point, rarely voiced but universally felt: bans demand trust; baselines build it. A ban assumes virtue—that states will voluntarily restrain themselves. A baseline assumes self-interest—that states will follow minimal procedures because the alternative is instability, suspicion, or reciprocal escalation.

Trust built on virtue collapses quickly. Trust built on shared self-interest is remarkably durable.

A rival may not believe your speeches, but they will believe your audit logs. They may not admire your morality, but they will respect your system design if it prevents accidental escalation. In strategic technology, predictability is the closest thing to peace.

Some argue that baselines are too weak, that the world needs the symbolic power of a ban. But symbolic power is cheap. Administrative power is priceless. The first cyber norms did not begin with sweeping treaties; they began with phone calls between security chiefs, informal rules of engagement, and quiet understandings about critical infrastructure. Years later, those unwritten baselines hardened into diplomatic language.

The future of AI autonomy will repeat this story. A cluster of pragmatic commitments—test-before-deploy, incident reporting thresholds, human override for protected targets, cryptographic provenance for high-risk models—will gradually form the skeleton of global norm-making. Some states will adopt them publicly. Others will adopt them silently. A few will resist until an accident forces their hand.

No one will call these changes revolutionary. They will be administrative, incremental, and utterly transformative.

The great irony is that baselines often achieve what bans promise. They reduce harm, prevent escalation, and enshrine accountability. And they do so without demanding that nations abandon self-defence, secrecy or strategic ambition. The law does not need to convert the world; it only needs to constrain it.

The deeper risk is not that baselines are too weak. It is that they arrive too late—after a catastrophic misfire, after a machine makes a decision that no diplomat can explain, after escalation outruns negotiation. The world has a narrow window to normalise safety before fear replaces reason.

Which leaves an urgent, unanswered question: will states choose the unglamorous work of building baselines now, or wait until tragedy forces them into existence?

In the theatre of arms control, bans make headlines. Baselines make history.

## Confidence-building for code

On a grey morning in 1983, a Soviet early-warning system reported five incoming American missiles. The alert chain jolted awake. Consoles flashed. Protocol demanded immediate retaliation. But the duty officer, Stanislav Petrov, hesitated. The data felt wrong. It was too small an attack for a real first strike. He overrode the warning. The missiles never arrived; the machines had misread reflected sunlight. One decision, taken by a single sceptical human, averted a war.

That moment lives in strategic folklore. Yet its lesson is rarely understood: what prevented catastrophe was not a dazzling treaty or a perfect machine. It was a fragment of trust—an instinct that the other side would not strike without warning, that missile trajectories meant something, that signals, however noisy, usually told a story.

In the age of autonomous models and algorithmic command systems, we need something stranger: confidence-building for code. Machines do not feel instinct. They do not sense when something is "too small" or "too strange". And adversaries cannot rely on a Petrov-style intervention when decision cycles shrink to milliseconds. If deterrence is to endure, nations must build technical rituals of reassurance: notifications, hotlines, shared signals, and lists of digital no-go zones. In other words, they must teach their code to do what Petrov did—signal, hesitate, and let cooler minds intervene.

The first and most basic tool is notification. During the Cold War, states used "nuclear notifications" to announce missile tests or satellite launches, preventing misinterpretation. A modern equivalent must operate at software speed. When a state spins up a high-risk autonomous model—say, an AI-enabled missile defence network or an autonomous maritime swarm—it could send a brief, cryptographically signed notice to a secure diplomatic channel. The message need not disclose architecture or purpose.

It can simply flag that a new model is being trialled in a region where sensors might misinterpret behaviour.

Sceptics will argue that no great power will tip its hand. Yet the logic cuts both ways. An unexpected spike in activity—a thousand new inference nodes activating across a border cloud—can be more alarming than a short, factual heads-up. Transparency becomes a tool of self-interest. You do not share secrets; you share context. And context prevents panic.

Hotlines extend this logic. Military hotlines already exist between major powers, but they are built for commanders, not engineers. A code hotline connects technical officers: cybersecurity specialists, model-risk leads, telemetry analysts. If a rival system behaves erratically—say, a rogue drone swarm drifts across a border due to a GPS spoofing incident—engineers can talk directly, explain anomalies, and coordinate safe disengagement. The mere existence of such channels changes incentives. It signals that neither side wants a training glitch to become an international crisis.

The most powerful confidence-building tools are not diplomatic at all. They are operational: common no-go targets for models. States could agree that certain categories of infrastructure—nuclear command nodes, hospitals, humanitarian corridors, civilian airliners—are off-limits for autonomous targeting, even indirectly. This does not require trust in virtue. It requires each state to embed "dumb" tripwires in their models: classification checks that simply refuse to lock onto protected classes, regardless of higher-order logic. A model that cannot target a hospital, even under spoofed data, reassures rivals without revealing architecture.

These agreements are not utopian. They already exist in softer form. Maritime law protects hospital ships; humanitarian zones are marked on military maps; nuclear early-warning networks use distinct identifiers to prevent spoofing. The shift is to encode these norms into machine logic rather than human memory.

Of course, no-go zones require verification. Rivals will not trust claims of constraint unless they can see evidence when something goes wrong. This is where shared incident taxonomies matter. Instead of each state inventing its own language—"anomaly", "misfire", "operator error"—they create a common vocabulary for failures. A Category-1 incident might mean a model acted outside human intent but caused no harm. Category-2 could involve civilian risk with near-misses. Category-3 could denote unintended lethal engagement.

A shared taxonomy does two things. First, it reduces ambiguity. When a state announces a Category-2 incident, rivals know exactly what that means, how serious it was, and what remedial steps follow. Second, it signals honesty. A state that publicly acknowledges low-tier incidents before they spiral into scandal shows seriousness. Silence is suspicious. Routine disclosure becomes a badge of responsibility.

The most ambitious step is shared telemetry. Rivals will never exchange raw training data or weights. But they can exchange provable summaries of behaviour: cryptographic proofs that a model passed a regulatory test suite; hashes of audit logs that can be inspected after a dispute; stimulus-response traces from controlled challenge trials. In nuclear arms control, satellites and seismic stations substituted for inspectors. In AI arms control, behavioural telemetry substitutes for code access.

The logic is the same: observe the surface to infer the core.

Critics scoff at these mechanisms, insisting that hard power will always trump procedure. They are half-right. No state will surrender a strategic edge. But history shows that confidence-building is not a gift to rivals; it is insurance for oneself. When machine-mediated systems interact—autonomous drones shadowing submarines, defensive models tracking missile launches—the greatest danger is not malice but misunderstanding.

Consider cyber warfare. Major powers now maintain "deconfliction channels" to prevent escalations triggered by malware spillover. Not because they trust each other, but because they distrust software. Autonomous models will require the same humility. A state may deploy a reconnaissance AI near a border. Local sensors, detecting unfamiliar patterns, might classify it as a strike preparation. Without a pre-agreed signal—an explicit message that the model is unarmed, unautonomous, or limited to observation—the risk of miscalculation rises.

Transparency does not invite attack. Opacity invites paranoia.

There is a deeper philosophical shift underway. Cold War confidence-building rested on human judgement. Diplomats understood coded language. Generals recognised ritual signalling: bomber overflights, naval transits, missile tests. Today's signals are invisible—model updates, data pipelines, cloud deployments. Reassurance must move into the technical substrate. The audience for confidence-building is not only politicians; it is monitoring algorithms, anomaly detectors, and alert filters on both sides.

That creates a peculiar demand: protocols that machines can parse. Notifications must be machine-readable, cryptographically signed, and automatically ingested into rival early-warning systems. No-go zones must be encoded as model constraints, not policy papers. Incident taxonomies must be formatted so automated monitors can detect when a rival shares a breach.

In short, confidence must be computable.

This may be the most radical departure from previous arms control. The architecture of trust becomes a software stack: notification schemas, proof-of-behaviour formats, hotline APIs, shared classification glossaries. Nations may fight over geopolitics, but their code will speak a common technical language. Many already do in cybersecurity: malware signatures, CVE numbers, and threat-intel feeds cross geopolitical divides because everyone fears the same catastrophic bugs.

AI autonomy will produce its own shared technical dialect. The earliest versions already exist in safety labs: red-team playbooks, interpretability metrics, adversarial stress tests. The challenge is exporting these from research to diplomacy.

None of this eliminates conflict. Rival states will still shadow each other; military AI will remain a tool of power. But confidence-building for code recognises a humbler truth: you cannot deter what you cannot understand. You cannot negotiate with telemetry you cannot read. And you cannot prevent an accident if you cannot distinguish an accident from an attack.

The opposite of trust is not hostility; it is confusion.

This is why the smallest signals matter. A brief notification before a risky model test. A public admission of a minor failure. A hotline call between engineers. These gestures buy time, reduce panic, and let humans intervene when the machines falter.

Petrov's instinct saved the world once. In the future, engineers will not be at the console. Models will observe models. Detectors will watch detectors. In that world, confidence-building is not diplomacy—it is survival.

The unanswered question is whether states will invest in these invisible guardrails while the window is still open, or whether the first catastrophic misunderstanding will force them into existence after the damage is done.

## Verification without X-rays

A curious contradiction sits at the heart of modern arms control: the most dangerous systems are the hardest to inspect. If a state fields a ballistic missile, satellites can count the launchers and watch the tests. If it stockpiles fissile material, inspectors can swipe for isotopes. But an autonomous weapons model leaves no plume, no reactor heat, no tell-tale signatures. Its capabilities are buried in patterns of weight matrices and training data—an arsenal that fits on a handful of encrypted drives. You cannot fly a drone over a data centre and "see" whether the models inside can decide life or death without human oversight. The world needs a way to check compliance without demanding source code or handing away strategic secrets. In other words, verification without X-rays.

Arms control has faced this riddle before. In the 1980s, when the United States proposed banning space-based missile defence systems, negotiators realised there was no reliable way to inspect satellites for hidden lasers. The answer was behavioural: prohibit certain test actions, monitor telemetry from launches, and watch for anomalies in orbital behaviour. If a satellite behaved like a weapon, it would be treated as one. You did not have to open the casing. You watched what it did.

Autonomous systems call for the same logic. You verify capability through behaviour, not disclosure. And you verify intent through provenance: where the model was trained, which datasets shaped it, what constraints were applied, and whether it can still be traced after deployment. The state keeps its intellectual property. The world keeps some guardrails.

The simplest form of behavioural verification is the challenge trial: a supervised test where a model is exposed to controlled scenarios known to provoke unsafe behaviour. Nuclear treaties use on-site missile inspections; pharmaceutical regulators use double-blind trials. For autonomy, inspectors could provide standardised adversarial stimuli—spoofed sensors, civilian look-alikes, ambiguous combatants—and record the model's choices. A model that refuses to fire on a hospital ship even in deceptive conditions demonstrates a constraint that matters far more than a promise. A model that escalates when communications are jammed reveals a risk that demands correction or containment.

Critics warn that challenge trials can be gamed: a state might tune a model to pass the test suite while remaining dangerous in the field. But this fear underestimates the difficulty of masking behaviour under stress. If tests are adaptive—tailored to the observed responses—and if inspectors can introduce randomised stimuli, the model must generalise safety, not memorise the exam. The very act of testing forces states to engineer robustness. It becomes easier to build constrained systems than to hide reckless ones.

Behaviour alone is not enough. A state could deploy a compliant model for inspection, then use a different model in conflict. This is where provenance matters. A well-designed model leaves a trail: hashes of weights, cryptographic fingerprints of training datasets, and secure audit logs of fine-tuning steps. These artefacts can be sealed at the time of challenge trials and later compared with deployed systems. If a model used in an incident does not match the sealed fingerprint, the discrepancy is clear. No need to reveal the contents—just the continuity.

This resembles how supply-chain security works for critical software today. Open-source communities already publish reproducible build hashes so anyone can verify that a binary matches the public source. States can adopt the same discipline for autonomous systems: reproducible weight builds tied to audit trails. The inspection body never sees the code. It merely checks whether two sealed signatures diverge. Verification becomes arithmetic, not espionage.

A subtler tool is behavioural attestation: cryptographic proofs that a model meets particular constraints, without revealing the constraints themselves. Zero-knowledge proofs—once a mathematical curiosity—now underpin commercial privacy systems and cryptocurrency protocols. They allow one party to prove that a secret satisfies a rule without exposing the secret. A nation could produce a zero-knowledge proof that its targeting model cannot initiate lethal force without human confirmation, or that it refuses to classify entities drawn from a protected no-strike list. Rivals gain assurance without access. Intellectual property remains untouched.

Sceptics argue that such proofs cannot capture the complexity of dynamic models. Yet techniques evolve rapidly. Hardware enclaves can execute sensitive code and produce attested logs. Formal verification methods already certify aircraft software and cryptographic protocols. If aviation can verify autopilot logic to safety-critical standards without publishing its source, defence systems can do the same for autonomy. The barrier is not mathematics; it is will.

There is an older analogue. Throughout the Cold War, the superpowers used "tags and seals" to track warheads without opening them. Inspectors affixed tamper-proof seals to missile casings. If a seal was broken, the weapon was presumed altered. Verification was symbolic but powerful: the seal's integrity mattered more than its contents. Cryptographic sealing of model provenance is the digital heir to this tradition.

Not all verification needs fancy cryptography. Some of the most effective tools are procedural. States can agree to maintain controlled copies of their deployed models in escrow—held by a neutral party or within a secure enclave—so that, if an incident occurs, the implicated model can be re-run against the scenario to investigate whether it behaved as designed or was tampered with. This mirrors flight data recorders in aviation: they do not reveal trade secrets but reconstruct what went wrong and why. The knowledge that a model could be replayed after the fact deters reckless design, just as the black box deters cutting corners in the cockpit.

Similarly, routine transparency reports matter. Autonomous models should produce machine-readable logs of key decision points: when they detected threats, how they scored targets, when they deferred to human operators. Logs need not reveal the inner logic. They only need to preserve enough context for analysts to trace a chain of events. International humanitarian law demands foreseeability and accountability. A model that cannot explain its choices cannot satisfy either.

Of course, logs can be forged. But cryptographic timestamping and cross-checking across redundant systems make forgery costly. States already use secure logging to track access to nuclear materials and sensitive cyber infrastructure. Extending these habits to autonomy is not speculative; it is a matter of copying best practice.

The thorniest problem is on-site access. Traditional arms control relies on inspectors visiting facilities. Yet no state will allow foreigners to wander through its AI labs. The alternative is remote verification through cooperative tests: the state spins up the model in an accredited cloud environment, controlled by its own security team, while inspectors observe inputs and outputs through a secure API. This is not science fiction. Financial regulators already run stress tests on banks using remote data feeds. Cybersecurity accreditors perform penetration tests on cloud services without seeing source code. Diplomats should adopt the same mindset: treat autonomous systems like critical infrastructure, not mystical secrets.

One might ask why any of this would work when geopolitics is driven by deception. The answer is simple: verification mechanisms are not for saints; they are for rivals who would rather avoid catastrophic surprises.

Behavioural audits reduce misinterpretation. Provenance trails expose covert escalation. And the knowledge that a model's misdeeds can be replayed later raises the political cost of reckless action. Verification is not trust; it is insurance against panic.

Yet a final paradox lingers. The very systems we seek to control are opaque even to their creators. Deep learning models cannot be perfectly explained. Interpretability is advancing but remains partial. If we cannot "open the box" ourselves, how can nations verify each other?

The answer lies in humility: stop pretending verification means omniscience. A pilot cannot see every line of code in an airliner, yet certification bodies verify its safety through rigorous trials and telemetry. Doctors cannot see every interaction in a drug, yet regulators verify its effects through clinical trials and pharmacovigilance. Behavioural verification is enough—if it is systematic, adversarial, and recorded.

The deeper question is whether states will accept verification that works like a defence in depth: behavioural challenge trials, sealed provenance logs, cryptographic attestations, and post-incident replays. No single mechanism suffices. Together, they create a chain that is hard to break and harder to fake.

That chain will be tested. States will attempt to cheat. Rogue actors will try to mask dual-use models as benign. But a world without verification is more dangerous than a world with imperfect verification. Great powers once learned to live with satellites watching every missile silo. They may have to learn to live with auditors watching their code's behaviour.

Some future crisis will hinge on these guardrails. A swarm of drones veers off course; a defensive system misclassifies a civilian airliner; a rival protests that a no-strike list was ignored. In that moment, logs, provenance trails, and sealed fingerprints may decide whether the world believes a system failed or a state lied. Verification without X-rays is not a luxury. It is the minimum price of peace in a world where arsenals are invisible.

And the question that remains, unsolved and urgent, is whether nations will build these mechanisms before the first accident forces them to—or after.

## Regional regimes

A small delegation gathers in a conference room on the outskirts of Brussels. No flags, no translation booths, no press. Just procurement officers, lawyers, and a handful of military technologists comparing notes on autonomy in weapons systems. Their governments are not negotiating a treaty—there is neither appetite nor leverage for that—but they are aligning procurement standards: what a defensive system must log, how human override must work, when a model must refuse to fire. No communiqué will be issued. Yet what happens in such rooms can shape the future of autonomous warfare far more than grand speeches at the United Nations.

This quiet diplomacy embodies a paradox. Global rules are ideal, but regional compacts get written. Universal treaties promise harmony, but club models—small groups of states that set shared standards—are often faster, tighter, and harder to water down. Arms control history is full of solemn declarations that never made it past the signing ceremony, yet procurement standards, export controls, and interoperability rules quietly remade the world. The airliner you board, the pharmaceutical you take, the encryption your bank uses—many of these are governed not by universal treaties, but by clubs that set tough standards and let the market enforce them.

Autonomous weapons are heading down the same path. Universal consensus is elusive: great powers distrust each other's motives, middle powers fear losing leverage, and non-aligned states resent being lectured. But regional regimes—coalitions bound by shared procurement rules—can move. If a dozen technologically advanced democracies require strong safety logs and human-on-the-loop overrides, any defence contractor selling into those markets must comply. Standards travel because supply chains do.

Club models are often derided as exclusive, but they sometimes become de facto global rules. Consider aviation. The International Civil Aviation Organization sets universal targets, yet the most demanding safety regulations originated in blocs such as the European Union and the United States. Manufacturers could not afford separate aircraft for permissive markets and strict ones. The stricter regime won by economic gravity. A similar dynamic played out in data privacy; European GDPR rules influenced software design worldwide. States that never voted for GDPR received stronger defaults because technology companies would not maintain two versions of their systems.

The same logic will apply to lethal autonomy. Most defence contractors sell to multiple governments. If several major buyers demand audit trails, no-strike list lockouts, and reproducible build signatures, contractors will bake those features into core designs. A regional regime becomes a global safety ratchet.

Still, club models have legitimacy challenges. States outside the club may claim they are being subjected to "norms by ambush": standards written without them, then exported through trade and interoperability. They may also fear dual-use constraints that strangle their own innovation. A club model must therefore strike a balance: strict enough to matter, open enough to attract new members, and transparent enough to avoid accusations of cartel behaviour.

One answer is procurement-aligned pledges: governments commit to buying only systems that meet certain safeguards, regardless of the supplier. These pledges are attractive because they are self-binding. No one forces a state to adopt them. But once adopted, market logic does the rest. Even firms outside the bloc will alter their products to compete. The pledge travels, step by step.

Universal compacts look more inclusive on paper. They aim to bind all states to a common floor of behaviour. Yet universality comes with a cost: the rules must be broad and vague enough for everyone to sign. Language that pleases diplomats may not constrain engineers. Some states will view universal agreements as a stage for propaganda, much as certain Cold War treaties accumulated impressive signatures and feeble enforcement.

Despite those weaknesses, universal compacts still matter. They draw a moral line in the sand. A state that violates a universal rule invites opprobrium and isolation. The Chemical Weapons Convention has not prevented every atrocity, but it has made chemical attacks rare, high-risk moves that attract global condemnation. If a universal compact on autonomous weapons established a prohibition—say, against systems that target humans without human authorisation—violators would pay a reputational price. Reputation is currency in geopolitics.

The tension, then, is between speed and scope. Club models move fast but lack broad legitimacy. Universal compacts move slow but create a shared ethical frame. The world may need both: clubs to raise practical baselines, and universals to articulate ideals.

Regional regimes can also serve as laboratories for policy. A small bloc can pilot mechanisms that would be unwieldy globally: shared incident taxonomies, common challenge trials, joint no-go target lists, or crisis hotlines for model malfunction. If those tools work, they can be offered to a wider audience. If they fail, their lessons will be absorbed quietly. Universal treaties rarely allow such experimentation. Clubs can afford to learn in public.

A striking example comes from cybersecurity. The Budapest Convention on Cybercrime has not been ratified by all, but it created a template for forensic cooperation and evidence standards. Meanwhile, regional blocs developed faster operational norms: breach notification rules, joint response teams, and shared threat databases. Over time, these club innovations influenced broader practice. The same dynamic could shape autonomous systems: a coalition could agree to share technical incident reports under strict confidentiality, creating the first trusted repository of failure modes. Other states, hungry for safety lessons, may follow.

The politics of exclusion is a risk. If a club appears to impose values rather than solve problems, it will struggle. The most successful regional regimes signal openness: membership grows with compliance, not ideology. The Nuclear Suppliers Group, though controversial, gradually attracted members by offering predictable access to sensitive materials under strict controls. Those who joined gained credibility and supply-chain security. Those who stayed out bore higher transaction costs. Even imperfect clubs can pull global practice toward safer norms.

There is a deeper philosophical question beneath all this: should rules about lethal autonomy arise from those who have the most power, or from those who have the most to lose? Universal compacts reflect the second view; club regimes, the first. The risk is that smaller states feel the world is being arranged without them. The danger is real. When powerful states dictate standards, resentment grows, and norms fracture.

One remedy is transparency. Clubs should publish their safeguards and allow external audits—not of their systems, but of their processes. They can host open technical workshops, share redacted lessons from incidents, and invite observers to challenge drills. This is not charity; it is strategy. Norms that are visible are norms that can spread.

Another remedy is modularity. Regional regimes need not demand full alignment overnight. A state might sign onto procurement pledges for logging first, then join challenge-trial exchanges later. Incremental entry lowers the political barrier. A modular club becomes a ladder, not a wall.

A final, understated weapon in regional regimes is interoperability. If armies want to fight alongside allies—and most do—they must adopt compatible standards. Interoperability becomes a Trojan horse for ethics. If a coalition requires that all partner systems maintain machine-readable logs of lethal decisions, any newcomer must upgrade to join. A state may not care about transparency for its own sake, but it will care about interoperability for operations. Ethics sneak in through the back door of logistics.

Yet there is a counterpoint. Regional regimes can harden geopolitical divides, creating a technological Iron Curtain. If one bloc adopts stringent safeguards and another rejects them, the gap becomes a fault line. Rival models may escalate in capability and risk. The world then faces a split: one side governed by safe defaults, the other racing without brakes. That scenario is not hypothetical. It has already played out in cyber operations and surveillance technology. The same could happen with autonomy.

This is the unresolved tension: club models may be the only path to rapid safeguards, but they may also deepen divides. Universal compacts may create shared principles, but they may arrive too late to prevent disaster. Somewhere between them lies a hybrid: regional pilots, global fora, and market incentives that let safety travel even where diplomacy stalls.

For the moment, the quiet rooms in Brussels—and in Singapore, Canberra, and Ottawa—matter more than the grandiose declarations. Procurement officers talking about log retention windows may do more to restrain dangerous autonomy than a thousand speeches. The question is whether the world will scale these experiments before the next crisis forces its hand.

## Path to incrementalism

A diplomat once joked that arms control only has two speeds: stalemate and crisis. Autonomous systems are testing that pattern. The world senses danger, yet sweeping treaties remain politically impossible. So policymakers have reached for a different instrument—the slow, meticulous art of incrementalism. Not grand bargains, but small steps that change what is normal to build, buy, and deploy.

Consider the first time a major coalition quietly agreed that any autonomous defensive system must store machine-readable logs of its targeting decisions. No cameras, no fanfare. Just a procurement note: no logs, no contract. Within months, contractors retrofitted models with audit trails because losing a buyer meant losing a market. A tiny rule achieved what no sweeping ban could: visibility. And visibility became habit.

This is the heart of incrementalism. You do not demand the world's militaries abandon autonomy overnight. You ask them to test before they deploy, to publish high-level safety summaries, to retain logs for independent review. You make compliance cheaper than defiance. And each new baseline raises the floor.

Incrementalism begins with transparency. Not transparency of source code—few states would accept that—but of behaviour. Militaries already publish declassified versions of missile tests to reassure allies and deter adversaries. Autonomous systems can follow the same pattern: states could release redacted summaries of failure modes, patch logs, or incident classifications. These disclosures need not reveal intellectual property; they simply show that someone is counting misfires.

A coalition of states could standardise this process. Shared taxonomies would allow meaningful comparison: near-misses, override activations, friendly-fire risks, sensor hallucinations. Today such terms vary between programmes. One military's "anomaly" is another's "catastrophic abort." A common vocabulary is a small step, yet transformational. It lets states compare notes, spot systemic weaknesses, and argue from evidence rather than speculation.

Transparency also forces internal discipline. When a ministry expects to publish a yearly safety briefing—even one scrubbed of secrets—programme managers take testing seriously. Politicians become aware of risks, parliaments ask sharper questions, and militaries budget for patching and retraining. A habit of disclosure begets a habit of caution.

The objection is familiar: transparency gives adversaries intelligence. That is partly true, but the risk can be managed. Nuclear-armed states share missile test notifications without describing warhead yield or targeting doctrine. They broadcast enough to avoid miscalculation, not enough to undermine defence. Autonomous systems can follow the same logic. Transparency is not confession; it is calibration.

After transparency comes testing—and not just laboratory testing. Models behave differently in the world than they do in simulation. Fog, smoke, rain, or cluttered electromagnetic environments can trigger bizarre classification errors. Autonomy needs operational stress tests: challenge trials that probe for brittle edges, deception resistance, collateral risk, and override responsiveness.

Who conducts such trials? Ideally, a mixed panel of engineers, lawyers, operators, and ethicists. Their job is not to veto autonomy; it is to map its limits. A system that performs perfectly against uniformed combatants might behave dangerously around civilians carrying metal tools. Another might struggle when adversaries deploy decoys or spoofed heat signatures. These vulnerabilities are discoverable—but only if someone bothers to look.

Coalitions can run joint challenge trials. Invite allied units to bring their systems to a secure range, share test scenarios, and pool lessons. Even without sharing code, you can share outcomes: which models hesitated, which misidentified, which asked for human confirmation. Over time, those lessons form a body of safety evidence more persuasive than diplomatic speeches.

Challenge trials also reveal an uncomfortable truth: some systems will fail. A responsible coalition does not hide that. Instead, it documents failure, patches models, and tests again. Better to find the bug at a range in Utah than on a street in Mosul. Incrementalism means accepting imperfection, then iterating until imperfect becomes tolerable and tolerable nudges upward to safe.

The hardest step is thresholds: deciding when autonomy is allowed and when it must yield to a human. These thresholds will never be fully universal, but regional convergence matters. One coalition might require human confirmation for any lethal action within range of civilians. Another might insist on human oversight when models classify potential combatants with less than a certain confidence score. A third could mandate automatic abort if a system detects ambiguity in sensor fusion.

Thresholds need not be moral sermons. They can be operational logic. A commander wants assurances: under what conditions might the system misfire? How often does it request human guidance? How does it behave when sensors degrade? Thresholds are simply rules that convert uncertainty into procedure.

The most realistic approach is progressive tightening. Initial deployments may allow autonomy in purely defensive roles, such as countering incoming munitions or drones far from civilians. Later, coalitions could require that any offensive autonomous system demonstrate traceability: the ability to explain why it fired, using logs retained for independent review. As models improve, thresholds can rise. The point is not perfection on day one, but steady attrition of unsafe behaviours.

Critics claim incrementalism is too slow. They are right to worry. Arms races move quickly, and norms move slowly. Yet incrementalism is not passive. It can accelerate through coalitions.

A coalition pilot compact is a powerful idea: a group of states voluntarily binds itself to transparency, testing, and thresholds. They agree to share redacted incident reports. They adopt common procurement standards. They establish a hotline for malfunctioning systems that could trigger escalation. They pledge not to purchase systems that lack machine-readable logs or override features. None of this requires the United Nations. It simply requires states with leverage choosing to use it.

Such compacts create a ratchet. Firms that want access to the coalition market must adopt its safeguards. Even sellers in non-member states face pressure; their buyers want interoperability. Over time, the compact becomes a magnet. States join not because they love norms, but because they need technology.

Critics will also argue that incremental safeguards are fig leaves—that they legitimise autonomy rather than restrain it. The counterpoint is pragmatic: autonomy is coming whether diplomats approve or not. The choice is not autonomy versus no autonomy; it is autonomy with brakes or without. Incrementalism installs brakes.

Incrementalism also recognises domestic politics. Leaders cannot always sign sweeping treaties without triggering backlash at home. But they can order their militaries to publish safety summaries. They can fund challenge trials. They can require procurement certifications. These measures are small enough to avoid political drama, yet substantive enough to matter.

History offers analogies. The most successful arms control has rarely come from the dramatic handshake. Radiation safety improved because regulators demanded shielding, containment, and monitoring. Aviation safety improved because investigators required black boxes, reporting obligations, and human-factor training. None of these reforms relied on perfect consensus. They relied on accumulating habits until they became normal.

Incrementalism thrives on boring details. Log retention windows. Override latency. Confidence thresholds. Human-on-the-loop doctrines. To the untrained eye, these are footnotes. To engineers and commanders, they are safety rails. When a coalition enshrines these rails in procurement rules, it forces industry to meet them. When industry meets them, norms silently spread.

There is, however, a danger in celebrating incrementalism: complacency. A world that grows comfortable with small steps may avoid larger ones. Transparency is reassuring, but transparency without accountability can become theatre. Challenge trials matter, but only if failures lead to real consequences. Thresholds are useful, but not if they are riddled with exceptions. Incrementalism must not become a ritual to pacify critics while systems remain dangerous.

Another danger is exclusion. Coalitions must be careful not to create a technological caste system. If well-resourced states adopt strong safeguards while poorer states cannot afford them, autonomy may become bifurcated: safe systems for the rich, risky ones for the rest. Incrementalism must therefore include capacity-building—sharing redacted test data, offering training, subsidising safety infrastructure. Norms spread faster when participation is possible.

A final tension is strategic timing. If one bloc advances safeguards while another ignores them, the safe bloc may lose confidence in restraint. Leaders may fear falling behind. Incrementalism is most effective when coalitions represent a critical mass of capability—large enough that defectors lose access to core supply chains or training networks. Norms enforced by markets are harder to escape.

Yet despite these risks, incrementalism remains the most credible path. Sweeping bans appeal to moral intuition but collapse under geopolitical stress. Vague universal agreements create symbolic legitimacy but weak operational discipline. Incrementalism is not utopian; it is practical. It accepts mistrust, rivalry, and technological flux—and builds rules that survive them.

Transparency, testing, thresholds: each step small, each step reversible, yet each step raising the cost of recklessness. A coalition pilot compact is not a treaty, but it is a scaffold. If it succeeds, it becomes a template. If it fails, others can learn from its mistakes. Incrementalism scales by imitation.

Somewhere in a classified testing ground, engineers are already conducting the next challenge trial. Somewhere in a ministry, lawyers are drafting the next procurement clause. These acts will not make headlines. But they will decide what future wars look like—and what they avoid.

The central question remains unresolved. Will incrementalism move fast enough to matter, or will crisis arrive first? The answer depends less on diplomats and more on those quiet clauses, those pilot compacts, those stubborn habits of caution. And habits, once woven into the machinery of war, can outlast the politics that created them.

# Chapter 10

# Strategy for the Long Game

In military history, the greatest errors rarely came from weak weapons. They came from confident leaders who thought they could win everywhere at once. The Maginot planners feared a repeat of trench warfare and fortified the wrong front. The Soviet Army in Afghanistan believed sheer numbers would overpower a decentralised foe. Power was not their problem. The strategy was. They fought the war they expected, not the war they faced. The future of AI systems invites the same trap: spreading effort thin across every trend, chasing headlines instead of advantage.

Early adopters of autonomous tools have already learned that the field punishes generalists. One small Baltic state, lacking the budget for grand fleets of drones, focused instead on something almost boring: navigation that could resist jamming. They poured talent and procurement into signal resilience. The result was modest, quiet, and decisive. When neighbouring exercises flooded the spectrum with interference, their drones kept flying. Allies took note. For a country with limited means, that niche advantage turned into leverage. It is a lesson that echoes beyond war rooms: strategy is not about doing everything—it is about choosing your hill and holding it.

Yet knowing which hill to choose requires rehearsal. Not once, but continually. The most successful militaries treat exercises not as theatre for journalists but as laboratories. They red-team assumptions, simulate sabotage, set traps for their own AI tools, and catalogue every failure. A quarterly red-team league inside a defence ministry sounds unglamorous. It is, however, a compounding asset. Each round reveals a brittle interface, a miscalibrated override, a tactic that no longer works. Over time, rehearsal becomes an intelligence system, one that exposes weaknesses before adversaries do.

There is a deeper logic here. Rehearsals are not add-ons; they are strategy's engine. Nations that practise relentlessly develop muscle memory for crises. They know what breaks when fog, sand, or corrupted GPS signals disrupt autonomy. They learn exactly when a drone pauses for human confirmation or when it attempts a fallback plan. These insights, accumulated through repetition, become as valuable as the hardware itself. You can buy technology; you cannot buy experience.

The coming decades will reward those who treat guardrails not as regulatory burdens but as strategic tools. A state that can demonstrate its autonomous systems are predictable, traceable, and testable has more credible deterrence. It can reassure allies, calm public opinion, and spread its systems across coalitions. Publishing a redacted test suite—a list of stress scenarios a system must survive before deployment—creates confidence at home and sends a signal abroad: we know what our machines do, even when the battlefield is ugly.

This is a quiet revolution. For decades, safety was seen as the domain of ethicists and lawyers. Now it is becoming a currency of power. A nation that offers autonomous systems with robust safeguards will find buyers; a nation that sells opaque systems may see them banned from joint operations. Guardrails become strategy, not compliance.

Another shift is underway inside capitols and parliaments. Leaders no longer want glossy briefings that promise miracles. They want governance. They ask which models escalate risk, under what conditions they fail, and how to communicate those realities to citizens who are both wary of AI and dependent on it. Teaching leaders to distinguish hype from capability becomes essential. Simple tools—risk ladders, confidence scores, operational thresholds—turn technical realities into comprehensible choices. Without that translation, politicians either panic or overcommit. Both are dangerous.

Publics matter too. Democracies cannot field systems their citizens do not trust. At the same time, governments cannot drown the public in jargon. Good governance means telling the truth about what autonomy can and cannot do. It means owning failure, not burying it. It means preparing society for a world in which machines act at machine tempo, and humans must set the rules in advance.

The most effective organisations are creating a new class of practitioner: part strategist, part engineer, part educator. Their job is to challenge extravagant claims, demand evidence, and insist on rehearsal. They treat every glossy presentation as a hypothesis to be tested. They ask simple, ruthless questions: what could go wrong, who is accountable, where are the logs, how fast can we shut it down? These are not the questions of sceptics. They are the questions of stewards.

This chapter offers something unusual in defence literature: a field manual for judgement. Not checklists that reduce complexity to tick-boxes, but frameworks that sharpen thinking. When a vendor touts breakthrough autonomy, you will know how to examine the capability stack. When an ally claims its system is fail-safe, you will know what evidence to demand. When your own organisation debates investment, you will know how to choose the hill that matters, rather than the hill that flatters your ambitions.

Across this chapter, the pattern repeats: smaller, smarter bets outperform sprawling wish-lists; rehearsal compounds faster than hardware; guardrails are signals of maturity, not weakness; and governance beats hype. It is the long game, played with discipline.

The real question is whether leaders will adopt this mindset before crisis forces it upon them. Because once conflict begins, the window for careful choice narrows. Those who practised will improvise. Those who guessed will learn in public. The reader now enters the practical core of the chapter—the place where theory meets planning, and planning meets reality.

## Choose your hill

The first mistake of ambitious nations is wanting everything. New sensors, new drones, new satellites, new doctrines—an arms race of catalogue shopping. Yet the states that quietly outperform their rivals tend to do the opposite. They pick one narrow problem, master it, and turn that mastery into influence.

A small Baltic defence lab demonstrated this with almost comic understatement. While regional militaries poured money into long-range strike drones and flashy autonomous swarms, the lab focused on something unglamorous: keeping aircraft on course when the sky is hostile. They studied signal spoofing, GPS corruption, terrain shadowing, and the sort of radio trickery that never makes headlines. After three years of stubborn iteration, their drones could navigate in environments where stronger nations' aircraft simply fell out of the sky. Engineers from larger states visited to learn how. The country went from consumer to teacher—without buying a single "game-changing" platform. They chose their hill, held it, and made it matter.

The lesson is older than AI. Strategy is not a talent for appetite, but a talent for exclusion. In complex competition, the side that tries to win everywhere often wins nowhere. Intelligence services call it prioritisation; militaries call it massing effects; economists call it comparative advantage. In modern autonomy, the stakes are sharper. Building a competent general-purpose system is ruinously expensive. Building a specialised, sovereign capability that no one else can easily copy is a bargain.

Most leaders know this in theory. The difficulty is emotional. Nobody enjoys admitting that their country or organisation cannot dominate every category of emerging technology. Yet the physics of time, talent, compute, and money do not bend. The question becomes: which hill is worth dying on? And the sharper question: which hill will your opponent ignore long enough for you to own?

Some nations choose terrain denial—making their airspace toxic to hostile autonomous systems through deception, electronic warfare, or cheap swarms of attrition drones. Others focus on logistics: routing autonomous convoys, maintaining fuel autonomy, or securing repair depots that keep machines alive. These are not cinematic priorities, but wars are won by movement and resupply, not glamour.

A country with extraordinary mathematicians but a small industrial base might specialise in cryptographic resilience: encrypted command channels, hardened mission data links, and tamper detection. Another with skilled machinists and a proud tradition of mechanical engineering might pursue modular drone chassis designed for fast field repair. Specialisation is not settling for less. It is deciding where you will outpace the world.

There is a philosophical thread beneath these examples. Autonomy is power, but power diffuses. Thirty years ago, only major powers could afford precision munitions. Today, garage workshops can produce loitering drones with frightening reliability. The arms race moves faster every year, and advantage evaporates unless someone slows the game and chooses carefully. The smartest states ask: where can we build an advantage that does not fade the moment a rival buys the same system from a vendor?

Consider anti-jam navigation. It sounds dull. Then imagine a crisis in which satellite signals are scrambled across a theatre, commercial receivers go blind, and autonomous patrol craft drift helplessly. One navy retains position because it invested in inertial backups, celestial correction, and terrain-matching algorithms. The difference between getting home and being lost at sea is not a miracle technology, but thousands of hours of disciplined focus.

Now contrast this with the impulse to build everything: swarms, hypersonics, cyber tools, deepfake operations, undersea robots, satellite constellations. Ambition becomes a quilt of half-built prototypes, a force structure full of demos that never matured. Defence ministries quietly admit that most of these projects will never see combat. They were procurement theatre, not strategy.

The fairest criticism of specialisation is fear of over-commitment. What if the hill you choose turns out to be irrelevant? What if a breakthrough renders your advantage obsolete? These are real risks. But they underline a brutal truth: generalisation does not save you from obsolescence; it only guarantees mediocrity in more places. A focused capability may be overtaken, but until then it wins real battles. And if the hill stops mattering, a focused organisation pivots faster than a scattered one.

Even superpowers benefit from focus. The United States Navy, faced with escalating drone threats, recently emphasised shipboard electronic warfare over more expensive missile-first responses. Israel's edge in air defence does not rest on purchasing every system, but on layered orchestration—radar, interceptors, electronic disruption, and short-range autonomous guards, tuned relentlessly in live conflict. China's hypersonic programme did not sprawl across every aerospace frontier; it moved stepwise on a small number of solvable technical questions. Nobody is too large to specialise.

Choosing a hill is not only technical. It is strategic storytelling. When a nation signals where it has chosen to excel, allies adjust their own investments, adversaries plan around it, and markets form supply chains. Specialisation attracts partners. A state known for robust navigation might collaborate with one known for resilient communications. A nation that perfects drone countermeasures might join coalitions that need its expertise. In a fragmented world, being indispensable is better than being impressive.

The temptation to skip this discipline is strongest during peacetime procurement. Officials want to show voters tangible progress: shiny drones, new cyber centres, glossy AI labs. But procurement theatre cannot hide the battlefield. When a crisis strips away illusions, only the things that work matter—and those things are usually the result of unglamorous, narrow grind. The future of conflict is a contest of robustness, not spectacle.

This subchapter lives in the human world as much as the technical one. Leaders who lack the courage to choose create organisations that cannot learn. Engineers who attempt to build everything produce fragile complexity. Analysts who track all threats become experts in none. The humility to specialise is a form of intellectual honesty: an acceptance that mastery has borders.

So how should a nation—or an organisation—choose the right hill?

Start with geography, doctrine, and identity. A coastal state with shallow waters might choose autonomous mine-hunting and port protection. A country with mountainous terrain might build terrain-following drones that can survive radar shadows. A landlocked power might prioritise cyber-physical resilience: keeping autonomous ground vehicles alive when satellites fail. The point is not fashion; the point is fit.

Next, resist the glamorous. A hypersonic programme might win headlines, but could swallow decades and deliver marginal advantage. Anti-jam navigation, precision logistics, autonomous repair, hardened sensors—these are the capabilities adversaries hate because they cannot be easily copied. When a specialist hill becomes a chokepoint in the battlespace, everyone suddenly wants a road through it.

Finally, measure progress ruthlessly. The danger of specialisation is believing your own myth. A nation that claims excellence must prove it continually: stress tests, red-teaming, hostile trials, open demonstration of performance under deception and jamming. Quiet mastery is powerful; self-flattery is fatal.

There is an old infantry lesson: if you defend everything, you defend nothing. Autonomy makes the lesson harsher. If you build everything, you understand nothing. Specialisation forces clarity. It forces research programmes to abandon vanity projects. It forces commanders to adjust doctrine around real strengths. It forces politicians to face trade-offs instead of slogans.

And in a world where small states now wield influence, the logic becomes democratic. A nation that picks a hill well can shape a region's security. A company that picks a hill well can shape an alliance's procurement. A research lab that picks a hill well can shift global standards. Power no longer belongs only to the biggest budgets; it belongs to those who are unreasonably good at something that matters.

There is tension here. Every leader fears choosing wrong. Every engineer fears backing the wrong architecture. But the deeper danger is paralysis. In a competitive world, refusing to specialise is itself a choice—one that hands advantage to those who dare to focus. The question is not whether you can afford to choose a hill. The question is whether you can afford not to.

The next crisis will not give anyone time to rediscover priorities. Drones will fall from the sky. Signals will jam. Clouds will blind satellites. Machines will act faster than committees. When that moment comes, the winners will be those who made their narrow strengths unavoidable.

Somewhere right now, a small lab is grinding quietly on a problem that looks boring until the day it is existential. The hill seems insignificant—until every other hill collapses. The only real uncertainty is whose hill that will be.

## Invest in rehearsal

The first autonomous convoy ambushed in a desert wadi did not fail for lack of hardware. Its sensors worked. Its communications link held. Its mapping software was flawless. What broke was the human layer above it. Commanders froze in uncertainty, operators hesitated, and legal advisers could not agree whether the convoy was authorised to fire back. The machines waited. By the time a decision arrived, the ambush was over. Systems built to move faster than human reaction were stopped not by enemy action, but by the absence of practice.

This is the paradox of technical power: without rehearsal, advanced capability shrinks to zero. Militaries know this in theory; organisations rarely absorb it in practice. They buy new autonomy, new simulation suites, and new decision-support tools, then deploy them into the field with only a sprinkling of training hours. What they lack is not software but muscle memory. The unit that rehearses more—red teams itself harder, fails faster, fixes ruthlessly—will defeat a superior machine that never learned to fight.

Rehearsal is not preparation for war; it is the first stage of it. When live ordnance is too expensive, when cyber tools are too sensitive, when autonomous systems cannot be tested on populated streets or crowded coastal waters, exercises become the battleground. Software learns. Operators learn. Command structures stretch, break, and rebuild stronger.

Some countries have understood this earlier than others. One northern state built an "autonomy league" hosted every quarter: three days of live-fire testing, urban navigation, jamming, deception, and cross-unit hacking. Engineering teams rotated between playing blue force and red force, attacking their own systems with malice and humour. After a year, the performance gap between units that attended and those that did not was unmistakable. Decision cycles shrank, failure modes were catalogued, and software updates became smarter, not heavier. Rehearsal compounded.

Another example came from an air force that lacked the funds for real missile testing. Instead, it built a digital twin of its radar and fire-control network, fed it modelled attacker behaviour, and forced its officers to fight simulated raids every week. Officers who once issued commands in calm, deliberate tones began to treat the simulation as a real crisis: shouting, reprioritising, making trade-offs. When a live incident finally came—an unexpected intrusion of hostile drones—responses were fast, disciplined, and boringly effective. Not because of new technology, but because of rehearsed minds.

There is always resistance. Rehearsal invites embarrassment. It surfaces flaws. It reveals friction between departments that prefer to avoid each other. It forces legal, political, and ethical questions into daylight: what rules govern an autonomous counterstrike when communications are jammed? How should a human override be invoked when the operator cannot see the target? Exercises produce the arguments that peacetime tries to hide.

Yet this pain is the asset. A system that has never been forced to fail will fail when nobody is ready. The most dangerous sentence in strategic planning is: "We will decide on the day." No adversary will give you that luxury. Autonomy compresses time. Decision points that once took thirty minutes may now take thirty seconds. Only rehearsal teaches an organisation how to think quickly without collapsing into panic or politics.

Red-team cultures are central. Not polite red teams that circulate PDF reports, but aggressive internal adversaries who try to break vehicles, spoof sensors, poison data, hijack command channels, and confuse human operators. The best militaries treat red teams as heroes, not annoyances. They court humiliation early so they can claim competence later. Some even publish the results openly, not to boast but to signal seriousness: *we find weaknesses faster than you can exploit them.*

Civilian infrastructure can learn the same lesson. Autonomous port cranes should be tested under neural-network misclassification attacks. Self-driving ambulances should be stress-tested in GPS-denied zones with unpredictable civilian patterns. Rail networks that use autonomous routing must practice failure: disabled trains, jammed signals, compromised control rooms. The more vital the service, the more rehearsal should feel like ritual.

A philosophical truth underpins all of this. Human beings learn through friction. We become agile by having our assumptions broken. An organisation that cannot tolerate rehearsal cannot tolerate reality. The rehearsal is not a luxury for large states; it is a strategic equaliser for small ones. Nations that cannot afford the largest drone fleets can build the fastest-learning ones. Red-team leagues, simulated crises, and rotating duty cycles cost little compared to a single precision munition.

There are objections. Rehearsals take time from real operations. They cost money. They risk public embarrassment if failures leak. They create legal headaches when autonomous systems and live personnel mix. All of this is true. And yet, every real conflict shows the alternative is worse: untested systems improvising under fire; commanders discovering basic truths at the worst possible moment; civilians paying the price of institutional denial.

There is an institutional trick to making rehearsal durable: treat it as a standing appointment, not an emergency project. Quarterly leagues. Monthly drills. Rapid post-mortems. No exceptions. Performance tracked, not as a box-ticking exercise, but as data for improvement. Units that fail to attend should have to explain why under calm scrutiny. The goal is not punishment—only continuity.

Some states are now experimenting with shared exercises across borders. Coalition red-team tournaments, joint cyber-autonomy drills, and spoofing contests where each participant must break and defend. Such cooperation reduces costs and spreads best practice. It also builds trust: if nations can rehearse crisis messaging or autonomous deconfliction under controlled stress, the risk of real miscalculation shrinks.

Notice what rehearsal does to culture. Engineers stop promising perfection. Commanders stop assuming clarity. Analysts stop treating data streams as gospel. Operators learn humility about their own machines. Everyone becomes suspicious of the easy answer. This scepticism is not pessimism; it is discipline. Rehearsal teaches that a system works only when it works under adversity.

But there is a deeper benefit still. Rehearsal exposes the human seams inside autonomous operations. It makes visible the moment when a lieutenant hesitates to authorise defensive fire, the moment when a political adviser fears headlines more than outcomes, the moment when an engineer distrusts their own algorithm. These moments can be studied, discussed, and resolved long before they unfold in battle. The psychological bandwidth of a crisis is finite. Rehearsal saves lives by pre-spending the uncertainty.

If there is a universal rule in autonomy, it is this: someone, somewhere, is rehearsing harder than you. The nation that treats rehearsal as a compounding asset will eventually outlearn its rivals. The unit that treats rehearsal as theatre will collapse the first time the lights go out.

The most sobering insight may be that rehearsal never finishes. Every software patch introduces new behaviours. Every adversary introduces new deception. Every battlefield introduces new geometry. The organisation that keeps practising learns how to adapt in motion, not on paper. That is power.

And so the uncomfortable question lingers: when the next crisis arrives, will your systems fail gracefully because they practised failing—or catastrophically because they never learned how?

## Guardrails as strategy

The most dangerous myth in autonomous defence is that restraint signals weakness. History suggests the opposite. The states that prove they can control their weapons—can switch them off, throttle them back, document what they did and why—are the ones others dare not provoke. Power without discipline invites gamble. Power with guardrails creates something sharper: credibility.

A decade ago, a small coastal nation demonstrated this in a way no summit speech could. After a neighbour probed its airspace, the nation's autonomous air-defence network surged to alert. Algorithms tracked the intruders, predicted flight paths, and queued fire-control authorisations. But instead of unleashing volleys, the system paused. For ninety unnerving seconds, every battery held fire while human oversight checked cross-border trajectories and civilian patterns. The aircraft drifted away. No shots fired. No lives lost. Yet every regional intelligence service noticed something more important: the system worked under pressure *without losing its temper*. It was not a hair-trigger; it was a scalpel.

This is the paradox at the heart of guardrails: safety becomes deterrence. If adversaries believe your autonomous systems will behave exactly as you claim—no accidental escalation, no catastrophic overreaction—you close the door to cheap coercion. They can no longer gamble on provoking a malfunction, or hide behind plausible deniability. Guardrails are not altruism; they are armour.

The trouble is that most governments speak about safety as if it were a press release topic, not a strategic asset. They promise "responsible AI" while fielding black-box systems that cannot be interrogated, audited, or trusted by partners. When a crisis arrives, allies hesitate. Who wants to stand next to an opaque machine that might misread a radar reflection and launch? Deterrence collapses partly because the system might misfire, and partly because no one can prove it didn't.

What does credible restraint actually look like? Start with the unglamorous: *publishable test suites*. Weapons and autonomous decision tools should be stress-tested against known failure modes—civilian decoys, spoofed targeting data, GPS denial, edge-case behaviours—and those results should be shareable, at least with allies and legislative oversight. A navy that publishes its autonomous mine-clearance benchmarks sends two signals at once: to partners, that cooperation is safe; to adversaries, that deception has already been anticipated and will likely fail.

Next, guardrails demand *predictability*. A system that overrides human command because of an unexplainable internal policy is not advanced; it is brittle. Commanders need documented trigger conditions, escalation ladders, and abort logic. When these rules are clear—and externally verifiable—others can model your behaviour. Strategic stability thrives when surprise shrinks.

Some will object that transparency reveals weaknesses. Why advertise how your autonomous missile evaluates jamming? Why release the adversarial tests your drone fleet survived? But secrecy is overrated. The world's major actors already test against each other's systems through cyber probing, sensor illumination, and electronic warfare. What secrecy preserves is not strength, but doubt. Doubt leads to miscalculation. Miscalculation fuels conflict.

Guardrails are also moral infrastructure. Autonomous systems will make mistakes. They will misclassify patterns no human can see. They will behave strangely after software patches or sensor degradation. The only responsible answer is *traceability*: every autonomous action must leave a trail—logs, telemetry, decision snapshots—that can be inspected after the fact. Not because we enjoy bureaucratic archaeology, but because accountability deters recklessness. Defence ministries that know their decisions will be reviewed internally and, at times, externally are less likely to gamble.

One country quietly implemented this. Before a new class of autonomous surface vessels went into fleet service, it mandated a forensic logging standard. If a vessel ever engaged a target without explicit human authorisation, engineers could reconstruct the full chain of perception, classification, and decision within minutes. Most analysts ignored it. Only when an exercise revealed that the vessels rejected a spoofed distress call—because they recognised suspicious telemetry gaps—did observers grasp the significance. The real innovation was not the sensors, but the guardrail that made trust measurable.

Trust is contagious. It spreads outward. Coalitions form around those who can demonstrate control, not merely advertise it. Arms races accelerate when doubt reigns; they slow when verification is cheap and diplomacy is informed. Guardrails bend the curve.

Strategists often imagine deterrence as a matter of possessing the biggest weapon or the cleverest algorithm. But in autonomy, deterrence is also behavioural. If your systems are known to pause when civilian signatures are detected, or to reroute rather than crash through jamming corridors, your adversary can no longer bluff with human shields, data poisoning, or chaos-on-demand. They cannot provoke you into a massacre that delegitimises you. In this sense, guardrails are political armour: they pre-empt the propaganda victory an adversary seeks when they try to bait an autonomous system into a tragic mistake.

The philosophical heart of guardrails is humility. Humans design systems they do not fully understand. We build neural networks whose latent states we cannot fully audit, then place them in weapons that move at supersonic speeds. Pretending that "trust us, it will behave" is enough is absurd. Strategic maturity demands acknowledging that machines fail—and that *how* they fail matters as much as how they succeed. A missile that gracefully aborts is safer, and therefore more strategically useful, than one that presses forward through corrupted data.

Safety culture has an unlikely champion: insurance mathematics. A growing number of defence contractors have begun pricing liability into autonomous platforms. A system that logs poorly, that lacks fail-safe behaviour, that cannot survive red-team testing without spinning into chaos, becomes more expensive to insure. In effect, guardrails create a financial gravity pulling manufacturers towards integrity.

There is a deeper human reason, too. Democracies are fragile. The public will tolerate high-tech defence only if they believe it aligns with their values. Whenever an autonomous system causes civilian harm, the strategic fallout is national, not technical. Legislatures launch inquiries. Allies distance themselves. Critical technologies face moratoriums. The long-term cost of a single ungoverned failure can dwarf the price of rigorous guardrails. No commander has ever regretted investing in restraint; many have regretted failing to.

Guardrails also change adversary calculus. When a state can prove its systems reliably avoid escalation, adversaries lose a favoured tactic: the manufactured incident. In the Cold War, pilots flirted with each other's airspace hoping to trigger overreaction. In the autonomous age, a hostile drone may mimic civilian signatures or attempt to force an automated counterstrike. Guardrails defang these gambits. They turn the aggressor into a visible provocateur while the restrained actor keeps legitimacy.

Some innovators now publish adversarial challenge sets—open technical trials where external researchers attempt to mislead, poison, or spoof a defence algorithm. Passing these trials becomes a badge of honour. Failing them becomes data, not scandal. A few militaries have gone further, releasing versioned safety benchmarks much like pharmaceutical regulators publish trial outcomes. The public sees not perfection but willingness to learn. In geopolitics, that transparency is strength.

The tension is obvious: can anything be both secret and trustworthy? Must a state reveal all to prove control? Not at all. Guardrails focus on behaviour, not code. A nation can keep its source private while showing that its systems abort cleanly under defined stress, that logs are retained and auditable for a fixed period, that independent observers have witnessed drills. Just as nuclear treaties evolved from intrusive inspections to seismic and atmospheric monitoring, AI governance will rely on external inference: if the system consistently behaves as promised, verification becomes pragmatic.

There remains a cultural barrier: many engineers and generals still view safety work as bureaucratic ballast. They want speed, novelty, dominance. But the world is littered with brilliant technologies that failed because the inventors treated discipline as an afterthought. In autonomy, the first state that fuses aggressive capability with visible restraint will define the global standard. Others will follow because they must, not because they wish to.

The lesson from every high-stakes domain—aviation, nuclear energy, cryptography—is that trust and power are not rivals. They are twins. One without the other collapses. The aircraft that flies fastest is useless if passengers refuse to board. The reactor that produces the most energy is worthless if no community accepts it. The autonomous weapon that terrifies its owners inspires no confidence abroad.

Guardrails are strategy. They lower the temperature of crises. They bind coalitions. They reduce escalation risk. They turn mistakes into learning, not catastrophe. They transform deterrence from a threat into a promise: *we are powerful, and we are sane.*

But the hardest question is never technical. It is political. Who demands guardrails? Who enforces them? Who pays, who inspects, who admits when a system failed? Without answers, even the best frameworks remain paper.

Sooner or later, a state will suffer a near miss—a missile that aborted inches before tragedy, a drone swarm that halted because civilian signatures were detected. If that state can prove *why* the system held, rivals will take note. The future of deterrence may belong not to those who fire fastest, but to those who can show they almost fired—and chose not to.

So the next time a government boasts about its "unstoppable" autonomy, listen for silence where discipline should be. Ask the only question that matters: under stress, under deception, under fear—does the machine stop?

## From hype to governance

When the first autonomous air-defence platforms were shown to a national cabinet, the presentation lasted seven minutes. There were glossy renderings, a dramatic video of simulated interception, and a bold claim: *zero collateral risk.* The room applauded. Funding was approved. Two years later, during a live exercise, a software fault misidentified a returning friendly aircraft. The strike was aborted only because the human overseer happened to be cautious. In the subsequent inquiry, ministers admitted the same truth: they had never understood how the system reasoned, what conditions triggered target lock, or how risk was controlled. They approved a capability, not a strategy.

The modern world is drowning in AI hype. Defence vendors overpromise, politicians under-question, and the public swings between fear and fascination. But autonomous systems are not magic; they are engineered hierarchies of assumptions. If national leaders cannot distinguish between a probabilistic classifier and a deterministic safety fuse, they cannot govern. If the public hears only slogans—"smart weapons", "no human needed", "zero mistakes"—trust erodes the moment reality intrudes. Hype is not a victory. It is a liability.

The only antidote is disciplined translation: turning technical risk into language leaders and citizens can act upon. That means abandoning superlatives and replacing them with structured, comprehensible frameworks. Among the simplest is a *risk ladder*: a plain-spoken breakdown of what the system might do, why, and under which stressors it becomes unreliable. When a minister hears "misclassification rate under sensor spoofing rises from 0.1% to 15%", the number means little. When they hear "in heavy jamming, this drone could mistake a fishing boat for a fast-attack craft one time in seven", the stakes become obvious. Governance begins when abstraction ends.

Most defence organisations still brief AI like consumer tech—slides of innovation, not risk geometry. That is a category mistake. A missile that misfires is not a product failure; it is a strategic crisis. Leaders must be shown *how* a system breaks. Under what edge cases? Which redundancies catch failure? What data fingerprints signal manipulation? Without this information, oversight bodies cannot set limits, and legislatures cannot legislate. Every profession with lethal stakes—aviation, medicine, nuclear energy—evolved rules for translating technical complexity into governance clarity. Autonomy must do the same.

Clarity starts with honesty. Engineers know that models behave differently in the wild than they do in constrained tests. They know that domain shift—weather, terrain, sensor ageing—silently erodes performance. They know that adversaries actively probe for blind spots. Yet briefings too often present controlled-lab excellence as field reality. The responsible path flips the script: assume adversarial pressure, assume data corruption, assume imperfect communication channels. Present risk ladders that escalate: *baseline, degraded, hostile*. Let leaders choose what failure probabilities are politically and ethically tolerable.

The public deserves equal candour. Any nation deploying autonomous force in its name must be prepared to explain why. It is not enough to claim that machines are "cleaner" or "more precise". The public needs to know who remains accountable, what oversight exists, and which lines the system will not cross. When governments stay silent, conspiracy thrives. When governments speak clearly, democratic legitimacy strengthens.

Consider a recent example. A European state announced a new class of defensive autonomous drones designed to intercept incoming missiles.

Predictably, the headlines focused on the futuristic. But the defence ministry did something rare: it released a simplified briefing for the public. It laid out the drone's decision logic in plain terms. It explained how the system aborted if it lost positive identification, how logs were stored for review, and what human override looked like. Far from panicking people, transparency earned support. Polling later showed higher trust not in the drone, but in the ministry itself. Governance is not only about control; it is about credibility.

Hype does the opposite. It creates distorted expectations. Some leaders are convinced autonomy will remove the fog of war. Others fear machines will "go rogue" the moment their back is turned. Both beliefs are technologically illiterate. Autonomy is neither omniscient nor demonic. It is a fallible instrument whose reliability reflects how well it has been trained, tested, constrained, and supervised. The role of governance is to set those conditions.

In practical terms, briefing leaders and publics requires a new literacy—one that blends operational insight with technical realism. Three rules make this possible.

**First: describe capability as envelopes, not promises.** Every autonomous system has operating envelopes where it performs well, and edges where it falters. A risk ladder makes this explicit. In clear conditions, classification confidence is high; in heavy fog, it drops; in sensor jamming, it may collapse altogether. If leaders grasp envelopes, they will not deploy systems where they are weak.

**Second: translate uncertainty into action.** When a briefing hides uncertainty behind jargon—"probabilistic perception", "latent state divergence"—it kills understanding. Better to say: *when this system loses 40% of its visual data, it becomes unpredictable. At that threshold, it must abort.* Leaders can act on thresholds; they cannot act on mysticism.

**Third: make accountability visible.** Who signs off on deployment? Who inspects logs? Who audits incidents? Who updates the model when new vulnerabilities are found? Governance is not theory; it is paperwork, process, and consequence. If responsibility is vague, power becomes reckless.

Some defence ministries are beginning to institutionalise this literacy. They use red-team leagues—recurring exercises where independent teams attempt to trick and break systems—to generate evidence. They publish after-action reports with failure lessons, not just staged triumphs. They build civilian review panels with access to test logs. These steps do not weaken national security; they fortify it. An autonomous system that survives public scrutiny is harder to defeat than one hidden behind slogans.

The hardest audience is neither politicians nor the public. It is the senior leader who is convinced complexity is beneath their attention. Generals and ministers who cut their teeth on hardware—tanks, jets, submarines—often assume autonomy is just another platform. They forget that software can mutate, that models can drift, that decision-rules can be poisoned without a single visible scratch on the metal. Persuading them requires stories, not spreadsheets. Engineers must show how adversaries can exploit false radio signals, how a small change in training data can produce catastrophic misclassification, how a swarm can collapse from a single clever packet injection. The point is not to scare, but to illuminate: in this domain, governance is strategy.

Philosophically, hype is comforting because it removes responsibility. If AI is unstoppable, leaders need not think. If AI is terrifying, they need not act. Both positions absolve them of stewardship. Governance demands the opposite. It insists on human ownership. It says: yes, these systems are powerful; yes, they are fallible; therefore, we must build rules that survive failure.

Those rules matter beyond the battlefield. As autonomy spreads into policing, border security, emergency response, and critical infrastructure, the public's instinctive question will be the same: *who controls the machine, and who controls the people who control it?* Nations that cannot answer will face backlash. Nations that answer well will find society less fearful and more resilient.

There is a quiet geopolitical dividend. States that master responsible communication build coalitions faster. Allies are more willing to integrate systems they understand. Procurement becomes interoperable. Training can be standardised around shared checklists and risk ladders. When crises erupt, partners already speak the same conceptual language. The alternative—coalitions held together by marketing slogans—is brittle.

In the long run, hype is unsustainable. Reality will arrive. A system will fail publicly. A misclassification will cause damage. The only question is whether society is prepared. When failure occurs in a framework of transparency and governance, it becomes a lesson. When it occurs in a vacuum of hype, it becomes a scandal.

So the task is not to persuade the world that autonomous systems are flawless. The task is to show that they are governable. That risk can be bounded. That accountability exists. That human judgment remains sovereign.

When leaders are briefed honestly, they stop treating autonomy as magic and start treating it as infrastructure. They ask disciplined questions. What is the system's abort behaviour? What are the false-positive penalties? What is the model update protocol? What is the outer limit of safe deployment? In those moments, governance displaces hype.

And for the public, the most powerful message is humility. Not the promise of perfection, but the commitment to improvement. A government that can say "here is what we know, here is what we do not know, here is how we monitor risk" earns permission to innovate. Secrecy breeds paranoia; transparency breeds resilience.

The world is about to witness the first autonomous incident that unfolds under global scrutiny—a drone misfire, an algorithmic misread, a defensive system that holds fire when a human might not. When that day comes, society will not judge only the technology. It will judge whether leaders understood its risks, whether they prepared oversight, and whether they spoke honestly about its limits.

Hype is theatre. Governance is civilisation. And the future will belong to nations that can tell the difference.

Because the next time a brilliant engineer stands in a cabinet room and promises "zero risk", someone needs to answer with the only responsible question: *show the ladder.*

## A reader's field manual

The first rule of modern strategy is simple: never trust a slide deck with fireworks. Every ambitious AI weapons proposal arrives wrapped in superlatives—"game-changing", "autonomous edge", "zero human burden". Yet when disaster strikes, the post-mortem almost always reveals something painfully mundane: a missing fail-safe, an unseen constraint, a forgotten dependency. The gulf between promise and practice can be measured not in slogans, but in checklists.

Serious strategists do not ask whether a system is impressive. They ask whether it is *coherent*. Does each promised capability rest on a foundation of verified components? Who operates it, who maintains it, and what happens when something breaks? Hype has a short half-life. A field manual outlives it.

Consider the capabilities that defence firms tout most aggressively: autonomous navigation, precision targeting, coordinated swarming, rapid re-tasking. Impressive on paper, seductive on stage. But beneath every headline capability sits a stack: sensors, perception models, comms links, encryption, control logic, power management, field repair, and human override. If any layer is brittle, the entire architecture becomes a liability. The most lethal weapon in a war room is not a missile; it is a broken assumption.

A field manual offers something rarer than slogans: disciplined evaluation. It is the intellectual equivalent of a pre-flight inspection. Pilots do not rely on persuasion; they rely on procedure. They do not ask whether the aircraft "should" work. They ask whether it *does*, under the conditions that actually matter. Defence leaders need the same mindset for autonomous systems.

Three clusters of questions should guide every reader who confronts a new AI military claim: *capability*, *control*, and *consequence*.

Capability sounds obvious—what does the system do? But genuine scrutiny asks: under what conditions, with what stressors, and with which dependencies? When a vendor claims "50 km autonomous navigation", the only intelligent response is: *how many hours of sensor life? What happens when GPS is denied? What is the error margin under spoofing?* Systems do not fail in laboratories; they fail in dust, rain, jamming, and cluttered terrain.

Control matters more. Who commands the system? Who supervises escalation? Who decides when autonomy disengages? A drone that can identify a hostile radar site is impressive. A drone that can identify a radar site and knows when *not* to fire—because civilians are present, because positive ID is lost, because sensors are degraded—is a strategic asset. In autonomy, the most important capability is restraint.

Consequence is governance in motion. When a system makes a mistake—and it will—how is the error detected, recorded, investigated, and corrected? The public will accept neither a black box nor an untraceable machine. Nations that deploy autonomous systems must be able to reconstruct decisions. That means logs with timestamps, sensor snapshots, decision trees, and trigger thresholds. Without provenance, accountability disintegrates.

To turn these principles into practice, a field manual must offer concrete tools. One of the simplest—and most revealing—is the capability stack worksheet. Every claim of significance can be broken into layers, each of which must stand on its own: sensing, perception, fusion, decision, action, recovery. When any layer is untested, untrusted, or opaque, the claim above it becomes fiction.

Take a hypothetical autonomous underwater vehicle that promises persistent harbour surveillance. Its brochure highlights intelligent patrol patterns and anomaly detection. A capability stack worksheet asks harder questions: what sensors operate in murky water? How is noise filtered? How does the system handle power scarcity? What happens if communication is lost for six hours? What redundancy exists if a propeller fails or a biofouling patch blinds a camera? A real capability lives in details, not abstractions.

Checklists are not bureaucracy; they are civilisation's memory. Every major safety regime—aviation, nuclear, medicine—grew from the ashes of preventable disasters. AI warfare must not wait for its own historic tragedy. It needs discipline before devastation.

A second tool in the reader's manual is the **trust map**. Every complex autonomous system is a partnership between machine and operator. Trust does not mean faith. It means calibrated confidence: knowing when to rely on automation, when to supervise, and when to intervene. A trust map forces designers and commanders to specify where human authority sits. Does the operator monitor or command? Can they override instantly, or only after a delay? What is the workload when dozens of systems run concurrently? A system that demands superhuman attention is not autonomous; it is a liability wearing a mask.

Another tool is the **failure inventory**. Every AI model has failure modes: adversarial spoofing, data drift, sensor freeze, hardware degradation, comms denial. Yet vendors rarely present them. Failure inventories insist on transparency. They list known weaknesses, tested edge cases, mitigation steps, and remaining unknowns. It is the difference between an honest partner and a naïve evangelist. Leaders cannot govern what they cannot foresee.

The field manual also includes **deployment thresholds**. Capabilities mature incrementally, not instantly. A state may approve a model for reconnaissance before approving it for targeting; approve semi-autonomy before full autonomy; approve low-risk environments before high-risk ones. Thresholds turn ambition into sequencing. They turn reckless rollout into controlled evolution.

These tools are not theoretical. Some nations have quietly begun to adopt them. In parts of Asia, procurement agencies require vendors to submit red-team reports alongside marketing claims. In Scandinavia, military auditors demand replayable logs for every autonomous mission. In North America, certain labs share challenge-trial results with oversight committees. None of this slows innovation. It strengthens it. Systems that barely survive scrutiny will collapse in combat. Better to discover flaws in a conference room than over a contested coastline.

Philosophically, a field manual returns power to the reader. It strips away mystique. It reminds us that machines do not cleanse war of human responsibility. They amplify it. A disciplined checklist exposes whether a system has a soul of engineering or a shell of marketing. It leaves no room for wishful thinking.

There is a subtle moral dimension as well. When a nation deploys autonomous force, it does so in the name of its citizens. That is a sacred delegation. Checklists protect that legitimacy. They stop hubris masquerading as strategy. They ensure leaders ask the questions the public would ask if they had the technical vocabulary. In that sense, a field manual is democratic: it turns complexity into accountability.

Yet there is a tension. Too much scrutiny can suffocate progress. Too little invites catastrophe. The art lies in balance: strict evaluation, not paralysis; transparency, not self-exposure; humility, not fear. A capability stack worksheet does not demand perfection. It demands honesty. It demands evidence. It demands the courage to say "not ready" when ambition outpaces reliability.

In the years ahead, autonomous systems will expand from battlefield airspace into maritime choke points, satellite constellations, logistics convoys, border monitoring, and critical infrastructure defence. The claims will become louder. The promises will become bolder. The risks will become greater. By then, every responsible reader—minister, analyst, officer, investor, journalist, student—must have a field manual in mind. Not to dismiss hype, but to interrogate it. Not to resist innovation, but to civilise it.

There is no glamour in checklists. They are dry, repetitive, and relentless. And yet they are the scaffolding of trust. They protect lives without applause.

They turn messy complexity into manageable reality. They prevent the kind of avoidable disaster that writes headlines in blood.

Any nation can buy an autonomous drone. Few can build a regime that keeps it honest.

And the next time a glossy demo promises "precision without supervision", the field manual's first question will cut through the spectacle: *show the stack.*

# About the Author

Dr. Karim Bellarte is a geopolitical analyst and AI policy scholar who studies how code, chips, and institutions reshape power. Raised between Beirut and Milan, he writes with the sensibility of borderlands, where rules meet realities and every system is tested by people under pressure. As a former adviser at an international cyber futures forum, he has worked at the seam of defence, diplomacy, and digital infrastructure, translating complex technology into clear strategic choices. His mission is simple: strip away hype, foreground accountability, and give readers tools to interrogate any claim about autonomy, targeting, or control. A thread he returns to is the Mediterranean's history as a crossroads of empires: a reminder that lanes, cables, and ports still decide who sets the tempo. He believes durable security depends on transparent practice, not theatrical promises.